HISTORICAL
ATLAS
OF
EXPLORATION
1492 ~ 1600

INFANTE
D'HENRIQUE
V CENTENÁRIO DA SUA MORTE
1460 - 1960

HISTORICAL
ATLAS
OF
EXPLORATION
1492~1600

Angus Konstam

Checkmark Books™

An imprint of Facts On File, Inc.

Historical Atlas of Exploration

Text and Design © 2000 Prima Editions, England

Checkmark Books
An imprint of Facts On File, Inc.
11 Penn Plaza
New York, NY 10001

Library of Congress Cataloging-in-Publication Data available on request.

Checkmark Books are available at special discounts when purchased in bulk quantities for businesses, associations, institutions or sales promotions. please call our Special Sales Department in New York at (212) 967-8800 or (800) 322-8755.

You can find Facts On File on the World Wide Web at: http://www.factsonfile.com

For Prima Editions:
Series Editor: Lucian Randall
Jacket Design: Keith Williams, Roger Kean
Illustrations: Oliver Frey
Copy Editors: Warren Lapworth, Neil Williams
Four-color separation: Prima Creative Services, England

Printed and bound in Spain

ISBN: 0-8160-4248-9

Picture Credits
Picture Research: Nathan Grainger of Image Select International, London
Aisa: 16, 17, 33 (right), 79, 86, 92, 123, 131 (bottom), 141; AKG London: 9, 19 (top), 21 (left), 21 (right), 25, 46, 50, 53 (bottom), 54, 55, 63, 64, 68-69, 73, 76, 96, 98, 100, 115, 119 (top), 120, 121 (top), 121 (bottom), 136, 149, 151, 156, 187 (bottom); Ann Ronan: 8, 11, 20, 34, 42, 47 (bottom), 48, 49, 51, 53 (top), 56, 62, 72, 80 (left), 81 (top-right), 81 (bottom-right), 84 (left), 85 (right), 87, 92, 93 (top), 93 (bottom), 97, 99, 101, 106, 117, 118, 126, 127 (top), 128 (bottom), 129, 131 (top), 133 (top), 138, 146, 147, 148, 150 (top), 150 (bottom), 153, 154, 155, 160, 161, 167, 171 (top), 184, 185, 187 (center), 188; British Embassy, Mexico: 119 (by kind permission of Miss M.L.A. Strickland); British Library: 94, 172, 173, 174, 175, 176, 178, 179; CFCL: 105; City Art Museum, Bristol: 77; Delaware Art Museum: 143; E.T. Archive: 128, 134; Fresh Manor, Bath: 170; Gamma: 15, 24-25, 28-29, 31, 58, 59, 66, 82, 83, 95, 182, 183 (bottom), 186; Lima Cathedral: 101; Lienzode Tlaxcala: 117; Mariners' Museum: 10, 39 (top), 40, 42-43 (top), 43, 127 (center), 183 (top); Mary Evans: 116; National History Museum: 71; National Maritime Museum, Greenwich, London: 41, 114; Pictor: 83, 70, 79, 107, 155, 156, 161, 169; Pier Point Morgan Library: 65; Prima Editions: 71 (bottom), 130, 132 (bottom-left), 132 (bottom-right), 137 (bottom), 185 (top), 189 (top), 189 (bottom); Prima Editions/Oliver Frey: 2-3, 6-7, 35 (top), 39 (bottom), 57 (center), 67, 68, 106 (top), 134, 166 (left), 166 (right), 168 (left), 168-169; Prima Editions/Martin Teviotdale: 188-189; Royal Armouries: 88; Scala: 89, 137 (left); Spectrum Colour Library : 1, 14, 30, 35 (bottom), 38, 47 (top), 70, 135; Superstock: 87, 163-164; Werner Forman: 26, 27 (left), 27 (right), 32, 33 (left), 102, 103 (top), 103 (bottom), 104, 105, 110, 111 (top), 111 (bottom), 112 (top), 112 (bottom), 113, 137 (top), 139, 140, 164, 165 (top), 165 (bottom), 171 (bottom)

Previous pages: Through almost continual fogs, Ferdinand Magellan works his ships and men through the strait that now bears his name, during the first circumnavigation of the globe. Painting by Oliver Frey.

Contents

INTRODUCTION

In October 1492, to the amazement of the Arawak inhabitants of a small island off the American mainland, Christopher Columbus raised the Spanish standard and named his discovery San Salvador. He thought he had found a new route to the fabled Indies, instead he had opened up a New World. Painting by Oliver Frey.

On a summer morning in 1492, a group of three small ships raised their anchors and sailed out of the southern Spanish harbor of Palos. They followed the Tinto estuary to the sea and set a southward course. Their departure went largely unnoticed in the town, whose inhabitants went on with their daily lives, landing fish for sale in the markets of Seville and repairing their nets, unaware that they were witnessing an event of crucial importance to the future of mankind. Even the fleet commander's diary entry was understated: "On Friday the third day of August of the year 1492, at eight o'clock, we set out from the bar of the Saltés. We went with a strong sea breeze sixty miles to the southward, that is fifteen leagues before sunset; afterwards, to the southwest and south by west which was the course for the Canaries." The diary entry was written by Christopher Columbus. In just over two months he would discover the New World.

The first voyage of Christopher Columbus did not mark the start of the period known as the "Age of Discovery," nor was he the first European to set foot in America. When he died he still refused to believe that the lands he found were anything other than a part of the Far East. The continent he discovered was named after another explorer, Amerigo Vespucci, and Columbus died a frustrated and broken man, spurned by the Spanish crown that had given him his golden opportunity. Despite this, of all the voyages of discovery made in the 15th and 16th centuries, that first voyage made by the Italian-born mariner is the one best remembered today. It has been hailed as a defining moment in world history, marking the end of the Middle Ages in Europe and ushering in a new era of scientific and geographical discovery. The name Columbus will remain well to the fore in popular imagination for centuries to come.

The chain of events that culminated in Columbus's voyage began in the late 1300s, when European mariners took advantage of improved sailing craft and ventured further than they had before. A few modest Portuguese discoveries led to royal encouragement of further voyages of exploration, a policy supervised by Prince Henry the Navigator. More than any other, he became known as the person who initiated the "Age of Discovery." The first phase lasted for a little over a century, as Portuguese and Spanish mariners mapped routes around Africa to the Far East and sailed west to find the two great continents of the Americas. Within a century of Columbus's voyage, the old maps of the medieval world had been replaced by global maps whose features were largely accurate. But there was still much to explore. While the French and English tried to find an alternative route to the Orient through the Arctic, the Spanish reached it by sailing around South America.

This book traces the story of the Age of Discovery by following each of the major explorers on their voyages. It shows how, in a period characterized by the Renaissance, the attitude of the explorers toward the people they came across was far from enlightened. Recurring themes run through these accounts: greed, lust for gold, vanity, national pride, and callousness. These mingle with more admirable traits, including maritime skill, bravery, resourcefulness, and vision.

More than in any other period in history, a handful of men made an impact far beyond the achievements of their fellows. Their story is one that still fascinates us in an era when transatlantic journeys are routine, and the exotic spices they sailed the world to find can be imported from those distant lands in a matter of hours.

The AGE of DISCOVERY

In 1522, a small ship called the *Victoria* sailed into the southern Spanish harbor of Sanlucar de Barrameda, thus ending the world's first voyage of circumnavigation. This was one of the high points of the Age of Discovery, the end of a remarkable expedition begun three years before by Ferdinand Magellan. Although the Portuguese captain was killed in a clash with natives in the Philippines, the return of his expedition is now regarded as one of the defining moments in world history—the culmination of a century of Portuguese maritime exploration that transformed mankind's knowledge of the world.

When the Roman Empire collapsed in the fifth century AD, Europe was divided up between tribes of barbarians, and entered an historic period known as the "Dark Ages." Much of the trappings of Roman civilization were destroyed, including urban settlement, organized trade, and specialized agriculture. Christianity survived the fall of Rome and slowly gained popularity among the peoples settled inside its former frontiers, while gradually a new social order based on feudalism emerged in Western Europe. Further to the east, in Greece, Asia Minor, and parts of the Middle East, a portion of the Roman Empire survived, largely influenced by Greeks, and was renamed the Byzantine Empire. During the seventh century a new force emerged to threaten Byzantium and the emerging feudal states of Western Europe. The new religion of Islam was founded by Mohammed in Arabia, and Muslim Arabs embarked on a holy war to spread the influence of the new religion as far as possible. By the middle of the eighth century the Arabs (or Moors) occupied all of the North African coast, the Middle East, and Asia Minor. They occupied half of Spain and Portugal and even reached as far north as France before they were repulsed.

The Byzantine Empire acted as a bulwark against further Muslim expansion, and continued to impede its advance until it collapsed in 1453. While the Spanish were left to reconquer their own lands from the Moors, the rest of Christendom (the Christian states of Western Europe) decided to turn the tables on the Muslims and launch their own holy war.

West meets East

The first of these Crusades was launched in 1096, and for the next two centuries European Christian armies battled the forces of Islam in the Middle East. The perceived need to spread Christianity was later used as a catalyst for the

Below: Arab traders sailed far and wide over the Indian Ocean in their dhows. Their influence left a strong Muslim culture throughout many of the territories the European explorers would later claim for their own.

Right: 16th-century Arab scientists studying with the use of astronomical and navigational instruments.

Portuguese voyages of discovery.

Although ultimately a failure, the crusades brought Europeans into direct contact with the Arab world. The Arabs possessed goods that were unheard of in Europe such as spices, silks, and ivory, in addition to vast supplies of gold. By the 13th century, Venetian and Genoese merchants regularly traded with Arab merchants and brought their luxuries to Europe where they could be sold for a phenomenal profit. When asked where the goods had come from, the Arabs said that they originated in the Orient. The Venetian traveler Marco Polo journeyed to China at the end of the 13th century, and returned with tales of the wonders of Cathay (China). The faceless Orient described by the Arabs was placed into context, and the account of Marco Polo's travels was circulated to an eager audience.

However, Christian Europe was separated from the Orient by a wide band of Muslim lands. The only access was through the trade links established between Italian and Arab merchants. After four crusades, and only temporary successes, the crusading movement was abandoned with the exceptions of Spain and Portugal, where Christians and Moors had been locked in conflict since the seventh century. As the Spanish recovered territory from the Moors they captured Arab universities and found copies of Greek scholarly works that had long been considered lost. These were translated into Latin at the same time as the influential books on geography arrived in Europe from Byzantium. Many of these works contained technology that would prove vital to the Age of Discovery: astronomy, cartography, mathematics, and navigation. The fact that the earth is a sphere had been proven by the Greeks centuries before, but this only emerged in European texts in the late 14th century as a direct consequence of this process. Old medieval superstitions were challenged by the newly found scientific knowledge that allowed Europeans to take a step into the unknown.

67 BC	AD 14	42	106	137	c.215	271	c.300
Roman general Pompey the Great eliminates the Cilician sea raiders.	The Romans build an aqueduct at Pont du Gard, France.	St. Peter is made the first Pope.	Greek sea captain publishes a guide to the Indian Ocean and Red Sea	A road is constructed to link the Nile to the Red Sea.	Decline of trade between China and the Roman Empire.	Magnetic compasses are used in China.	Cargo vessels in use throughout Europe in Roman trade boom.

Above: *A 16th-century depiction of Ferdinand Magellan's vessel the* Victoria *surrounded by a shoal of flying fish.*

Below: *Science versus superstition—strange sights seen by Marco Polo, in the* Livres des Marvelilles.

The catalyst for exploration

This fresh scientific knowledge, together with improvements in European shipbuilding, made the Age of Discovery possible. While a century before, European shipbuilders had produced clumsy coastal craft that were unsuited to long voyages, recent improvements led to the production of a new kind of vessel. An amalgam of north European and Mediterranean shipbuilding techniques resulted in the

production of the caravel, a small and responsive vessel that was well suited to the challenges of 15th-century expeditions. The Portuguese perfected this vessel type, and it remained in use as the principal ship of exploration until augmented by the larger carrack (or nao) during the last quarter of the 15th century. Portuguese mariners had the ships required for the job, while the nation's universities contained the scientific information mariners needed to chart their way through unknown waters.

What Europe needed now was to marry this new scholarship with enterprising mariners and their ships. This was achieved by a member of the Portuguese royal family, Prince Henry the Navigator (1394–1460), who saw a way to combine the crusading ethos with the old desire to bring spices to Europe without having to deal with the Arabs. Since Portugal was the leading maritime nation in Europe, excepting Italy, Prince Henry was ideally placed to achieve his goal and to launch the world onto a new course.

Because Spain was still locked in a deadly struggle against the Moors in the south of the country, and the Christian Byzantine Empire was in the last throes of its collapse, with a resurgent Ottoman Empire dominating the eastern Mediterranean, Prince Henry was accused of diverting Portuguese resources into exploration and away from the Christian assault on Muslims. Henry countered criticisms by declaring that the voyages he organized *were* a crusade, seeking to attack the periphery of the Moorish realm along the coast of West Africa.

Science versus superstition

He faced another problem. In some quarters, medieval Europe feared that the use of Arab scientific knowledge might place the teachings of the Church into question. By choosing non-controversial works on scientific subjects, Prince Henry was able to deflect such criticism. As for banishing medieval superstition, he saw that as a necessary part of his mission. One such belief was the notion that the Earth was flat. When Ptolemy's *Geography* was translated into Latin, Europeans were exposed to his

AD 610	630–40	700	711	c.800	896	c.1000	13th century
The Grand Canal is completed, linking the Yangtze and Yellow rivers.	Arab pirates prey on ships in the Red Sea.	Polynesians settle on the Cook Islands.	Southern Spain is invaded by Muslim armies.	Settlers from Polynesia reach New Zealand and Easter Island.	King Alfred of Wessex, England, repels a Danish invasion.	Greenland colonized by Vikings.	"Reprisal" contracts given to wronged mariners starts privateering.

theories that the Earth was round and, contrary to current popular belief, many were convinced of this concept long before Columbus sailed in 1492. What Europe now needed was for mariners to sail far enough to prove the theory, and to discover whether any lands lay undiscovered in uncharted waters.

When Henry the Navigator established a navigation school at Sagres in southern Portugal, his aim was to teach the latest scientific skills of navigation and astronomy to the best mariners available. He drew upon the merchant traders who had already made Portugal a leading maritime power by the early 15th century, but he also looked further afield, to Venice and Genoa. Sea captains were offered incentives to work for the Prince. These men had made a living trading commodities between one port and another, and were materialistic rather than idealistic. In order to maintain the concept of the venture being a crusade, Henry frequently appointed Portuguese noblemen to command these expeditions; men who would make the decisions but leave the operation of the ship to experienced mariners.

When a local potentate asked Vasco da Gama why he had come to India, he replied that he had come in search of spices and Christians. Although the profit motive was a major factor in the impetus for the explorations of the Age of Discovery, the desire to outflank the Muslim world and to spread Christianity was never far behind. The diary kept by Columbus contains observations sprinkled with references to the possibility of finding gold and of converting the people he encountered. The accounts of the pioneers of exploration speak for themselves, but in almost all cases, greed and religion appear to have been the prime motivating influences behind the men who initiated the Age of Discovery.

Above: *Prince Henry the Navigator, the visionary who almost single-handedly launched the Age of Discovery.*

1206	1241	1295	c.1300	15th century	1405	1453	1479
The Mongols begin their conquest of Asia, led by Genghis Khan.	Hanseatic League is formed to supervise maritime trade.	Marco Polo returns from the Far East.	The League of the Cinque Ports develops British trade and protects the Channel.	Carvel-built ships replace the "clinker built" craft that cannot be fitted with artillery.	The Chinese voyage around the Indian Ocean.	The Byzantine Empire ends as Ottoman Turks take over Constantinople.	Venice pays the Ottoman Empire for trading rights in the Black Sea.

CHAPTER ONE

EUROPE *in the* 15*th* CENTURY

The continent Christopher Columbus sailed from in 1492 was in a period of immense change. For centuries, a society based on feudal obligation had dominated Europe, but over the previous century, the growth of a merchant class threatened to disrupt the older order. Cities were increasing in size, and commerce had replaced land and agriculture as the principal source of wealth for kingdoms such as England and Portugal. Technological improvements in farming ensured that the population of these growing cities could be fed, while the development of ship design was making maritime trade vital to national economies.

In 1492, Spain saw the end of the Moorish (Islamic) presence after centuries of warfare between Christians and Muslims. The Church was all-powerful, and demonstrated its muscle when it arranged for the expulsion of all Jews from Spain in the same year. In Italy, the cultural phenomenon known as the Renaissance was in full bloom, and people were beginning to challenge the old medieval values and superstitions that abounded throughout Europe. While this was beginning to create problems for the Church, it also created an atmosphere in which people began to wonder what lay beyond the boundaries of the known world.

Portuguese mariners had already explored much of the African coast. It was now up to explorers, such as Christopher Columbus and Vasco da Gama, to take up the mantle and push further into the unknown. Within a few short years, their voyages of discovery would alter European perception of the world forever.

SCOTLAND
Allied with France
Edinburgh

IRELAND

ENGLAND
Strong trading links with Portugal
Bristol
London

Atlantic Ocean

English Channel

Brittany
(France from 1491)

Loire

FRANCE
Allied with Scotland

Bay of Biscay

La Coruña

Bordeaux

Santander

Oporto

SPAIN
Controls southern Italy, Sicily, Sardinia, and the Spanish Netherlands

PORTUGAL
Strong trading links with England

Navarre
(Spain from 1512)

Tagus

Madrid

Barcelona

Lisbon

Aragon
(Spain from 1479)

Castile
(Spain from 1479)

Strong trading links with England

Córdoba

Seville

Balearic Islands (Spain)

Granada
Spain recaptures from the Moors 1492

Cartagena

Málaga

Tangier Ceuta
Portuguese influence after capture of Ceuta, 1414

Melila
Spain captures from the Moors 1497

Orán
Spain captures from the Moors 1509

Algiers
Spain captures from the Moors 1510, loses to Ottomans 1555

Canary Islands (Spain)

Marrakech

AFRICA

Las Palmas

North Sea

Christiania

Stockholm

SWEDEN

Estonia

MUSCOVY

Baltic Sea

Livonia

Courland

Riga

Moscow

DENMARK–NORWAY

Copenhagen

Prussia

Vilna

Minsk

Danzig

Hamburg

Amsterdam

NETHERLANDS
(Spain from
1477)

Berlin

Vistula

Warsaw

Brussels

POLAND – LITHUANIA
Struggle to maintain territory against
Muscovite and Ottoman aggression

Picardy
ce from 1482)
aris

Elbe

Prague

Kiev

Seine

Strasbourg

**HOLY ROMAN
EMPIRE**
A disjointed dormant power
comprising numerous small states
and principalities

Rhine

Burgundy
(France from
1482)

Imperial Hungary
(Austrian Hapsburgs from 1526)

Transyvania
(Ottoman Empire
from 1541)

Basel

**SWISS
CONFEDERATION**

Vienna

Buda

Rhone

SAVOY

Milan

VENICE

Hungary
(Ottoman Empire
from 1541)

OTTOMAN EMPIRE

Venice

MILAN

Avignon

Provence
(France from 1481)

Genoa

Ravenna

Belgrade

Bucharest

Danube

Black Sea

BATTLE OF
PAVIA 1525

Florence

Adriatic Sea

Sofia

Corsica
(Genoa)

**PAPAL
STATES**

Rome

NAPLES

Northern Italy is a
power vacuum and
becomes a
battleground in
1494, as Charles VIII
of France invades as
far south as Spanish-
held Naples.

Naples

(Spain)

SARDINIA

(Spain)

Mediterranean Sea

Aegean Sea

**OTTOMAN
EMPIRE**

Constantinople

Izmar

Tunis

Spain
captures
from the
Moors 1535

SICILY
(Spain)

Malta

(Knights of St.
John 1530)

Athens

13

DYNASTIC PORTUGAL

P ortugal, a small kingdom on the periphery of Europe, was bounded on one side by a hostile larger power and on the other by the Atlantic Ocean. Her development during the 15th century was a balance between maritime expansion and the need to keep an eye on her old enemy, Castile. Between these forces she emerged as a powerful country and led Europe in maritime exploration. More than any other European nation, Portugal launched the Age of Discovery.

Portugal was one of dozens of feudal kingdoms that developed throughout Europe in the 11th century. Portugal survived the Muslim invasion, assisted by her own military skill and religious armies such as the Knights of Calatrava. The process that ended in the expulsion of the Moors also hastened the amalgamation of feudal territories under royal control. With the removal of the direct threat of Muslim attack, Portugal's next biggest threat was the neighboring Iberian province of Castile. The overwhelming military power of Castile was in part offset by the emergence of diplomatic links between Portugal and the neighboring kingdoms of Aragon and Navarre. However, Castile would continue to threaten the security of Portugal, especially when the union of Ferdinand and Isabella united Castile and Aragon in 1479.

Below: The Cape of Good Hope, Portugal's gateway to the East.

GALICIA

Vigo

ATLANTIC OCEAN

By 1492 Portugal also controlled the Canary Islands, the Cape Verde Islands and had settlements on the West African Coast.

Oporto

Major shipping trade with England, the Low Countries, and France (spices from the Orient).

PORTUGAL

Salamanca

Spices sold to Spain and other European countries by land trade as well as sea routes.

Coimbra

Tagus River

Abrantes

CASTILE

Lisbon

Estremoz

SPAIN

Sines

Lagos

Huelva

Seville

Sagres

Faro

CAPE ST. VINCENT

By 1492, Portugal was the largest European importer of spice and was growing rich on the proceeds of her Indian trade routes.

Cadiz

Cueta

Tangier

During the 14th century, external attack was not the only threatening prospect for Portugal. The century was marked by a series of conflicts between factions within the Portuguese ruling family, and internal political discord among the nobility, with the divided factions being supported by Portugal's powerful Iberian neighbors. The problems arose when King Alfonso IV of Portugal (1325–57) quarreled with his son Pedro. Pedro was married to a Castilian princess, but preferred the company of a mistress. Alfonso had the mistress killed, which prompted the first of several Portuguese dynastic wars. Pedro was assisted by Castile

1097	1128	1415	1434	1441	1458	1494	1495
Alfonso VI of Leon (Spain) gives son Henry of Chalon the hereditary county of Portugal.	Alfonso Henriques defeats Teresa, his mother, at São Mamede, gaining control of Portugal.	Ceuta is captured, Portugal's first territory in Africa.	Portuguese round Cape Bojador, off West Africa.	Slave trading begins between Portugal and West Africa.	Diogo Gomes rounds West Africa, reaching slave and gold areas of Guinea.	The Treaty of Tordesillas divides the world between the Spanish and the Portuguese.	Jews are expelled from Portugal.

and, following the death of his father, he was crowned as King Pedro I (1357–67). By the time he was succeeded by his son Ferdinando (1367–83), Castilian influence in the Portuguese court was pronounced. A fresh marriage alliance between Ferdinando's daughter and King Juan I of Castile prompted a popular uprising. After Ferdinando's death, João (John), the son of Pedro's murdered mistress, became John I (1385–1433), crowned following a wave of anti-Castilian feeling. This prompted a Castilian invasion, and Portugal asked for help from England, her principal trading partner. English troops helped the Portuguese defeat the Castilians in the Battle of Aljubarotta (1385), and the new alliance was further cemented by a marriage between King John I and the daughter of England's virtual regent, John of Gaunt. The couple produced four sons, Duarte, Ferdinand, Pedro, and Henry.

Portugal comes of age

Castile signed a peace treaty in 1411, and this freed Portugal to pursue her own quest for military glory. Under the pretext of launching a campaign against a possible Moorish assault on Portugal, King John attacked and captured the African port of Ceuta on the southern side of the Strait of Gibraltar. This gave Portugal a foothold in Africa and, more importantly, served as the impetus for the John's fourth son, Henry, to expand the Portuguese sphere of influence southward down the West African coast.

Meanwhile, the power struggles surrounding the Portuguese continued. When King John died in 1433, he was succeeded by Henry's brother Duarte (Edward) who reigned for five years. One brother helped another, and while Edward diverted profits from trade with Madeira to fund Henry's maritime adventures, his brother helped to extend the Portuguese domain, and for which he earned his name

"the Navigator." Ferdinand was captured by the Moors in 1437, so when Edward died the following year he was succeeded by his six-year-old son, Alfonso V (1438–81), with Prince Pedro as regent. When Alfonso came of age in 1448, a fresh civil war erupted between the young monarch and his regent, and Pedro was

killed in battle the following year.

It was fortunate for Portugal that despite dynastic struggles, a succession of her 15th-century rulers actively encouraged maritime exploration. When John II (1481–95) succeeded to the throne he was already heavily involved in the encouragement of voyages of discovery, and it was under his sponsorship that Bartolomeu Dias discovered the Cape of Good Hope, and that Portugal won her monopoly of trade around Africa to the Indies. By the time Columbus sailed on his transatlantic voyage in 1492, Portugal was well on her way to establishing her trading empire, and within a decade would become one of the richest countries in Europe.

Above: The port of Lisbon, a 16th-century engraving by Theodore de Bry.

1498	1500	1511	1517	1518	1529	1578	1581
Vasco da Gama becomes first to make a return voyage from Europe to India.	Pedro Cabral discovers "Terra da Veracruz," later renamed Brazil.	Malacca is captured by the Portuguese.	Fernão Pires de Andrade is the first modern European to reach Canton, China.	Magellan joins Charles of Spain, after falling out with Manuel of Portugal.	The Portuguese at Malacca are first attacked by Achenese Muslims.	Sebastian I of Portugal is killed at al-Qasr al-Kabir (Alcazarquivir), Africa	Philip II of Spain annexes Portugal.

FRAGMENTED SPAIN

Opposite: King Ferdinand and Queen Isabella entering Granada after its capture from the Moors in 1492. From a tomb relief in Granada.

Below: Seville, seen here in 1503, became Spain's main embarkation point for the New World.

Spain during the 15th century was, like most European countries, a state in the process of creating itself. In the century that ended with the voyages of Columbus, much of Spain was unified under Ferdinand and Isabella, a regional alliance that made Spain a major European power. Her conquest of Granada in 1492 consolidated Spanish power in the Mediterranean, and freed Iberia of the Moors for the first time in centuries. Spain was now able to compete with Portugal on the vanguard of exploration and discovery.

From a narrow northern frontier backed by

Muslim realm, and Moorish influence left its mark in the region. The presence of non-Christians in Spain was anathema to the northern Spanish feudal states, and a war that lasted for centuries was fought for control of the peninsula. From these campaigns the province of Castile emerged as the strongest Christian state. By the early 15th century, Castile had expanded south and added the province of Andalusia to the kingdom. This region became New Castile, and Castilian settlers ensured it would remain Christian. Castile went on to secure the port of Seville, a Moorish city that

became the residence of the Castilian court. The Castilians also expanded to the southeast, capturing Murcia and driving a wedge between Christian Aragon and Muslim Granada.

Consolidation

While a hiatus in the centuries-long religious war allowed both sides to draw breath, the Castilian nobility secured political and economic control over their new territories, a policy of conquest, settlement, and then administration that was repeated by Castilian conquistadors in the New World. The Castilian domination of Iberia also ensured that the Castilian language would become the dominant tongue in Spain. By the mid-15th century, having emerged from a period of bitter civil war, internal dispute, and a failed invasion of Portugal, Castile was ready to resume the attack on Muslim Spain. A marriage alliance between Aragon and Castile in the late 14th century helped to bring the two kingdoms together, and Henry III (1390–1406) and his son John II (1406–1454) considered themselves

mountains, through an arid central plateau interspersed with more mountain ranges to a temperate Mediterranean and Atlantic coastline, Spain is a land of great geographical diversity. Mountains and rivers divided Spain in the Middle Ages into several regions, each with its own urban administrative center: Toledo, Bilbao, Barcelona, Seville, and Valladolid. The same geographical barriers prevented Spain from being permanently overrun by the Moors. From the eighth until the 13th centuries, the southern half of the Iberian peninsula was a

1027	1062	1072	1469	1478	1492	1493	1494
Sancho the Great takes Barcelona, Castile, and León as he conquers Christian Spain.	Abu Bakr founds Marrakesh, Morocco, and invades Spain.	Sancho is assassinated and brother Alfonso VI becomes King of Castile and León.	Ferdinand of Aragon marries Isabella of Castile and promises to unify Spain.	The Spanish Inquisition is founded.	Spanish conquest of Granada, ending Muslim rule.	Founding of Hispaniola, the first Spanish settlement in the Americas.	The Treaty of Tordesillas divides the New World between Spain and Portugal.

diplomats on the European stage as much as crusaders against the Moors. The monarchs brought Castile a much-needed period of stability that included a more secure monarchy, a growing economy, and strong diplomatic support. Henry's brother Ferdinand I of Aragon (1412–16) was also a Castilian, which ensured a link between the kingdoms that would result in the union of Ferdinand and Isabella in 1479. This European interest involved strengthening links with the Papacy, keeping an eye on the rising power of France, and maintaining Aragon's influence over southern Italy.

The resumption of the war between Christian and Muslim in southern Spain also marked the end of centuries of religious tolerance in the Iberian peninsula. Muslims and Jews, who had long been tolerated in the conquered Christian provinces of Spain, became the victims of a new wave of intolerance. The worst came following the marriage of Isabella of Castile and Ferdinand of Aragon. Isabella was a devout and strong woman, who felt it her duty to cleanse her territory of non-Christians. Muslims and Jews were driven from Ferdinand and Isabella's territory; the last great Jewish expulsion took place in 1492, the year Columbus discovered America.

The Granada campaign began in 1482, and ten years later the province fell to the Spanish. Spain then looked toward Africa for more military conquests, but Columbus's discoveries and the French invasion of Italy forced a change of policy. The 1494 Treaty of Tordesillas allocated Spain as yet undiscovered territories in the New World. 1492, therefore, marked the year when Spain ended her centuries of crusading against the Moors in Europe and ushered in a new era of conquest and settlement in the New World.

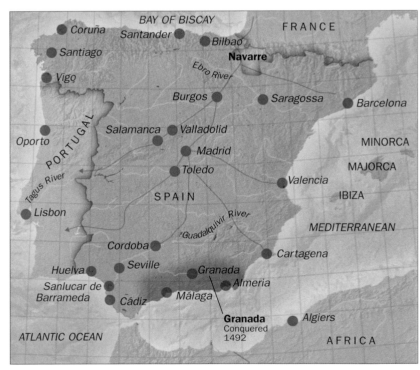

1500	1513	1521	1530	1533	1565	1568	1571
Juan de la Cosa publishes his "Mappa Mundi," the first map of the world.	Vasco Núñez de Balboa is the first European to see the Pacific Ocean.	Conquistadors conquer the Aztec Empire, renaming it New Spain.	The Spanish treasure fleets begin their annual trading voyages.	Francisco Pizarro completes his conquest of the Inca civilization.	From a base in the Philippines Miguel López de Legazpi conquers the archipelago.	Alvaro de Mendaña de Neyra discovers the Solomon Islands.	The Philippines are conquered by the Spanish.

ENGLAND *and* FRANCE

England and France were two of Europe's most powerful kingdoms and yet, in the late 15th century, they did not interfere when Spain and Portugal began to carve out vast territories in the New World and the East. Their occasional voyages of discovery lacked the zeal of the Iberian nations and, in the 16th century, they were unable to follow up on their modest successes. Both countries were wrapped up in their own affairs, but their reluctance to participate in the first wave of great discoveries involved more than simply domestic introversion.

By the late 15th century, England craved peace. In 1453 the French had driven the English from their last footholds on the continental mainland, bringing the conflict known as the Hundred Years' War to a close. Only the port of Calais remained in English hands as a reminder that she had once ruled half of France. Within two years a dynastic quarrel between the rival houses of York and Lancaster for the throne erupted into civil war. For 30 years, the War of the Roses devastated the economy. As central authority weakened and agriculture suffered, taxation and revenue declined. Unable to maintain a navy, the waters of the English coast became the haunt of pirates, who further damaged England's fragile trade links with the continent.

In 1485, royal contender Henry Tudor sailed from France with a force of English exiles and French mercenaries. Landing in Wales, he became the focal point for a revolt against the Yorkist king, Richard III. The decisive battle of the war came in late August 1485, when Henry defeated and killed Richard at Bosworth. Henry Tudor was duly crowned King Henry VII of England—the first Tudor monarch. The country needed time to recover, and Henry spent much of his reign uniting the land and repairing the economy.

When John Cabot approached him and suggested a voyage of discovery, Henry listened because the prospect of new territory meant greater national wealth. Although Cabot's discovery of Newfoundland led to a second voyage, Henry was unimpressed. Because fresh cartographic evidence suggested that the Orient lay thousands of miles to the east of Cabot's landfall, the monarch lost interest in further

Map (left)

SCOTLAND

Area around Dublin occupied by English, but country was in constant revolt.

Feudal factions in North still in revolt against Crown after the coronation of Henry VII in 1485.

REVOLT

IRELAND

IRISH SEA

Dublin

York

NORTH SEA

ENGLAND

REVOLT

WALES

Norwich

REVOLT

Wales was occupied but independent of England until 1536.

Bristol

London

Plymouth

Rye

SPANISH NETHERLANDS

ENGLISH CHANNEL

Cherbourg

Le Havre

Brest

Brittany 1491

Paris

ATLANTIC OCEAN

Nantes

FRANCHE COMTE

FRANCE

Many French regions still not part of France in 1492 (see map, right).

La Rochelle

SAVOY

Bordeaux

Provence 1481

Narbonne

Marseilles

SPAIN

Timeline

1003–1013	1066	1106	1309–77
The Danes, led by King Sweyn and son Canute, conquer England.	Viking presence in England ends with King Harald Hadrada's death at Stamford Bridge.	England and Normandy are reunited after King Henry defeats brother Robert at Tinchebrai.	Under the French monarchy, the Papacy is at Avignon; Great Schism follows.

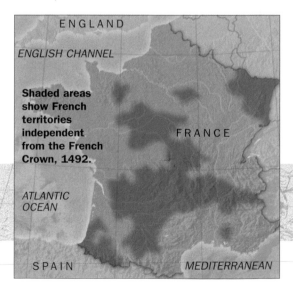

ENGLAND

ENGLISH CHANNEL

Shaded areas show French territories independent from the French Crown, 1492.

FRANCE

ATLANTIC OCEAN

SPAIN

MEDITERRANEAN

presided over two significant events. First, a post-war improvement in the French economy helped royal revenues and, happily for the monarch, because the regeneration was in the towns and centers of population, it did not contribute to the coffers of the feudal nobility. Second, Burgundy disintegrated following a disastrous war with the Swiss Confederation in 1476–7. An unpopular monarch, Louis was nevertheless successful in bringing many of the French feudal lands under royal influence. His successor, Charles VIII (1483–98), inherited a prosperous and partially unified kingdom, and was free to involve himself in military conquests. His invasion of Italy in 1494—which helped cause the Spanish to turn toward the New World—plunged Europe into a new dynastic war, and it effectively ruled out any allocation of French resources to exploration until well into the 16th century.

Left: King Francis I (1494–1547) commissioned the Italian Giovanni da Verrazano (see pages 88–89) to explore the coast of North America to find a northern passage to the Indies. When Francis lost to the Imperialists at the battle of Pavia (1525) and was captured, da Verrazano had to wait for the king's release before continuing with his second expedition.

Below: King Henry VII of England holding court in the tower of London, from a late 15th-century manuscript.

ventures. At the time, England was involved in a program of naval construction, and Henry was too shrewd a businessman to speculate with his nation's scant resources. When he died in 1509, he was succeeded by his son, Henry VIII, who was also too heavily involved in European politics and the problems of securing national stability to become involved in exploration. English involvement in the Americas would have to wait until the reign of Henry's daughter, Elizabeth.

Inner turmoil

In France, the end of the Hundred Years' War brought peace, but left King Charles VII (1422–1461) with a divided kingdom. To the east, Duke Phillippe of Burgundy maintained his lands in almost complete independence. Charles was mistrustful of Burgundy, which had sided with England in the last decades of the war. Similarly, many French nobles held their lands without owning them by royal consent, so the French monarchy was anything but an absolute power. Charles was succeeded by his son Louis XI (1461–83), who by good fortune

1323	1337–1453	1415	1429	1530	1535	1552	1554
Treaty of Edinburgh ends the wars between England and Scotland.	France and England fight the Hundred Years' War.	The English win the Battle of Agincourt.	The French, led by Joan of Arc, defeat the English in Orleans, France.	The Church of England is established by Henry VIII.	Jacques Cartier discovers Québec and Montréal.	The French invade Lorraine, causing a war with the Holy Roman Empire.	Richard Chancellor forms a trade deal between Muscovy and England.

The CHURCH and the POPE

A t a time when the Church was on the verge of splitting apart, religion was seen as a tool with which explorers and conquistadors could justify their actions. The Papacy acted as an arbiter, trying to hold the Christian kingdoms together while the medieval world was being splintered with new scientific and geographical discoveries.

When Europeans first came face to face with peoples of different cultures, the immediate response was to try to convert them to Christianity. Prince Henry the Navigator (1394–1460) saw his encouragement of Portuguese exploration as a crusade to drive the Moors from West Africa and bring Christianity to the heathen. The Pope, who was also committed to driving the Muslims from Africa, gave Portugal a monopoly over African trade in 1481.

Both parties were inspired by the legend of Prester John. It was said that a Christian country in central Africa ruled by the mysterious Prester John had been cut off from the rest of Christendom by the advance of Islam. The hope was to discover this kingdom and enlist the mysterious king's aid in driving the Moors from North Africa in a two-pronged assault. The Pope stepped in diplomatically between Portugal and Spain to smooth over any potential areas of conflict until contact could be made with these African Christians.

European concepts of just wars and crusades were also changing. Although Henry the Navigator represented a new breed of crusader who saw exploration and trade as religious tools as powerful as conquest, other European figures adopted more conventional views, since they were still engaged in direct religious conflict. These attitudes altered as the threat posed by the Moors diminished.

For example, Alfonso V of Portugal was preoccupied with attacking the Moors in North Africa, while his son John II saw the establishment of trading settlements along the African coast as the best form of attack. Similarly, as soon as Ferdinand and Isabella of Spain completed their conquest of Granada, Isabella authorized Columbus's first voyage of discovery and gave him a religious banner blessed by the Pope to plant on whatever lands he found.

The struggle for order

For 40 years, a split in the Church had led to there being two ruling Popes, one based in Rome and the other at Avignon, in southern France. The Great Schism, which ended in

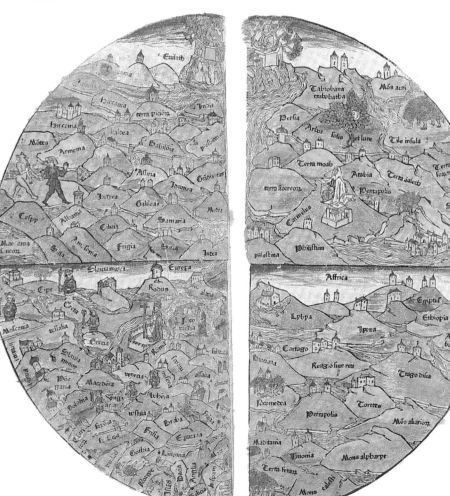

Below: Map of the world printed in the Rudimentum Novitorium *at Lübeck, the text of which was intended as education for young ecclesiastics.*

1095	c.1115–42	1190	1308	1317	1378–1417	1380	1469
Pope Urban begins the first Crusade to liberate the Holy Land from infidels.	Paris becomes a center of religious education thanks to the efforts of Peter Abelard.	Germany's Teutonic Knights defend Christians in Palestine and Syria.	The Papacy moves to Avignon, France.	Nomadic Muslim Arabs overthrow Christian Makkura, Africa.	The Papacy is split between Avignon and Rome in the Great Schism.	The Bible is translated into English.	Birth of Guru Nanak, founder of Sikhism.

1417 when Pope Martin V was elected as sole pontiff, devastated Christians and damaged the Papacy. The controversy led to a reappraisal of the Church, and reformers throughout Europe called for changes in its administration and privileges. These complaints would continue for another century, until they led to the Protestant Reformation. The Pope's approval of the crusading zeal of early explorers was one way to deflect criticism.

Criticism of Church taxation led to a conflict between the Pope and secular princes over revenue and the right to appoint bishops. By the mid-15th century this had been largely resolved, but in the process the Church lost both income and control over its appointees. By the time Pope Sixtus IV (1471–84) became involved in solving the disputes of the Portuguese and the Spanish, the Papacy was reeling from a series of defeats.

By involving European princes and academics in launching the Age of Discovery, the Papacy hoped to avoid further setbacks. The scheme may have had merit, but nobody could save the Papacy from itself. Pope Innocent VIII died in the year Columbus sailed for America, and his successor was Alexander VI

(1492–1503). This infamous Borgia Pope epitomized the corruption that had beset the Church, and even his participation in the discussions that lead to the ultimate Portuguese and Spanish deal—the Treaty of Tordesillas in 1494—failed to save the Church from its slide toward the Reformation.

Above left: Richard Haldingham's world map, which placed Jerusalem at the center of the world.

Above: Pope Alexander VI "The Borgia Pope," from a Vatican fresco by Bernardino Pinturicchio, c.1492.

1492	1494	1521	1530	1549	1551	1559	1562–1598
The Moors are driven out of Granada, Spain.	The Tordesillas treaty divides new territories between Spain and Portugal.	Protestant reformer Martin Luther is expelled from the Roman Catholic Church.	The Church of England is established by Henry VIII.	Christian Missionary Francis Xavier reaches Japan.	French Parliament refuses to let the Jesuits into France.	A Jesuit college is founded in Munich.	The French wars of religion.

CHAPTER TWO

An AFRICAN PRELUDE

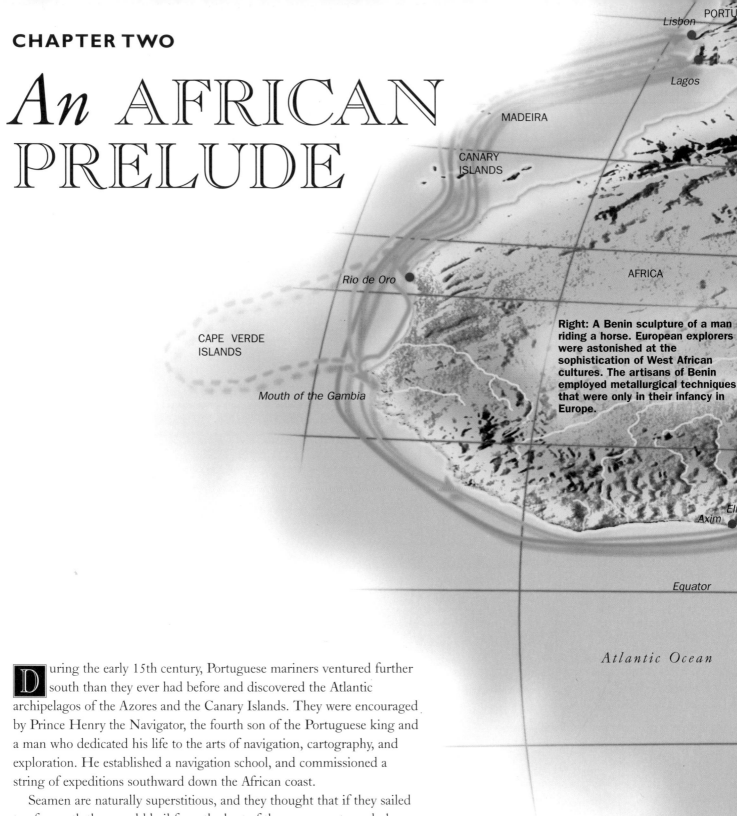

PORTUGAL
Lisbon
Lagos
MADEIRA
CANARY
ISLANDS
AFRICA
Rio de Oro
CAPE VERDE
ISLANDS
Mouth of the Gambia
Elmina
Axim
Equator
Atlantic Ocean

Right: A Benin sculpture of a man riding a horse. European explorers were astonished at the sophistication of West African cultures. The artisans of Benin employed metallurgical techniques that were only in their infancy in Europe.

D uring the early 15th century, Portuguese mariners ventured further south than they ever had before and discovered the Atlantic archipelagos of the Azores and the Canary Islands. They were encouraged by Prince Henry the Navigator, the fourth son of the Portuguese king and a man who dedicated his life to the arts of navigation, cartography, and exploration. He established a navigation school, and commissioned a string of expeditions southward down the African coast.

Seamen are naturally superstitious, and they thought that if they sailed too far south they would boil from the heat of the sun, or enter a dark world of treacherous seas—the underside of the earth. Gradually, they rolled back the curtain to reveal the African continent and, by 1450, they reached the tropical coast of West Africa. By 1487 they had ventured as far as Africa's southernmost point. They found a continent of great mystery.

If Victorian explorers saw Africa as the "Dark Continent" because of its vast tracts of uncharted territory, to the 15th-century Portuguese it must have seemed far more mysterious. The African people themselves were equally exotic, and these first Europeans encountered great empires, well-established cities, and a level of technical sophistication that surprised many observers. It is futile to speculate how these African cultures might have developed if they had been left in peace. Following the Portuguese voyages of exploration, Africa's fate was decided by Europeans.

The Expeditions

Gonçalo Cabral &
Gil Eannes 1432–35

Alvise de Cadamosto 1455–56
Diogo Gomes 1458–59

Diogo Cão 1482–85

Bartolomeu Dias 1487–88

PAIN

Mediterranean Sea

Mouth of the Niger

Mouth of the Congo

Right: King John II had stonemasons carve tall columns, topped by the royal coat of arms that his explorers could erect along the coast of Africa to claim the territory in the name of Portugal. Called a *padrão*, **this one, erected by Diogo Cão, was found at Cape Cross, and is also inscribed in the name of São Agostinho.**

Tropic of Cancer

Cape Cross

CAPE OF GOOD HOPE

INDIAN OCEAN

PRINCE HENRY
the NAVIGATOR

1394 to 1460

Below: Prince Henry the Navigator stands at the prow of a monument to Portugal's maritime past in the port of Lisbon.

More than any other Renaissance figure, Portugal's Prince Henry the Navigator personified the quest for geographical knowledge. Due to his encouragement, Portugal emerged as the leading maritime power of the time, and he has been credited with almost single-handedly launching the Age of Discovery.

During the late 14th century, the greatest threat to Portugal was the neighboring Kingdom of Castile (united with Spain in 1479). King John I of Portugal looked toward England, Portugal's most important trading partner for an ally. He married Philippa, the daughter of England's John of Gaunt, and the resulting defensive alliance secured Portugal's frontiers. The marriage also resulted in the birth of four sons: Duarte, Ferdinand, Pedro, and Henry. The princes were given a formal chivalric education, and were first-blooded in battle in 1414, when it was decided to launch an attack on the Moorish North African port of Ceuta. Prince Henry helped to organize the invasion fleet, and, in August, the Portuguese launched a surprise attack on the port, which fell after a fierce struggle. Ceuta lay on the edge of a trading network that spanned much of Muslim Africa. The Portuguese were able to gather valuable economic and geographic information that would help in their effort to extend the Portuguese trading sphere.

Prince Henry, imbued with the religious zeal of the crusader, saw a policy of Portuguese expansion as a way to continue the war against the

Moors. This crusade would be a maritime one, so he withdrew from court life and established himself at Sagres, a peninsula on the southwestern tip of Portugal. Here he turned the palace into the center of maritime study. A naval arsenal, a chapel, a library, and a "school of navigation" were added to his residential complex, and soon Sagres became a training ground for a new breed of Portuguese mariners. The aim was to provide a clearing house for information, supplied by a well-trained group of mariners. Master Jacome of Majorca was appointed royal cartographer, charged with transcribing the latest information onto a series of constantly updated charts. As such, Prince Henry's institution at Sagres was the first cartographic center in Europe.

The ships themselves were an equally vital part of the scheme. The caravel (*see pages 39–41*) was perfectly designed for the task: responsive, rugged, and capable of holding enough supplies for lengthy voyages. Most of Henry's voyages were trading ventures, designed to pay for themselves. In an effort to push back the boundaries of the known world, he offered incentives for discovery, and even underwrote unsuccessful voyages if they led to fresh information. He chose his sea captains wisely; only those who were prepared to risk venturing into the unknown, undaunted by medieval superstitions, were selected.

The most prevalent superstition centered around the "Sea of Darkness." The Canary Islands marked the boundary of the known world, and the region beyond Cape Bojador on the Moroccan coast of Africa was the beginning of this sea, a boundary between the living world and the underworld.

During the first years of Henry's maritime strategy, the Portuguese achieved a number of spectacular successes that increased their confidence. The Azores, Madeira, and parts of the Canary Islands were colonized, establishing bases from which further expeditions could be supported. In 1434 Gil Eannes passed the psychological barrier of Cape Bojador and proved that the "Sea of Darkness" did not exist. Alfonso Baldaya ventured even further in 1436, reaching Cape Blanc, more than 500 miles beyond Cape Bojador. Conflict with the Moors in North Africa, followed by a Portuguese civil war and the threat of a renewed war with Castile, served to halt Prince Henry's maritime strategy for almost 15 years from the 1440s, but peace allowed a resumption of his scheme. By the time a new wave of captains was dispatched in the 1450s, Prince Henry was old, ill, and frail. Before he died in 1460, his captains brought him two more successes: the discovery of the Cape Verde Islands and the passage of Cape Palmas, opening the way for the Portuguese development of the Gulf of Guinea. During his lifetime, Henry the Navigator had revolutionized Portuguese maritime affairs. After his death, the captains he encouraged would go on to make even greater discoveries.

Above: Prince Henry the Navigator encouraged his mariners to expand the boundaries of the known world.

NORTH *and* WEST AFRICA *in the* 15th CENTURY

When the Portuguese captured the North African port of Ceuta in 1414 they gained a useful foothold in Muslim Africa. The Portuguese portrayed the voyages of exploration as a crusade, a means to limit Muslim influence in Africa. But further south they discovered a continent of large empires, thriving cities, vibrant cultures, and wealth.

The North African coast was the springboard. Following the fall of the Roman Empire, the coast was settled by Vandals, who coexisted with the inhabitants of the former Roman African provinces until the late seventh century. In AD 622 Islam was founded in Mecca, and by the middle of the century the new religious movement had swept through the Middle East and Africa like a wave. Muslim rule was established in Tunisia in 670; 13 years later the Muslim vanguard had reached the Atlantic coast of Morocco. By the early eighth century the Muslims had crossed into Spain and Portugal, and reached France in 732.

What was even more remarkable than these conquests was the Moorish ability to stimulate the economy within years of settling in a province. While the Christians of Europe were thrust into the "Dark Ages," Islam was seen as a tolerant religion, encouraging religious diversity, education, and science. The people they conquered were offered new prosperity and membership of what would be described today as "a new world order." Unlike the later wave of European imperialism in Africa, Muslim domination involved participation rather than foreign imposition.

The unity of the Islamic world was short lived, however. By the 11th century it was divided into allied but distinct caliphates or regions.

A poor Christian kingdom

One of the driving forces behind Portuguese exploration in Africa was the desire to find the mythical Christian kingdom of Prester John. The legend stemmed from Christian settlements in the Upper Nile area that had been isolated from Christian Europe after the Arab conquests of the seventh century. Nubia remained a Christian region until the 13th century, when it fell prey to invaders. Further south, a Christian enclave continued in modern Ethiopia, whose kings traced their ancestry back to King Solomon. In 1488 Portuguese explorer Pedro de Covilham reached Ethiopia in search of Prester John, but he considered the communities there too impoverished to fit his concept of a rich Christian empire. The search continued into the mid-16th century, when it became apparent that no such place existed.

West Africa in the late 15th century was a complex region, where a collection of semi-independent coastal tribes such as the Mandinka, Akwamu, Yoruba, Benin, and Ibo peoples appeared willing to trade with the Portuguese and act as agents for the richer states inland. The main trading commodities were ivory, slaves, and gold, all of which had been traded to the north, but the establishment of coastal trading stations altered the economy of the coastal regions and the Niger basin.

Although the great Mali Empire was in decline by this time, the Wolof people and, to some extent, the Mandinka saw themselves as descendants of the once-powerful state based in the Senegal basin. By the time the Portuguese arrived, the Mali Empire had been replaced by

Below: *Terracotta head from Ife, Nigeria, c.12th–15th century.*

c.1070	1076	1135	c.1250	1317
Trans-Saharan travelers spread the Islam faith through West Africa.	The kingdom of Ghana is destroyed by Almoravids.	Northwest Africa and Muslim Spain are dominated by Almohads.	The Benin kingdom is founded.	Nomadic Muslim Arabs overthrow Christian Makkura, Africa.

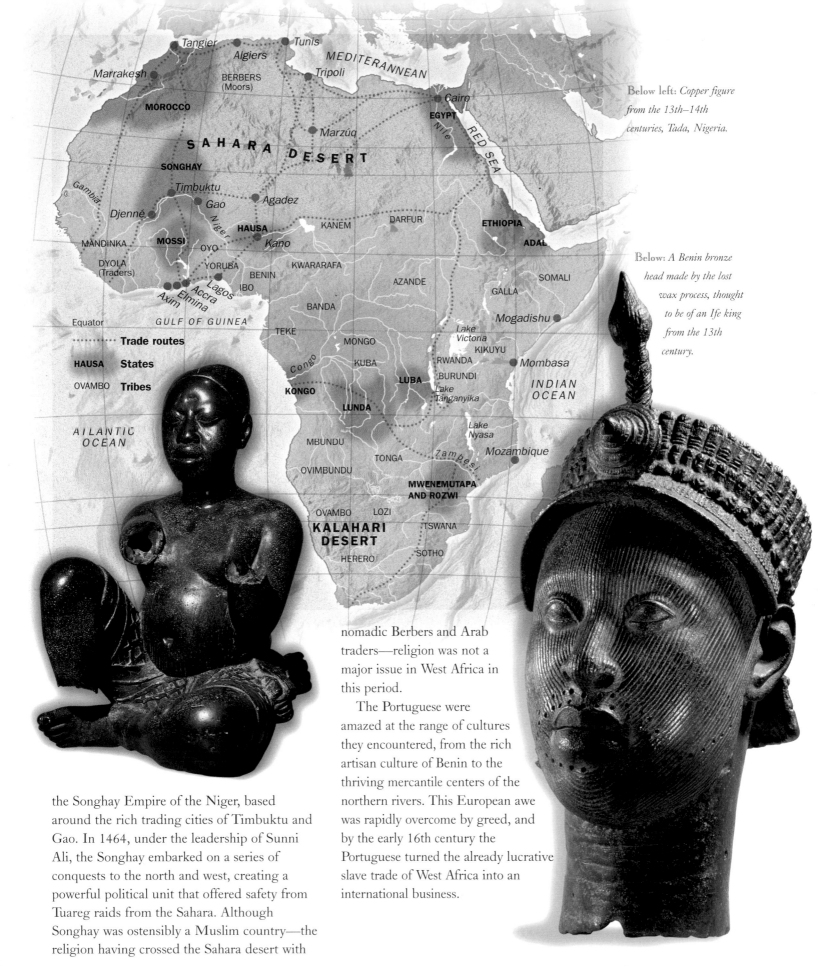

Below left: *Copper figure from the 13th–14th centuries, Tada, Nigeria.*

Below: *A Benin bronze head made by the lost wax process, thought to be of an Ife king from the 13th century.*

Trade routes ·······
HAUSA **States**
OVAMBO **Tribes**

nomadic Berbers and Arab traders—religion was not a major issue in West Africa in this period.

The Portuguese were amazed at the range of cultures they encountered, from the rich artisan culture of Benin to the thriving mercantile centers of the northern rivers. This European awe was rapidly overcome by greed, and by the early 16th century the Portuguese turned the already lucrative slave trade of West Africa into an international business.

the Songhay Empire of the Niger, based around the rich trading cities of Timbuktu and Gao. In 1464, under the leadership of Sunni Ali, the Songhay embarked on a series of conquests to the north and west, creating a powerful political unit that offered safety from Tuareg raids from the Sahara. Although Songhay was ostensibly a Muslim country—the religion having crossed the Sahara desert with

1352	1464	1508	c.1510	1570	1578	1580	1591
Ibn Battuta explores the Sahara Desert.	Sunni Ali, leader Songhay Empire, expands to the north and west.	The Portuguese begin to colonize Mozambique.	African slaves are first transported to America.	Kanem-Bornu becomes the major Niger-to-Nile power.	Portuguese areas in Northwest Africa are wiped out by Moroccans.	The Dutch make Guinea the site of their first African trading posts.	Spanish and Portuguese mercenaries destroy the Songhay Empire.

GONÇALO CABRAL *and*
GIL EANNES

c1386
to
c1447

c1395
to
c1445

Many of the most important mid-15th century discoveries were due to the encouragement of Portugal's Prince Henry the Navigator. In 1431 he sent Gonçalo Cabral west into the Atlantic in search of a mythical group of islands. He found nothing, so Prince Henry sent him back again. This time, in 1432, Cabral made a landfall on Santa Maria, one of the islands of the Azores. Subsequent voyages by Cabral revealed more of the island group. Together with the Canary Islands and Madeira, this important discovery provided the launching pad for many of the most important voyages of discovery.

Gil Eannes holds a particularly important place in the ranks of the Portuguese late-medieval maritime explorers. He was the first mariner to pass Cape Bojador (now in the Moroccan-occupied western Sahara), just past the Canary Islands, following the instructions of Prince Henry to probe south down the African coast.

Eannes was raised in the prince's royal household, where he served as a squire, indicating that he came from Portugal's leading nobility. In 1433 he was given command of a royal ship and ordered to sail it down the African coast and to round Cape Bojador. Until his expedition, the cape was feared by mariners, who told mythical tales of the people and creatures who lay further south, in the tempestuous "Sea of Darkness." It was difficult and extremely hazardous to navigate past because treacherous shoals and reefs extended far out into the rough seas.

Unlike later Portuguese explorers, Eannes was no seaman; his appointment was reflected by the later Spanish system where a nobleman was appointed captain of the ship and made all the decisions relating to the expedition, while a ship's master or pilot operated the ship and managed all the aspects of seamanship and navigation. It was only in the second half of the 15th century that a career as a mariner was seen as a suitable occupation for a young Portuguese nobleman, a change in outlook encouraged by Prince Henry the Navigator.

Sea of Darkness

During his first 1433 expedition, Eannes sailed down the Moroccan coast, then on to the Canary Islands, where he planned to take on provisions before continuing south to Cape Bojador. The young nobleman listened to the protests of his master and the crew, and gave in to pressure to return without attempting to pass the cape. When Prince Henry was told of the expedition's failure, he ordered Gil Eannes to undertake the voyage again, forbidding him to return until he had passed Cape Bojador.

The second attempt was undertaken in the following year, 1434, and Eannes pressed on to the waters around the cape. Assisted by a skilled pilot, the expedition picked its way through rough seas and treacherous shoals. Once past Cape Bojador, the Portuguese were surprised to find that the sea was extremely calm; its waters bore no relation to the "Sea of Darkness" of maritime myth. The coastline offered little in the way of vegetation or habitation, but Eannes gathered samples of an herb, which he named "Rose of Santa Maria," as evidence that he had sailed as far south as that. The expedition reversed course and followed its newly charted course through the Cape Bojador shoals, and returned to Lisbon. Prince Henry was delighted, since Portugal had broken through a psychological barrier imposed by medieval superstition.

Eannes was sent on a third expedition, to probe down the coast beyond the cape and report on what he found. He left Lisbon in 1435 with two ships, the second commanded by fellow explorer Alfonso Goncalves Baldaya. Eannes passed Cape Bojador, and this time continued south for just over 200 miles. He later reported that the coastline was bereft of life or vegetation.

Close to the Tropic of Cancer the Portuguese encountered a fishing settlement, the first sign of human habitation they had seen. They traded with the settlers, and then turned for home to report their findings. Gil Eannes returned to court duties, and his mantle as a maritime explorer was taken over by men like Dinis Dias, Diogo Cão, and Bartolomeu Dias.

15th century Portuguese mariners believed that a "Sea of Darkness" lay beyond then inhospitable Cape Bojador.

Inset: A rare statue to Gil Eannes celebrates one of Portugal's great unsung maritime explorers.

ALVISE *da* CADAMOSTO *and* DIOGO GOMES

c1432
to
c1480

c1440
to
c1482

For over 40 years during the 15th century, Prince Henry the Navigator encouraged Portuguese captains to explore ever further down the African coast, only temporarily halted by a Portuguese civil war. The death of Prince Pedro, Henry's brother, brought an end to the conflict, and the voyages recommenced in the mid-1450s, 20 years after the voyages of Gil Eannes. Prince Henry recruited a number of prominent sea captains, one of whom was Alvise da Cadamosto, a Venetian merchant, reputedly an Italian nobleman who became a trading captain to pay off his family debts. By entering the service of Prince Henry, he was also allowed to break into the virtual monopoly of Portuguese trade with Moorish African ports.

Da Cadamosto left Lisbon on March 22, 1455, setting course for Madeira. He continued to the Canary Islands and the African coast, sailing further out to sea than Eannes had, and made landfall at Cape Blanc, 300 miles south of the Tropic of Cancer. Further to the south he reached the island of Arguim, the most southerly point reached by Portuguese traders. There, a fort guarded the anchorage that served

as a trading post for gold and slaves, where Portuguese merchants traded with Arab merchants who traveled there from inland cities such as Timbuktu.

Da Cadamosto resupplied his ship and continued south into uncharted territory. He reached the mouth of the Senegal river, an area populated by people who traded with Arguim. He traded with the Senegalese, then moved south of Cape Verde to the mouth of the Gambia river. Slave traders provided the last of the human cargo he sought, and da Cadamosto returned to Lisbon. His voyage was a commercial success, and his detailed account of the journey ingratiated him with Prince Henry.

A year later, in May 1456, da Cadamosto set sail for Africa again, in command of three caravels, to combine trading with the gathering of information for Prince Henry. He led his ships past the Canary Islands and directly to Cape Blanc, where his small flotilla encountered a fierce storm. The ships, forced to run with the storm for a week, were swept away from the coast in a southwesterly direction.

When it abated they found themselves close

Right: *The Canary Islands became a vital jumping-off point for further southward exploration of Africa's western coast.*

to two hitherto-unknown islands, part of the Cape Verde archipelago. This important discovery would provide a useful landmark and watering place for future explorers. Although it is unclear if da Cadamosto was the original discoverer of the islands or not, he has generally been credited with the find. He gathered his ships and sailed west to the Gambia River. After trading up the river again, he sailed south for another 100 miles to the Bissagos islands before returning home.

Gomes sights Guinea coast

Diogo Gomes was the next of Henry's captains to extend Portugal's reach. In 1458 the Portuguese followed da Cadamosto's route to the Gambia River, then continued down the coast for another 900 miles. He passed the Bissagos islands and finally reached the point he called Cape Palmas, which marks the place where the coast curves east into the Gulf of Guinea and the Bight of Benin. For the first time, Portuguese mariners had rounded the corner of West Africa, and were able to penetrate the rich slave- and gold-trading areas of the Guinea Coast.

Gomes returned to Lisbon in early 1459 with his holds filled with both trading commodities. Unfortunately, on his arrival Prince Henry was

on his deathbed; the royal navigator died in the following year. Gomes went on to establish regular trading links with the Cape Verde islands and the Guinea Coast.

These last trading explorers, operating under the protection of Prince Henry, had finally reached the prime African coastal market places, and completely vindicated the monarch's policy of encouraging exploration.

Above: *In 1458, the Portuguese rounded the corner of West Africa and sighted the Guinea Coast for the first time.*

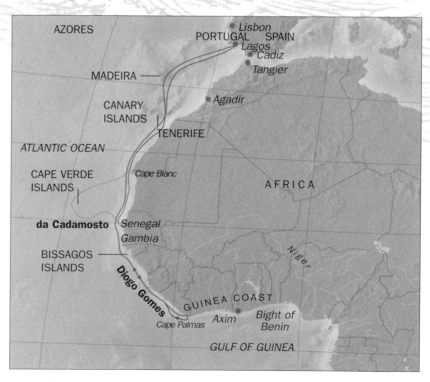

DIOGO CÃO

1450 to 1486

Below: A Benin-made ivory salt cellar depicting Portuguese noblemen around the base. The lid is surmounted by a Portuguese caravel.

When Diogo Cão discovered the Congo River, he had traveled further south than any other explorer of his day; his exploration formed part of Portugal's remorseless advance toward the southern tip of Africa and the riches that lay beyond it.

Although his roots are obscure, Cão was probably of humble origins, born the son of a soldier in the northern Portuguese garrison town of Vila Real. Around 1464, Cão joined the Portuguese navy as an apprentice seaman, and served in naval operations in the western Mediterranean, off the African coast, and in the Atlantic. By 1480, at the latest, he had risen to the rank of captain and was regarded as a skilled mariner.

As the Portuguese spread south to encompass the West African coast, Cão increasingly operated in African waters, fought off local tribal attacks, Spanish or Arab privateers, and ensured the safety of the embryonic Portuguese trading settlements that were being established along the coast. In 1482 Diogo Cão's repute was such that King John II of Portugal appointed him the commander of an expedition designed to extend Portuguese territory further south below the Bight of Benin.

In June 1482, Cão set sail from Lisbon in a single ship. Apart from supplies, the hold was filled with limestone pillars that King John had ordered Portuguese stonemasons to cut. Each the height of a man and topped with a cross, these *padrão*s were inscribed with the king's name, the date they were erected, and the name of the expedition leader. They were designed to be set at conspicuous points along the coast, to reinforce Portugal's claim to the territory they were erected in. Similar *padrão*s were carried by other, later Portuguese explorers.

Cão sailed to the Moroccan coast then on to the Canary Islands for reprovisioning. Passing around Cape Verde and Cape Palmas, Cão entered the Gulf of Guinea and followed the coast east, past the settlements on the Gold Coast, into the Bight of Benin. In October he reached the Cabo Santa Catarina (now Pointe Ste. Catherine), south of Cape Lopez in Gabon. This marked the most southerly point reached by a Portuguese explorer.

Lost beyond Cape Cross

Cão followed the coast for another 400 miles, until, in late December 1482, he came to the mouth of what was clearly a substantial river. He erected his first *padrão* on the southern shore of the river mouth. The local Bakongo called the river "Nzadi" (Great Water); Cão

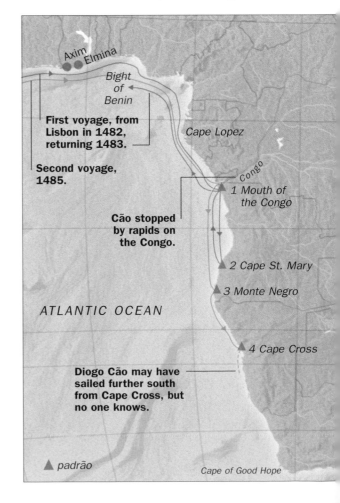

Axim Elmina
Bight of Benin

First voyage, from Lisbon in 1482, returning 1483.

Second voyage, 1485.

Cape Lopez

Congo

Cão stopped by rapids on the Congo.

1 Mouth of the Congo

2 Cape St. Mary

3 Monte Negro

ATLANTIC OCEAN

4 Cape Cross

Diogo Cão may have sailed further south from Cape Cross, but no one knows.

▲ padrão

Cape of Good Hope

believed it might lead to the mythical inland Christian kingdom of Prester John, especially when the Bakongo told of a royal city upriver, the capital of the Mani Kongo people, and their king, the Lord of the Kongo.

Cão named the river the Congo, dispatched slaves upstream with gifts, and spent months charting and exploring the lower reaches of the river and the coastline near its mouth before he continued to sail south. When he reached a headland he named Capo Santa Maria (Cape St. Mary), 500 miles south of the Congo in what is now Angola in August 1483, he erected another *padrão*, then returned to the Congo. He found no sign of his slave emissaries, so he captured Bakongo as hostages and returned to Lisbon, arriving in April 1484.

Delighted with Cão's accomplishments, King John II knighted the explorer and sponsored a second expedition. Cão set sail again in 1485 with the now-Christian Bakongo hostages. Once he arrived on the Congo, he sailed upstream for almost 100 miles to reach what is now Matadi, before rapids halted his progress. Returning to the sea, he sailed down the coast and reached Monte Negro and Cape Cross (in modern Namibia), some 1,200 miles south of the

Congo. It is not recorded if Cão returned safely to Lisbon, or whether he was lost in a shipwreck or died at the hands of tribesmen. We do know that he achieved the most southerly point at that time because of the two *padrão*s he erected at Monte Negro and Cape Cross. Since slaves captured by the expedition did reach Lisbon, historians consider it likely that Diogo Cão simply died of disease while at sea.

Above: King John II of Portugal, known as "El Perfecto," continued the promotion of maritime exploration after the death of Henry the Navigator.

Above left: A plaque depicting Benin warriors.

BARTOLOMEU DIAS

c1450 to 1500

Right: Dias named the southernmost point of Africa the Cape of Storms after the ferocious weather he encountered there. Ironically he drowned off the landmark in 1500 when his ship foundered in a storm.

etails surrounding the background of Bartolomeu Dias, the first European mariner to sail around Africa's Cape of Good Hope and into the Indian Ocean, remain obscure, although some historians insist he was related to a family that produced several leading mariners, including Dinis Dias, who reached Cape Verde (1455). Bartolomeu's first historical mention is in 1481, when he participated in an expedition to the West African coast. Five years later he was a part of the court of Portuguese King John II, with the responsibility of overseeing royal warehouses.

In 1487 Bartolomeu Dias was given command of a flotilla of three ships, with orders to find the southernmost tip of Africa, a point

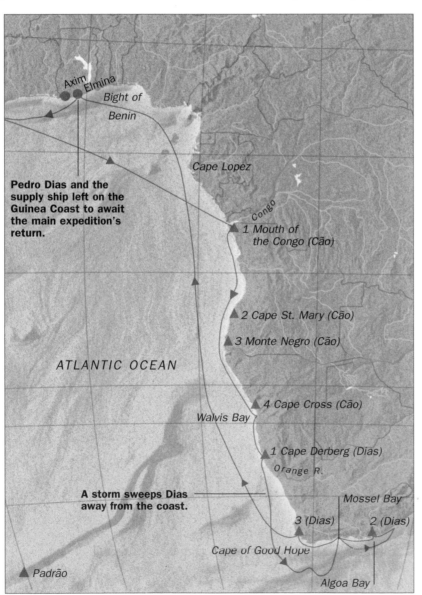

Pedro Dias and the supply ship left on the Guinea Coast to await the main expedition's return.

Axim Elmina
Bight of Benin
Cape Lopez
Congo
1 Mouth of the Congo (Cão)
2 Cape St. Mary (Cão)
3 Monte Negro (Cão)
ATLANTIC OCEAN
4 Cape Cross (Cão)
Walvis Bay
1 Cape Derberg (Dias)
Orange R.
A storm sweeps Dias away from the coast.
Mossel Bay
3 (Dias) 2 (Dias)
Cape of Good Hope
Padrão
Algoa Bay

referred to as *Prassum Promontorium*. Once it was found, he was to look for the land of Prester John, the mythical Christian king who supposedly ruled over large tracts of Africa.

The expedition sailed from Lisbon in late July 1487 with Bartolomeu in command; his brother, Pedro Dias, took charge of one of the three ships, a supply vessel. Bartolomeu carried African interpreters aboard his ship, and all down the African coast he anchored, traded with local Africans, and asked for information about Prester John and the *Prassum Promontorium*. The supply ship commanded by Pedro Dias was left on the Guinea Coast to provide provisions for the return voyage.

On Cape Cross, on what is now the coast of Namibia, they reached the stone cross (*padrão*) erected by Diogo Cão four years earlier. The marker indicated the most southerly point reached by Portuguese explorers. After a ladfall in Walvis Bay, Bartolomeu Dias and his men sailed on southward and he erected his first *padrão* near what is now Cape Dernberg.

By Christmas Dias had reached the mouth of a river (the Orange River) when a severe storm swept them south-southeast and away from the coast. The storm took two weeks to pass, and when it abated, Bartolomeu Dias sailed east, hoping to reach the African coast again. After a further two weeks it became apparent that they had been driven past the *Prassum Promontorium*. Dias changed course to follow a northerly heading until February 3, 1488, when he made landfall on the South African coast.

Confused by geography

Dias anchored in a bay he named Bahia dos Vaquieros (now Mossel Bay) and went ashore. A skirmish with local Hottentot tribesmen indicated that the anchorage was not safe, and Dias sailed further to the east. Ironically, he was not aware that he had rounded the *Prassum Promontorium* because he was confused by the geography.

A further 250 miles east, Dias reached the anchorage of Algoa Bay and landed on an island that he named Santa Cruz. By this time the crew of both ships were eager to return home, and it was only after great persuasion that Dias convinced them to continue a little further.

Approximately 50 miles beyond the bay he encountered another river, at a point where the coast started to curve to the northeast. Dias named the river Rio de Infante (now the Great Fish River), but its confluence marked the furthest Dias could go—his crew refused to sail any further. Dias turned his flotilla around and sailed west. After rounding Cape Agulhas (the southernmost point of Africa), Dias turned north, then saw the *Prassum Promontorium* ahead of him. It is said that he named it Capo Tormentoso, in recognition of the storms he encountered there and that it was King John II who named it the Cape of Good Hope. Certainly the latter name was being used soon after the return of Bartolomeu Dias.

When the expedition reached the Guinea Coast on the return voyage, Pedro Dias and the majority of his nine crew were found dead from disease, and local Africans had looted most of the provisions. The last leg of the voyage home proved uneventful, and Dias returned to Lisbon in late December 1488.

He continued to advise the crown on maritime affairs and, in 1497, he traveled with the da Gama expedition as far as Elmina on the West African coast, where he established a trading post. In 1500 he took part in Pedro Cabral's voyage, but his ship foundered in a storm off the Cape of Good Hope on May 24, 1500. For Dias, "Capo Tormentoso" was a more appropriate name for the headland.

Below: Bartolomeu Dias pushed Portugal's sphere of influence around the southern tip of Africa and into the Indian Ocean.

Below: The Cape of Storms (Capo Tormentoso) was renamed about 1490, with the more benign title of the Cape of Good Hope.

CHAPTER THREE

WIND *and* CURRENT

NORTH AMERICA

WEST
INDIES

SOUTH AMERICA

When Portuguese explorers discovered the Azores, Canary Islands, and the Cape Verde archipelago, they unwittingly found the perfect set of stepping stones to help future explorers span the Atlantic Ocean between Europe and the Americas. The islands' waters benefited from the winds and currents that were vital to help the frail sailing ships of the period make a safe and speedy transatlantic passage. Later, the North Atlantic equivalent of the same natural phenomenon was used to help ships make the return voyage. Within years, it became standard practice for vessels to sail to the Americas aided by the North Equatorial Current, and use the North Atlantic Drift to hasten the return voyage. Although the precise details of these currents were only understood in the 19th century, 16th-century mariners were aware of the basic principles behind them.

As European mariners reached even further afield, they became aware that the same pattern was repeated throughout the globe. A southerly route across the Pacific, passing through the South Sea islands, was complemented by a more northerly route from Asia to America, riding along the North Pacific Current. Similarly, Vasco da Gama and Pedro Cabral pioneered a fast route from Portugal to India by swinging well out into the South Atlantic to take advantage of the Trade Winds, before passing far south of Africa to head east, using the West Wind Drift.

Everywhere these explorers went, they looked for ways to take advantage of the phenomena of prevailing wind and current to assist them. They also learned the signs that indicated when nature would be less helpful, and came to understand the seasonal phases of Atlantic hurricanes and Pacific typhoons.

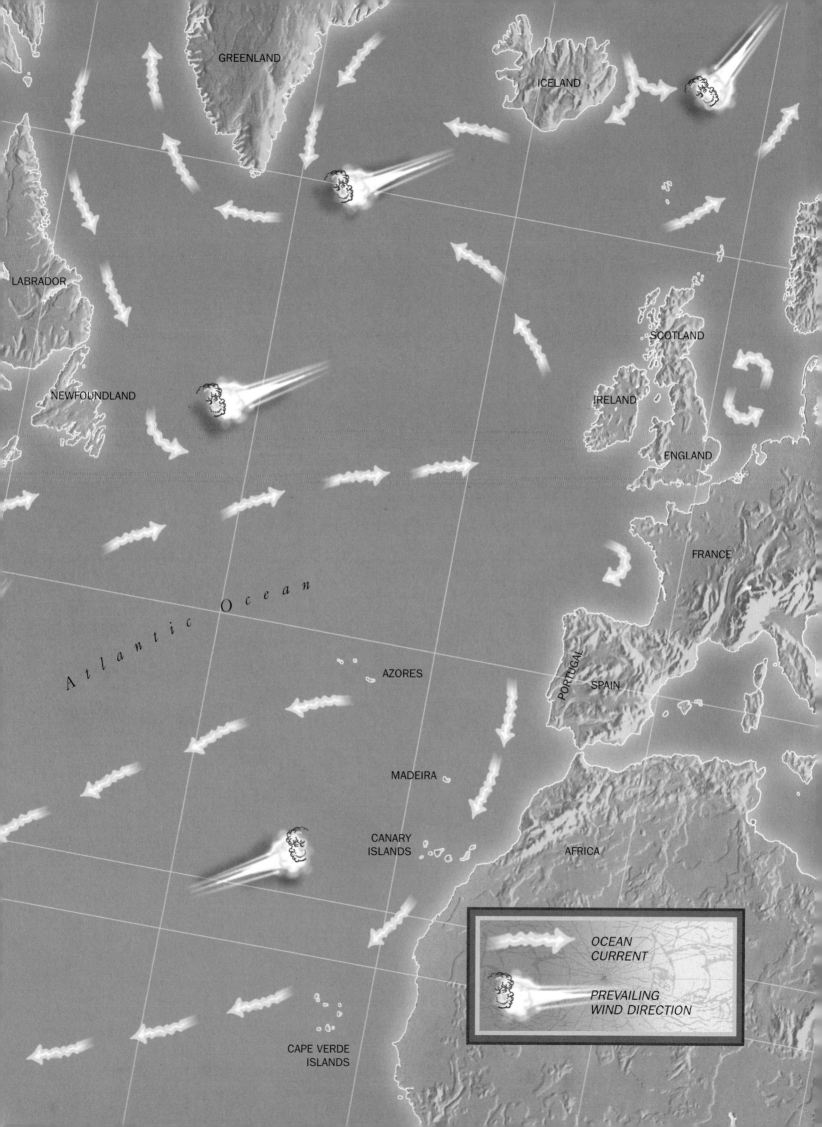

GREENLAND

ICELAND

LABRADOR

SCOTLAND

NEWFOUNDLAND

IRELAND

ENGLAND

FRANCE

Atlantic Ocean

AZORES

PORTUGAL

SPAIN

MADEIRA

CANARY
ISLANDS

AFRICA

CAPE VERDE
ISLANDS

OCEAN
CURRENT

PREVAILING
WIND DIRECTION

SHIPS *of* DISCOVERY

When Christopher Columbus sailed across the Atlantic in 1492, he did so in a vessel that was well designed for the task; a steady, seaworthy craft that could carry the large volume of stores needed for a transatlantic voyage. The *Santa Maria* and its two accompanying vessels were the result of a long evolution of European medieval ship types.

The cog

During the early Middle Ages, the standard merchant ship in northern Europe was the knorr, a vessel based on a Viking design. Originally pointed at both bow and stern, its hull was composed of overlapping strakes or planks riveted together in a method known as clinker building. It was open-decked, and used a single mast carrying a large square sail.

A single large steering oar near the stern acted as a rudder. By the 13th century the oar was replaced with a rudder and tiller, which meant the rounded stern had to be replaced by a square one. Raised platforms at bow and stern provided shelter, but principally they were fighting platforms and lookout positions. Hulls became deeper to enable larger cargoes to be carried and to improve seaworthiness. This form of craft, known as the cog, rapidly became the dominant ship type found in northern waters.

By this time, European shipbuilders were well aware of a Mediterranean style of shell-first construction, or carvel building. Planks were laid edge to edge on a pre-constructed series of frames and pinned together. The seams between planks were caulked to provide a watertight join.

These craft also used a large triangular sail, supported from a single mainmast. This lateen sail allowed Mediterranean ships to sail far closer into the wind than their square-sailed northern rivals. The cog developed throughout the Middle Ages, and superstructure height and hull size steadily increased.

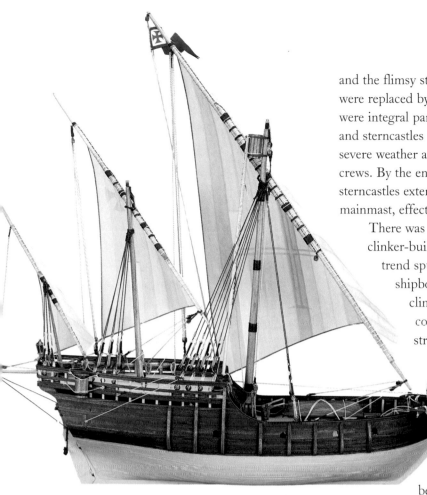

The caravel

By the start of the 15th century, ships combined features of both Northern and Central European design. The ultimate expression of the Mediterranean shipbuilding school of the time was the caravel, which relied heavily on Northern European features.

It combined the stern rudder and flat stern of the cog with a carvel-built hull and two or three masts carrying lateen sails. The caravel was the first of two main types of ship used for the discoveries of the late 15th and early 16th centuries—two of Christopher Columbus's ships were caravels.

At least in Spain and Portugal, caravels were also adapted to carry a square mainsail when required, which was faster when sailing with the prevailing wind and easier to handle. This lightly built, responsive variant—the caravela redonda—was widely used by the Portuguese during their explorations of the African coast and the Indian Ocean.

The carrack

The second major ship of discovery was grounded more in northern shipbuilding traditions. By the late 15th century, the cog had developed into a vessel capable of carrying two or three masts. Ships' hulls were more streamlined,

and the flimsy structures at the bow and stern were replaced by more substantial features that were integral parts of the hull. These forecastles and sterncastles made ships less vulnerable to severe weather and gave increased comfort for crews. By the end of the century some sterncastles extended as far forward as the mainmast, effectively an extra deck.

There was also a gradual shift from clinker-built hulls to carvel-built ones, a trend spurred on by the development of shipborne artillery. The integrity of clinker-built hulls was compromised by gunports, so strongly armed ships had to be carvel-built. These ships combined a strong frame with a streamlined hull and a cargo capacity greater than that of Mediterranean ships of the period. This type of vessel became known as a nao by the Spanish and Portuguese and a carrack by Northern Europeans.

Like the caravel, these ships used a combination of square and lateen sails, depending on the sailing conditions they encountered. The standard carrack sail plan used a square sail on the mainmast, flanked by a square sail on the foremast and a lateen sail on the mizzen mast (if a third mast was available). This combination helped when tacking, and allowed the vessel to sail in a variety of wind conditions. By the late 15th century a sprit-sail was added to the ship's bowsprit, and topsails were added to the fore and main masts.

Below: Sometimes called "the Chinese Columbus," Admiral Cheng Ho sailed on seven voyages of exploration 87 years before Columbus. He traveled as far afield as Mecca, using vessels that would dwarf Columbus's Santa Maria (85 feet). The treasure ship pictured is over 400 feet in length.

Ships fit for the Atlantic

In 1492, when Columbus sailed in search of a land beyond the Ocean Sea, his flagship was the nao *Santa Maria*. By this time the nao (or carrack) was a fully rigged ship capable of weathering ocean conditions and large enough to carry the men and provisions needed to undertake voyages of exploration. The caravel remained in use for short voyages and coastal trade, but the carrack became the premier ship of discovery during the 16th century. From a combination of contemporary descriptions and illustrations, archæological evidence, and even replica shipbuilding, we can gain a reasonable picture of what these ships looked like, how they

Right: A reconstruction of Columbus's flagship, the nao (or carrack) Santa Maria. *Her original appearance was never recorded, so all reconstruction is conjectural.*

operated, and the conditions onboard.

A typical carrack of the 1492–1550 period had a hull length of 85–100 feet and a burden of about 100 tons (91 tonnes). She was bulky, with a pronounced rounded hull that meant that she required a substantial spread of canvas to propel her through the water—her three masts carried a combination of square and lateen sails, providing a sail area of more than 2,000 square feet. In favorable conditions, speeds of about six to eight knots could be expected.

The same rounded hull that provided room for supplies also made these vessels very seaworthy, capable of riding the long surging waves encountered far across the oceans. In turn this also provided a stable weapons platform and, for the first time in history, late 15th century carracks were capable of carrying a powerful armament of naval artillery. Four or more large wrought-iron breech loading guns (bombardettas) were mounted on low wooden carriages, while lighter swivel guns (versos) were placed on the ship's rails and on her quarterdeck. When mariners were not expecting attack, these could be stowed in the hold, ready to be hoisted up if trouble threatened.

Uncomfortable, but practical

Wooden vessels were ravaged by marine worms such as the teredo; the concept of sheathing hulls in copper came later. Instead, ships had to be careened regularly, which meant beaching them so that marine growth could be scraped from the hull. It was regarded as inevitable that these craft would leak, and manning the pumps to remove excess water from the bilges was a daily task. On a ship taking part in a long voyage, whose planks had been sprung by constant battering from the waves, pumping out water was a near-constant occupation. In several voyages where expeditions contained a number of ships, there are accounts of less resilient craft being abandoned, their

crew and stores brought aboard one of the more robust ships in the fleet. Similarly, with little chance to repair cordage and sail spars so far from home, most ships of discovery had spare spars lashed to their decks, and extra rope coiled in their holds.

To say crew conditions were primitive would be an understatement. On most carracks and all caravels the only space for the crew to sleep was below deck, among the ship's stores. While the captain maintained at least a modicum of privacy in his cabin, other officers made do with bunks screened from the helmsman's position by canvas awnings. Sanitation was a problem, and disease could quickly ravage a vessel. A lack of medical and nutritional knowledge only exacerbated the problem.

By 1516, small caravels and even smaller brigantines were being built in the Americas by explorers such as Vasco Núñez de Balboa and Francisco Pizarro, who used them to explore the coast of the Southern Sea (Pacific Ocean). Meanwhile, carracks (or naos) were used by the Portuguese to transport spices from the Indies, and by the Spanish to bring the looted wealth of the Americas to Spain. Ferdinand Magellan used a fleet of small naos when he set sail in 1519 on his voyage of circumnavigation, and English and French carracks probed the icy waters of Newfoundland and the Gulf of St. Lawrence.

Although these vessels varied in style during the 16th century, the basic design remained the same. Warships became progressively sleeker and more specialized, and galleons were adapted to carry treasure by the Spanish, but the carrack and nao were the general workhorses of 16th-century shipping.

Above: *Building a caravel, from a 15th-century Portuguese illustration. Changes in shipbuilding technology allowed the construction of vessels capable of crossing the Ocean Sea (Atlantic Ocean).*

NAVIGATION *in the* AGE *of* DISCOVERY

hen Henry the Navigator launched his expeditions into the unknown reaches of the African coast, navigation was far from an exact science. The aim of his teaching school at Sagres was to improve the navigational, astronomical, and cartographic knowledge of his sea captains to a uniformly high level of expertise. Only by employing the best, most

Below: An 11th-century Arabic astrolabe. The European adoption of Arab scientific skills helped pave the way for the Age of Discovery

skilled people could Prince Henry be assured that the information they brought back with them was of the highest quality.

Navigation was something of a "black art," since there was no accurate means by which a mariner could determine a ship's position at sea. Even as basic a tool as a compass was far from properly understood; although the ability to find north was understood and utilized for at least five centuries before 1450, mariners did not understand the difference between true north and magnetic north. The problems this caused were accentuated the further north the explorer traveled. The marine compass in the 14th century was a simple affair, consisting of an iron needle which had been magnetized by rubbing it with magnetite, and then floated on a wooden raft in a bowl of water. By 1420 it had become more sophisticated, with the addition of a circular card marking the cardinal points of the compass and a brass center pin that held the needle. Despite its shortcomings, the mariners' compass could give a reasonably accurate indication of direction, and compared with other navigational tools, it was the personification of reliability.

Mariners had to rely heavily on astronomy to estimate their position. North of the equator, the Pole Star could be seen at night, indicating North. Similarly, in daytime, as long as the observer remained north of the Tropic of Cancer, the sun would lie to the south of the ship at noon. Its path through the sky was also understood, moving from east to west in hourly increments of approximately 15°. The sun could therefore be used to tell time using the same principle as that which governs the use of a sundial. An hourglass was used to provide some idea of the passage of time, and the ability to tell the time, however crudely, was a vital part of the navigation process. The ship's speed through the water was measured by "heaving the log," whereby a wooden float was cast overboard. A rope line of a set distance was attached to the "log," and as the log fell astern, the line was unwound from a reel. The line was knotted at measured distances along its length, and the number that were unwound in a set time was recorded. This produced a rough indication of the speed of the ship, measured in "knots."

Determining longitude

By the early 15th century, the system of determining a position on the earth that we still use today—by determining latitude and longitude—became prevalent. For longitude (that is the east-west element of the position) observers needed an accurate chronometer, none was yet available that could work efficiently at sea, and this was a major problem for navigators. Latitude, the distance north or south of the equator was an easier proposition because it was related to the movement of celestial bodies, principally the Pole Star and the Sun. In theory, by measuring the angle between the Pole Star and the

horizon, mariners could determine latitude by consulting astronomical tables known as "ephemeris," and cross-referencing the angle measured with the date. On land, astronomers regularly performed this calculation, using a device known as an "astrolabe." Invented by Arab scientists, this delicate instrument was used at sea from at least the early 16th century, but the rolling motion of a ship made calculation difficult. Two other tools were available. A rough indication of the height of the pole Star (or the Sun) could be found using the hand, but in the 1470s, the quadrant came into use, providing a relatively simple means of determining latitude. The Quadrant was literally that—a quarter circle of wood or brass, fitted with a plumb-line and marked in degrees. The observer sighted the celestial body along one edge of the instrument while an assistant recorded the angle of the plumb-line.

Although not as accurate as an astrolabe, the quadrant gave a reasonably accurate measurement if the instrument was accurately made. By the early 16th century another variant, the Cross-staff was introduced, which employed similar principles, but allowed for greater accuracy.

Above: *A navigational cross-staff, an instrument that provided mariners with an accurate method to determine longitude.*

Left: *A device invented to determine the magnetic variation of a compass, c.1610.*

43

CHAPTER FOUR

ACROSS *the* OCEAN SEA

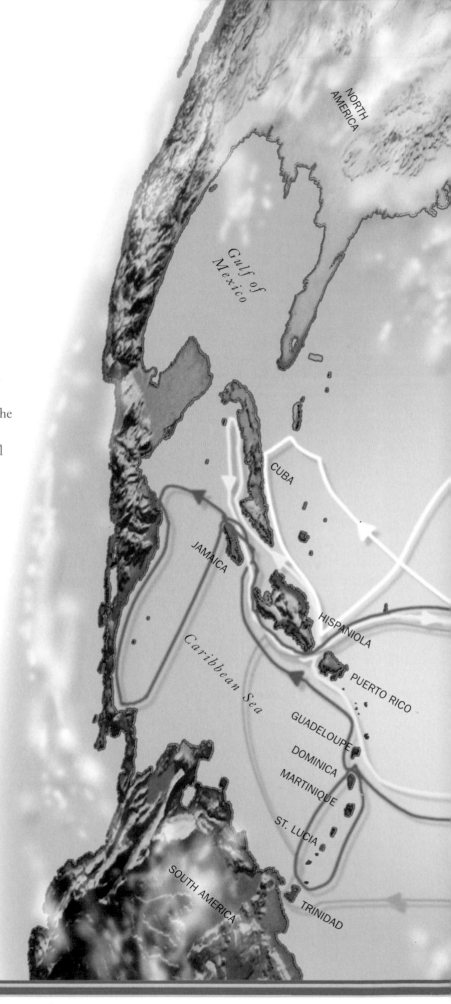

Although the myth that people in 1492 thought the world was flat has been disproved, the prospect of undertaking a voyage west into the Atlantic was still a daunting one. No vessel had ventured west of the Azores, and any such journey was a true voyage into the unknown, where anything might happen.

Although the explorers were prepared, and had theories about finding the Orient at the other side of the Ocean Sea (Atlantic), they still could not be sure of what they would encounter. In modern terms, where transatlantic air crossings occur a hundred times a day, the voyage undertaken by Columbus was more akin to space exploration than anything else we can imagine.

Columbus went to his grave convinced that he had discovered part of Asia, and had pioneered a sea route directly from Europe to the Orient. Within ten years of the return of Columbus to Europe in 1493, it was becoming obvious to all but the most stubborn that he had found a previously unknown continent, a "New World." Although a direct route to the Orient could still be found, explorers would first have to find a way around the landmass of America. This first contact with the New World would also have a devastating effect on the people already living there. Today, Columbus Day is a national holiday in the United States, but many Native Americans do not believe that they have anything to celebrate.

PORTUGAL

SPAIN

Palos
Cadiz

MADEIRA

CANARY
ISLANDS

AFRICA

Atlantic Ocean

CAPE VERDE
ISLANDS

*The Voyages of
Columbus*

1492–93

1493–96

1498

1502–04

CHRISTOPHER COLUMBUS

1451 to 1506

Columbus is the one explorer whose name and year of voyage everyone remembers, and he is the only one to have a national holiday named after him. Credited with discovering America, he didn't sight the American mainland until his third voyage in 1498, never reached the continent of North America, and died convinced that he had reached a part of the Orient. These points apart, his voyages of discovery rank among the most important ever undertaken.

Columbus was born late in 1451 in Genoa, a thriving Mediterranean seaport on the northwestern Italian coast. Some mystery surrounds his background. It has been suggested he was born into a humble family, and certainly Columbus had little formal education before he became a mariner—in later years he claimed that he was largely self-taught. Columbus went to great lengths to hide details of his early life, and some believe he may have had Jewish links in his family; details which would have prevented support from the Spanish crown if they had been made public.

In 1476 Columbus sailed to Lisbon to join an established Genoese maritime community in the Portuguese capital. For the next ten years he participated in Portuguese trading voyages east into the Mediterranean, north to England and France, and south to the newly discovered West African coast. There is even a possibility that he participated in a voyage to Iceland in 1477.

In 1479 he made a good marriage to a Portuguese noblewoman, Doná Felipa Perestrello e Moriz. Soon after moving to Madeira, the couple had a son, Diego, born in 1480. His wife died some time before 1485, Columbus returned to Lisbon.

About this time he conceived the idea that it was possible to sail to the Indies by sailing west across the Ocean Sea (Atlantic). He proposed an expedition to discover this sea route and sought sponsorship from King John II.

When the Portuguese monarch rejected the

Above: Christopher Columbus, painting by Sebastiano del Piombo.

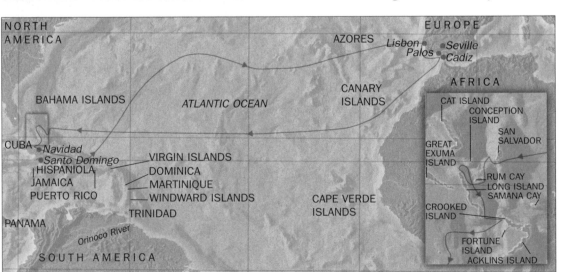

Although he set a westerly course, Columbus took advantage of the trade winds to speed his journey, which sent him on a west-southwest course. By 1492 the notion of a spherical earth was widely accepted, but Columbus miscalculated the size of the globe, underestimating the distance he expected to travel from Europe to Asia. By his calculations, the Orient would be encountered to the west of where the Bahamas are in fact situated, and he predicted a voyage lasting 21 days.

After 30 days the crew became restless, so he lied to them about the distance traveled each day to help allay their fears. On the night of October 11, Columbus thought he saw a light to the west, and early next night, a crewman on the *Pinta* sighted land. Columbus landed on the island the next morning, claiming it and all surrounding territory for Spain. He named his landfall San Salvador. The exact location is still in doubt, but the first island discovered was probably Samana Cay in the Bahamas. Columbus had discovered America.

Left: A modern reconstruction of the Santa Maria, *showing the quarters in the stern used by the "Admiral of the Ocean Sea."*

proposal, he moved to Spain to seek sponsorship from the Spanish court of Ferdinand and Isabella. He presented his proposal on two occasions but met with rejection both times. During this period he won the support of several influential Spanish courtiers, including Luis de Santangel, Chancellor of the Royal Household. As a result of their lobbying, Queen Isabella agreed to sponsor Columbus to undertake a voyage of discovery in 1491.

A lengthening journey

In the southern Spanish port of Palos, Columbus acquired and readied three ships: his flagship the *Santa Maria*, and the smaller caravels, the *Pinta* and *Niña*. They were manned by 90 seamen, including the captains of the caravels, Martín and Vicente Pinzón (*see pages 54–55*). Apart from finding an alternative sea route to the Indies, Columbus expected to encounter undiscovered lands, and therefore lobbied for authority in any new territory. As a result he was appointed "Admiral of the Ocean Sea" and governor of any territories he discovered.

On August 3, 1492, Columbus set sail from Palos, bound for the Canary Islands. The expedition was delayed while modifications and repairs were carried out on the two smaller vessels, and it was only on September 6 that the small fleet set sail on what was to become the most important voyage of discovery ever undertaken.

Below: Columbus soothes the restless crew, illustration published in London c.1910.

Above: An engraving showing Columbus aboard his ship during the voyage to America, being serenaded by sea nymphs blowing conch shells.

Avoiding the cannibals

The Spanish traded with the Arawak islanders, a people Columbus called "Indians," since he felt he was close to the Indies. Taking several Indians with him, Columbus left the island after two days and sailed southwest to "Fernandina" (probably Crooked Island), then north to "Isabella" (Fortune Island), both in the Bahamas archipelago. He was searching for a land of gold described by the Indians, but instead all he found were beautiful islands and an abundance of fish and timber.

About October 21 he sailed west-southwest to make landfall at what is now Bahia de Bariay, Cuba on October 26. Sailing southeast down the coast of Cuba, Columbus noted that the coast offered several good harbors and the land was fertile, but the local Carib Indians were unfriendly, and the Arawaks persuaded the crew that they were cannibals (a contemporary drawing shows the practice [*see page 53*]).

In late November, Martín Pinzón left the flotilla on his own authority to search for gold. Passing the eastern tip of Cuba, Columbus sailed southeast with the remaining ships, and reached what is now Haiti, a land Columbus named Hispaniola. He explored the northern

coast of the island until December 24, when the *Santa Maria* ran aground. The crew saved what they could, then abandoned their ship. Close to the wrecksite, Columbus established a settlement he called La Navidad (now En Bas Saline, Haiti). The local Indians appeared friendly and the chief, Guacanquari, even helped to establish the camp and provision it.

When the *Pinta* rejoined the expedition, Columbus sailed for Spain in the two caravels on January 16, 1493, leaving a colony of 40 seamen at La Navidad to await his return.

Although the ships were separated by a storm, they reached port safely, first Lisbon, then Palos. Soon after his triumphant return, Columbus planned a second voyage with the full support of the Spanish crown. On September 25, 1493, he set sail again, this time departing from Cadiz with 17 ships and 1,500 men—seamen, soldiers, priests, and settlers. The aim was to establish a permanent colony.

The massacred settlement

On November 3, landfall was made on Dominica, then he led his ships to the north along the chain of the Leeward Islands. Columbus explored (and named) Guadalupe

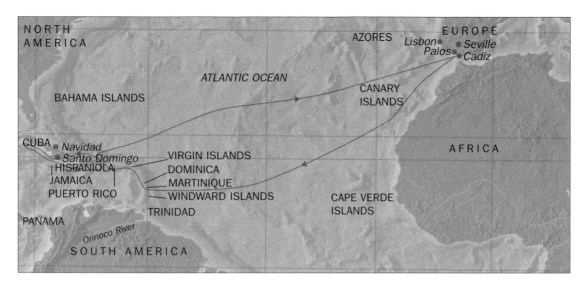

(Guadeloupe), San Martin (Nevis), and Santa Cruz (St. Croix). He next explored a group he named the Virgin Islands before sailing on to Hispaniola. He reached the settlement of La Navidad only to find that it had been destroyed and the settlers killed by Caribs. He chose not to rebuild but moved further east along Hispaniola's north coast to establish the settlement of Isabella.

Exploration revealed a small seam of gold, so Columbus began to pacify the region and enslave the Indians to use as gold diggers. He built a string of fortifications and collected all precious metal the slaves found. It is clear that Columbus had become disillusioned with the Indians he had encountered since the destruction of La Navidad, although he appeared to favor the more peaceful Arawaks over the aggressive and cannibalistic Caribs. Compared to later Spanish explorers, Columbus's attitude toward the region's natives was benign.

Twelve of the ships were sent back to Spain in mid-1494 with gold and orders to return laden with supplies, while Columbus set off toward Cuba with his remaining five vessels. Passing through the Windward Passage, he sailed along the southern coast of Cuba, noting the suitable harbor at what would become Santiago de Cuba. He continued as far as the Island of Pines (now, Isla de la Juventud) before turning back, convinced Cuba was a peninsula of the Asian mainland.

On the return journey he discovered Jamaica, but a severe fever prevented further investigation, and he returned to Isabella in time to meet the returning fleet carrying provisions. Following several months of illness, Columbus decided to return home to Spain to counter charges that were being brought against him. As it had become clear that Isabella was an unhealthy site, Columbus abandoned it and established a new colony—Santo Domingo—on the south side of the island. He returned to Spain with his fleet in early 1496, promising to send back fresh colonists and supplies at the earliest opportunity.

Below: This woodcut published in Florence in 1493, is said to be the first depiction of Columbus's discovery. It shows Ferdinand II of Aragon, Columbus's patron, pointing to Columbus in his ship Santa Maria, and the Pinta and Niña approaching land.

Above: Ferdinand and Isabella, seen here bidding Columbus farewell on his first voyage, supported the explorer for four expeditions, despite an enquiry into his handling of the Hispaniola settlement of San Domingo.

In Spain, Columbus found that although jealous courtiers and bureaucrats had tried to defame his character, he still enjoyed the support of Ferdinand and Isabella, so a further expedition aimed at finding mainland Asia was approved by the Spanish monarchs. Columbus left Seville in May 1498 with a meager two ships, plus three supply ships that were bound for Santo Domingo. His aim was exploration, not settlement.

Columbus parted from the supply ships at the Canary Islands and, as they headed for Hispaniola, he veered further to the south than he had before. On July 31, 1498, he sighted Trinidad, then circled around it into what is now the Gulf of Paria. He reached the mainland of South America at the mouth of the Orinoco River, the first European contact with the American mainland. Columbus still thought it was the mainland of Asia.

Heading north, he crossed the Caribbean Sea to Hispaniola, only to find the settlement at Santo Domingo was in revolt. He quelled the rebellion, but complaints about his heavy-

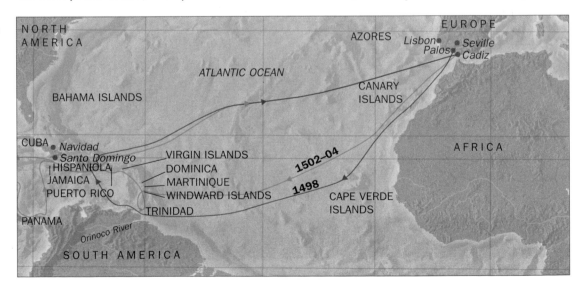

handedness reached Spain, and Francisco de Bobadilla was sent to investigate. In August 1500 de Bobadilla found Columbus guilty of usurping his authority. Columbus was arrested, put in chains, and sent home to Spain. The trial cleared him, but his authority over the Hispaniola settlement was revoked to avoid further clashes between the Admiral of the Ocean Sea and the Santo Domingo colonists.

Columbus now came under pressure from cartographers and other explorers who claimed that the lands he had discovered were not a part of Asia, but instead belonged to a new continent. Columbus remained adamant that he had discovered a sea route to the Indies, and lobbied Ferdinand and Isabella to sponsor another expedition that would settle the matter once and for all.

A troubled last voyage

On May 11, 1502, Columbus set sail on his fourth and last expedition, in command of four ships crewed by 140 men and accompanied by his son and brother. They made landfall at Martinique on June 15, and Columbus sailed north for Hispaniola, passing the string of the Leeward Islands for the second time. The new governor of Santo Domingo refused him permission to land, so Columbus continued west to pass between Jamaica and Cuba.

Early in August he reached the northern coast of what is now Honduras. Severe tropical storms prevented him from continuing north, so he sailed south along the coast of Central America, searching for a passage through the landmass. After passing the regions that are now the countries of Nicaragua and Costa Rica, he reached the isthmus of Panama, a place that the Indians told him lay between two great bodies of water. Firm in his belief, Columbus recorded that the land formed part of the Malay peninsula, north of where Singapore stands today. In his mind, Cathay (China) lay to the north, while a sea route to India could be found somewhere to the south.

In February 1503 Columbus tried to

establish a settlement, but the Indians proved too aggressive and he was forced to withdraw, abandoning one ship. He sailed for Jamaica to land at St. Anne's Bay after losing a second ship in a severe storm. His two remaining ships were too badly damaged to reach Santo Domingo, let alone Spain. In July he sent two canoes to Hispaniola for help, but the governor, Nicolás de Ovando, took almost a year to rescue the party, by which time they had been reduced to less than a hundred men.

Columbus returned to Spain in November 1504, disillusioned and in poor health. For the next two years until his death, he spent most of his time bitterly attacking critics and in litigation with the crown. He maintained that he had found the Indies rather than a "New World" until the day he died—May 20, 1506.

Today, Columbus is hailed as the man who discovered the "New World" of the Americas, two names that he refused to use. His discoveries began a new era on the American continent, and neither the Old World nor the New would be the same again.

Above: *A late 16th-century depiction of Columbus with his sons Diego and Ferdinand. After his wife died in 1485, Columbus never remarried, but he did take a Spanish mistress, Beatriz Enrique de Araña, who bore him the illegitimate Ferdinand in 1488 while they were living in Córdoba. In 1502, when Columbus sailed on his fourth voyage, he was 51; Ferdinand was only 13.*

Pre-Columbian CARIBBEAN CULTURES

The native peoples of the Caribbean were the ones who made the first contact with European discoverers in 1492. As a result, they were also the first group of American peoples to be decimated by disease, enslaved, and driven almost to extinction. Lacking the political unity of native societies in other parts of the Americas, they were an easy group of people for the Spanish to subjugate.

Anthropologists have grouped the native American civilizations of Cuba, Hispaniola, the West Indies, coastal Venezuela, and parts of Central America into a culture known as Circum-Caribbean. This grouping includes the Arawaks, Caribs, Ciboney, Taino, Mosquito, Cuna, and many other peoples who had interrelated social and economic structures. Cannibalism was widespread, but unlike the larger militaristic civilizations of Central America, human sacrifice was rarely practiced. Not all these societies functioned in the same manner, since coastal villages practiced an agrarian culture while further into the interior more nomadic people of the same ethnic groups acted as hunter-gatherers. There was no common language throughout the Caribbean, or even any shared mythological heritage, although certain tribes demonstrated strong cultural links with others. Anthropologists have discovered that the language of the Arawaks is related to those found in the Andean-Equatorial region, while the nearby Caribs spoke a Ge-Pano-Carib tongue similar to that used by tribes in modern-day Venezuela and Colombia. Chiefdoms helped to unite the peoples of a particular area, such as on Hispaniola, while larger alliances were unknown.

The earliest people in the Caribbean basin were hunters and foragers, and artifacts dating to 13,000 BC have been found in Venezuela. By about 4000 BC, these people turned to cultivation to help support themselves, and archæologists have traced the first Caribbean settlements to this period, principally on the Panamanian and Colombian coastlines. These early villagers had settled on the islands of the Caribbean and in the Florida Keys by 1500 BC at the latest, and the linguistic mix of the region has been partly explained by expeditions to the islands being launched from disparate points of the mainland during this period.

A fresh impetus to the settlement of the West Indies came in the first centuries AD, when Saladero Culture people from the Venezuelan coast moved north and brought their own innovations of ceramics and agriculture

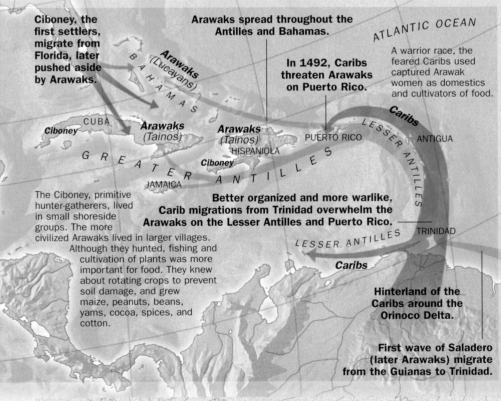

Ciboney, the first settlers, migrate from Florida, later pushed aside by Arawaks.

Arawaks spread throughout the Antilles and Bahamas.

ATLANTIC OCEAN

In 1492, Caribs threaten Arawaks on Puerto Rico.

A warrior race, the feared Caribs used captured Arawak women as domestics and cultivators of food.

Arawaks (Lucayans)

BAHAMAS

CUBA

Ciboney

Arawaks (Tainos)

Arawaks (Tainos)

HISPANIOLA

Ciboney

PUERTO RICO

ANTIGUA

Caribs

GREATER ANTILLES

LESSER ANTILLES

JAMAICA

The Ciboney, primitive hunter-gatherers, lived in small shoreside groups. The more civilized Arawaks lived in larger villages. Although they hunted, fishing and cultivation of plants was more important for food. They knew about rotating crops to prevent soil damage, and grew maize, peanuts, beans, yams, cocoa, spices, and cotton.

Better organized and more warlike, Carib migrations from Trinidad overwhelm the Arawaks on the Lesser Antilles and Puerto Rico.

LESSER ANTILLES

TRINIDAD

Caribs

Hinterland of the Caribs around the Orinoco Delta.

First wave of Saladero (later Arawaks) migrate from the Guianas to Trinidad.

c.AD 1	1400s	1492	1496	1510	1511	1511	1513
Farming people migrate from South America to the Caribbean islands.	Cultures in the West Indies are still in the New Stone Age.	Christopher Columbus sails to the West Indies.	Santo Domingo, heart of the Spanish Caribbean, is established.	The first slave voyage from Guinea reaches Haiti.	The Spanish take Puerto Rico.	Diego de Velazquez de Cuélla conquers Cuba.	Juan Ponce de León discovers Florida.

Left: *Terrified Arawaks convinced Columbus that the Caribs were cannibals. Although some authorities dispute the notion, this drawing of 1497 shows human flesh being eaten (top left), and part of a human body hanging from a beam (center top). The accompanying text states that Americans eat each other and live to be 150.*

square that contained a meeting house (or chief's house) and often a temple. In some low-lying areas such as the Venezuelan coast, houses were sometimes built on piles over a lake or lagoon, a style that prompted Amerigo Vespucci (*see pages 92–93*) to call the region "Little Venice."

About a century before the arrival of Europeans in the Caribbean, a further wave of conquest and migration altered the makeup of the region. Caribs from the Atlantic coast of South America invaded the West Indian islands settled by the Arawaks, and the more peaceful islanders were forced north from island to island by the Carib invaders. The lack of higher social organization of the Circum-Caribbean peoples made them susceptible to attack, and the Caribs took full advantage of this, as would the technologically advanced Spanish after 1492.

to the fishing communities already established in the islands. These people became known as the Arawaks, and their migration has been defined as a conquest rather than as a peaceful settlement. By the time Columbus arrived in 1492, the earlier and technologically more primitive Ciboney people were only to be found in the western corners of Cuba and Hispaniola.

Invasion of the Caribs

Throughout the Caribbean basin, villages increased in size and importance during the five centuries before Columbus came. As agricultural techniques improved, arable land was cleared and the settled coastal band crept inland. The type of food grown varied depending on location, with corn being the staple diet on the South American coast, and sweet potatoes, beans, and tropical fruit being prevalent in the Caribbean islands. Land was also turned over to the harvesting of cotton, and the Arawak people produced netted cotton hammocks (a bed never before seen by Europeans) and clothing, while mainland tribes used bark and wool to create clothes, although in most regions, simple breechcloths were the standard form of dress.

Construction techniques varied greatly throughout the region. People of the Tairona Culture in modern Colombia built structures similar to those produced by the Maya civilization, with temples, houses, paved roads, and irrigation canals. Elsewhere, structures were wooden, with villages clustered around a central

Below: *This copper-tinted engraving by Theodore de Bry, published in 1596, depicts the first contact between people of the Old World and the New. The Arawaks who met Columbus were too poor to present their visitors with gold and jewels as shown here.*

1514	1523	1524	1538	1562	1565	1625	1640
Panama colony is established; Panama City is founded five years later.	Pedro de Alvarado conquers Guatemala and founds a settlement there.	Nicaragua colony is established.	The Spanish gain control of Colombia.	Englishman John Hawkins runs his first slave-trading voyage to the West Indies.	The Spanish establish St. Augustine to stop French Huguenots colonizing Florida.	British begin to settle in the West Indies.	The West Indies' main business is in sugar plantations.

MARTÍN *and* VICENTE PINZÓN

1440
to
c1493

1463
to
c1523

The Pinzón brothers are best remembered for being the captains who accompanied Christopher Columbus on his first transatlantic voyage in 1492, in command of the caravels *Niña* and *Pinta*. Although Martín Alonso Pinzón's only opportunity for independent exploration came when he temporarily deserted Columbus, his younger brother, Vicente Yáñez, explored much of the Central and South American coast, voyages that helped undermine Columbus's claim that he had reached the Indies.

Born in the Andalucian port of Palos about 1440, Martín Pinzón became a mariner. The Pinzón family were ship owners and, as they grew up, younger brothers Francisco and Vicente followed their older brother to sea. When Columbus was campaigning for his first voyage, Martín was a strong advocate and when royal permission was granted Palos became the obvious choice for a port of embarkation. All three brothers accompanied Columbus, with

Below: Vicente Yáñez Pinzón followed his career with Columbus to become a renowned explorer in his own right.

Martín commanding the *Pinta* (accompanied by his brother Francisco) and Vicente the *Niña*. It was a crewman on Martín's *Pinta* who first sighted land on October 12, 1492.

Pinzón controversially abandoned Columbus once the expedition reached Cuba to explore on his own. Indians he encountered told of an island called Babeque, where the natives harvested gold on the seashore. He never found the island, but he did discover Hispaniola before Columbus and, exploring inland, discovered small amounts of gold in the "mountains of Cibao" (now the Cordillera Central range). Local Indians told him that Columbus had reached Hispaniola and was shipwrecked, so Pinzón rejoined the main expedition in January 1493.

Although Columbus forgave the desertion, Martín Pinzón tried to betray Columbus again by attempting to beat him home to be the person who broke the news of the expedition's discoveries. Contrary winds foiled his attempt, and Columbus and Vicente in the *Niña* reached Europe first. Soon after his return to Palos in 1489, Martín Pinzón died, probably from a combination of syphilis and tropical disease.

Local hero

Within six years, Vicente Pinzón, who had returned to Palos a hero, decided to undertake his own expedition to the New World. He left Palos in late 1499 with four ships, and made landfall on the easternmost point of Brazil in January 1500, a headland he named Santa María de la Consolación. It is still disputed whether Portuguese explorer Pedro Cabral (*see pages 68–69*), Amerigo Vespucci, or Vicente Pinzón reached Brazil first, but Cabral is generally credited with the discovery.

Pinzón then sailed northwest up the coast and passed the mouth of the Amazon, where fresh water was present so far out to sea that Pinzón named the estuary Mar Dulce (The Fresh Sea). Pinzón, alarmed by the currents closer to the river's mouth, avoided it, although

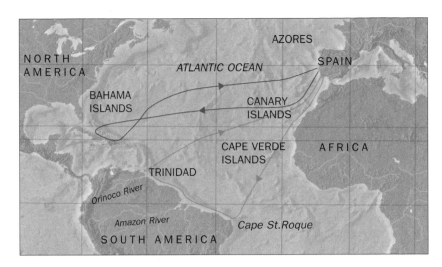

he raided a coastal Indian village and captured prisoners to learn more of the region.

Pinzón sailed on up the coast to the northwest, then turned north around the Guiana coast to cross the Caribbean Sea to Hispaniola. After watering his ship in Santo Domingo, he sailed through the Windward Passage and up the chain of the Bahama Islands before returning home in September 1500.

Vicente Pinzón undertook a second independent expedition two years later in search of precious metals. As before, he made landfall in Brazil and followed the same route. In Hispaniola he met Columbus, who was recovering from his shipwreck on Jamaica, and they most probably compared notes on their experiences.

A third expedition in 1506 was undertaken in association with the Spanish explorer and cartographer Juan de Solís. Pinzón retraced the route taken by Columbus in 1502–4, but this time the explorers made a detailed survey of the Yucatán peninsula and the coast of Honduras. Pinzón noted a natural harbor in Honduras that would be ideal for settlement (now the port of Trujillo).

Back in Spain, Pinzón was appointed Governor of Honduras, but he never returned to take up his commission. A final voyage to Brazil ended in failure after he and his partner Solís fell out, and, following his return, Vicente Pinzón retired from exploration to spend the rest of his life as a businessman.

Left: *Martin Alonso Pinzón deserted Columbus in the middle of his first voyage. He preferred to sail off on his own in search of gold.*

55

PÁNFILO *de* NARVÁEZ

c1470 *to* 1528

Pánfilo de Narváez is remembered as the conquistador who lost his entire expedition, but he made several contributions to contemporary understanding of the New World. His 30-year career in the Americas earned him a name for cruelty, bravery, and bad judgment in almost equal measure.

Born about 1470 in Spain, he emigrated to

Right: *An early engraved map of Cuba, c.1530, bore little relation to the actual geography of the island.*

Hispaniola in 1498—only six years after Columbus had discovered the island. He served on garrison duty and assisted in the subjugation of the local population until 1509, when he accompanied Juan de Esquirel to Jamaica. Instrumental in the conquest of the island, de Narváez was entrusted with his own independent command.

In 1511 he led an expeditionary force to Cuba with the twin aims of conquering the entire

island for Spain and conducting a thorough survey. While other Spanish forces secured the coastal settlements, de Narváez marched inland. For the next seven years, he undertook his task with such zeal that the Spanish missionary Bartolomé de las Casas, who accompanied the expedition, singled out de Narváez as one of the cruelest of the conquistadors. De las Casas reported that de Narváez's men massacred thousands of Indians.

By 1518 the few remaining indigenous people of Cuba were incapable of opposing Spanish rule. The other part of de Narváez's mission was also a success—Cuba was thoroughly mapped and its potential as a source of ore and food was reported to the Spanish Crown.

In late 1518, the Governor of Cuba, Diego Velásquez, appointed Hernán Cortéz (*see pages 116–119*) to lead an expedition to what would become New Spain (Mexico). Although de Narváez missed the chance to participate in the campaign, his opportunity came in 1520, when Velásquez considered that Cortéz had exceeded his authority. The governor sent de Narváez to take over command of the expedition. In April he landed at Vera Cruz and entered into negotiations with the conquistadors, as well as with the captive Aztec Emperor Montezuma. But prepared, Cortéz launched a surprise attack on de Narváez and, after defeating him, imprisoned his rival for the next two years.

Makeshift vessels

De Narváez returned to Spain and lobbied for the opportunity to lead new expeditions of conquest. In 1527 he was granted a charter to explore from La Florida (present-day Florida and Alabama) to the River of Palms (the Rio Grande). On June 27 he sailed from Spain with six ships and 500 men. On the way he lost one ship in a hurricane and 140 men through desertion on Hispaniola.

The reduced crew landed at what is now Tampa Bay in April 1528. De Narváez made the mistake of splitting up his weak force. He sent his five remaining ships up the coast to rendezvous with him later, while the conquistador led 300 men inland to the swampy

center of the Florida peninsula. On hearing rumors of a rich city, De Narváez headed northwest, crossed the Suwannee River, and captured Apalachen, near the modern Florida State capital of Tallahassee. There was little to eat and no gold, so the dwindling band of conquistadors headed southwest, to rendezvous with their fleet.

At the mouth of the St. Mark's River they realized they had missed the fleet (the ships, having patrolled the coast for a year without finding their companions, had gone on to Vera Cruz), so de Narváez ordered his men to build

barges to sail along the coast to New Spain. Just over two weeks later, five of these craft, roughly made from wood, crudely forged nails, animal skins for waterproofing, and clothing for sails, set sail on September 22, 1528 during the last few weeks of the hurricane season.

They should have waited. A tropical storm off the Mississippi delta scattered the barges, and when it was over, only two had survived. Somehow they reached Galveston Island in what is now Texas before being shipwrecked and, led by Alvár Núñez Cabeza de Vaca (*see pages 166–167*), the survivors began their long trek home to New Spain. Pánfilo de Narváez and the men on his barge were never seen again. It is believed they perished at sea off the mouth of the Mississippi River.

Above: Cuba provided a fertile soil for the establishment of Spanish colonies, farms, and plantations.

Left: Pánfilo de Narváez was known as being one of the cruelest of conquistadors. His flaming red hair matched his fiery reputation, but the blindness in one eye cannot have contributed to the shortsightedness he displayed in losing an entire expedition.

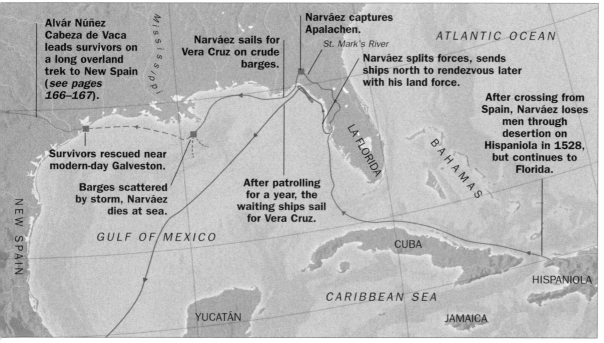

Alvár Núñez Cabeza de Vaca leads survivors on a long overland trek to New Spain (**see pages 166–167**).

Narváez sails for Vera Cruz on crude barges.

Narváez captures Apalachen.

St. Mark's River

ATLANTIC OCEAN

Narváez splits forces, sends ships north to rendezvous later with his land force.

After crossing from Spain, Narváez loses men through desertion on Hispaniola in 1528, but continues to Florida.

Mississippi

Survivors rescued near modern-day Galveston.

Barges scattered by storm, Narváez dies at sea.

After patrolling for a year, the waiting ships sail for Vera Cruz.

LA FLORIDA

BAHAMAS

NEW SPAIN

GULF OF MEXICO

CUBA

HISPANIOLA

CARIBBEAN SEA

YUCATÁN

JAMAICA

FOUNDATION *of the* EARLY SETTLEMENTS

Below: A Theodore de Bry engraving dating from 1592 shows natives of Hispaniola, surrounded by a growing ring of Spanish fortifications and settlements. In reality, many of the native population had been killed by disease within decades of the Spanish arrival.

L a Navidad, founded by Christopher Columbus in 1492, was the first European settlement in the New World, albeit a temporary one. Between that time and the establishment of the first permanent settlement on the North American mainland at St. Augustine in Florida in 1565, dozens of colonies sprang up throughout the Spanish New World.

As colonists and crops were gradually introduced into the Americas, diseases to which they had no natural defenses devastated the native population. Fatally weakened, they were unable to resist the European incursion. By examining the archæological evidence of two early settlements, we can trace the development of this process of conquest.

La Navidad was founded almost by accident, when Columbus's flagship *Santa Maria* ran aground on Christmas day, 1492 on the north coast of Hispaniola (Haiti), close to the present

c.1000 AD	1492	1503	1522	1529	1530	1535	1565
Vikings settle temporarily at L'Anse Aux Meadows in Newfoundland.	Columbus founds La Navidad, the first temporary Spanish colony in the New World.	Puerto Real is founded within a mile of La Navidad.	Mexico City is founded on the ruins of Aztec Tenochtitlán.	Pizarro conquers the Inca empire in Peru and founds the city of Lima.	Portuguese colonization of Brazil begins.	Cartier founds Montreal in Canada.	St. Augustine in present-day Florida is founded by the Spanish.

Cape Haitien. The local Arawak chief, Guacanacaric, offered the hand of friendship, and lent men and canoes to help rescue the ship's stores. Accounts indicate that the temporary settlement Columbus founded included a well, a watchtower, storehouses, living quarters, and a fortified palisade. As it was established at Christmas, the settlement was called La Navidad (the nativity).

When Columbus left for Spain, 39 men were left behind in the settlement with food and supplies to last a year. They included officers, a doctor, a boat builder, a gunner, and a barrel maker—a group with enough skills between them to ensure that the colony would be self-sufficient. Their instructions were to trade with the Arawaks for gold, and to await Columbus's return. When, after 11 months, he did return the men were dead and the settlement burned to the ground, along with most of the neighboring Arawak villages. It is unclear what had happened, although it is likely that the settlers provoked a war with their neighbors and were massacred. Columbus then sailed on to the west to found the new settlement of La Isabela. Although it was not much of a colony—more like a winter encampment—as the first settlement, and because of the mysterious circumstances surrounding its end, La Navidad continues to fascinate historians.

During the 1980s, a team from the University of Florida excavated a site at En Bas Saline in Northern Haiti, which is almost certainly the remains of La Navidad. Evidence of burned structures, an adjacent Arawak settlement, and a well containing European objects dating from before 1500 all provide clues about the destruction of the colony, but a definitive report has still to be produced.

A permanent settlement

In 1503 a new Spanish colony, Puerto Real was founded within a mile of La Navidad, and this was designed to be permanent. It was sited to take advantage of a good harbor, but its primary economic use was as a mining town. In its early years the settlement of about 100 households

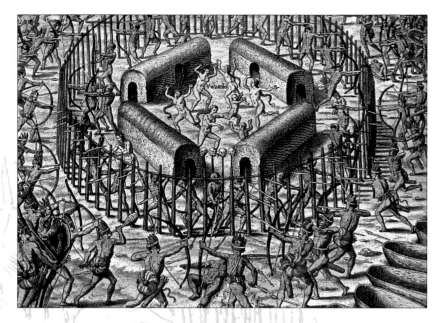

prospered, especially after the local Arawak villages were subjugated and made slaves or, more euphemistically, "Indios de Servicio." Disease decimated the potential pool of slave labor for the region's silver mines and they became unproductive by the 1520s. Increasingly, slaves imported from Africa were used in the colony, which had to turn to agriculture to sustain itself. An earthquake damaged Puerto Real in 1562, and two years later the settlement was attacked, looted, and burned by French sea rovers. With a stagnant economy and no funds to rebuild, the Spanish finally abandoned Puerto Real in 1578.

An archæological investigation of the remains of the town was started in 1979, and has provided fascinating information about the format of early Spanish settlements in the Americas. A substantial stone "cathedral" stood on a central square, reminiscent of Spanish towns in the Old World, while the remains of stone buildings suggested, unsurprisingly, that they were built on traditional Spanish lines. Other less substantial buildings housed slaves. Ceramics and domestic items indicated that the settlement continued to rely on Spain for basics well into the 16th century. The devastated first settlement and the failed colony reflect two phases in Spanish settlement in the New World, the first exploratory and the second based around extraction of local resources and use of native slave labor.

Above: A Theodore de Bry engraving of 1592 shows a native attack on an Arawak village. The first Spanish colony of La Navidad was built alongside a similar village.

CHAPTER FIVE

SEA ROUTES *to the* INDIES

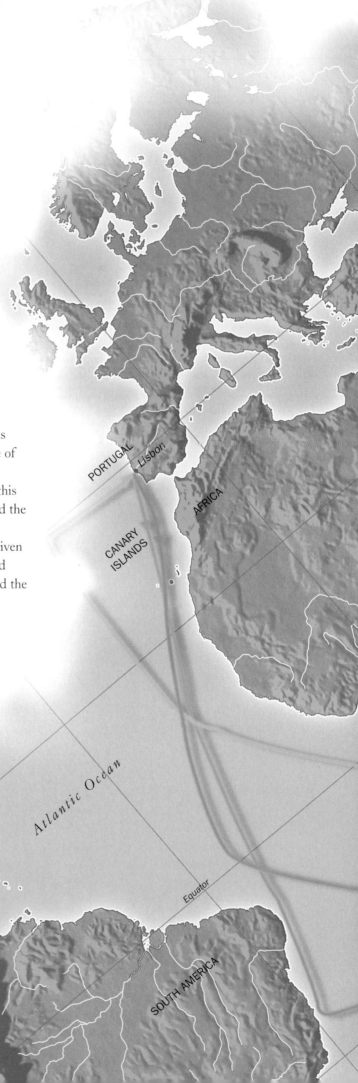

When Vasco da Gama entered the Indian Ocean, he broke into a fabulously lucrative trading monopoly that had eluded Europeans for centuries. Until his voyage, spices from the Far East were highly priced luxuries brought to Europe by Italian merchants who traded with Arabs. Da Gama was followed by Portuguese conquerors who broke this Arab monopoly and established Portugal as the premier source of spices in Europe, making the small country one of the richest in Europe and the envy of all.

The Treaty of Tordesillas (1494) ensured Portuguese control over this trade, and throughout the Age of Discovery her merchants maintained the flow of spice, while her soldiers and mariners fought to maintain her preeminent position in the Indies and the Indian Ocean. Although driven by a desire for profit more than knowledge, Portuguese merchants and explorers ventured deep into the waters of southeast Asia and provided the first European trade links with China and Japan.

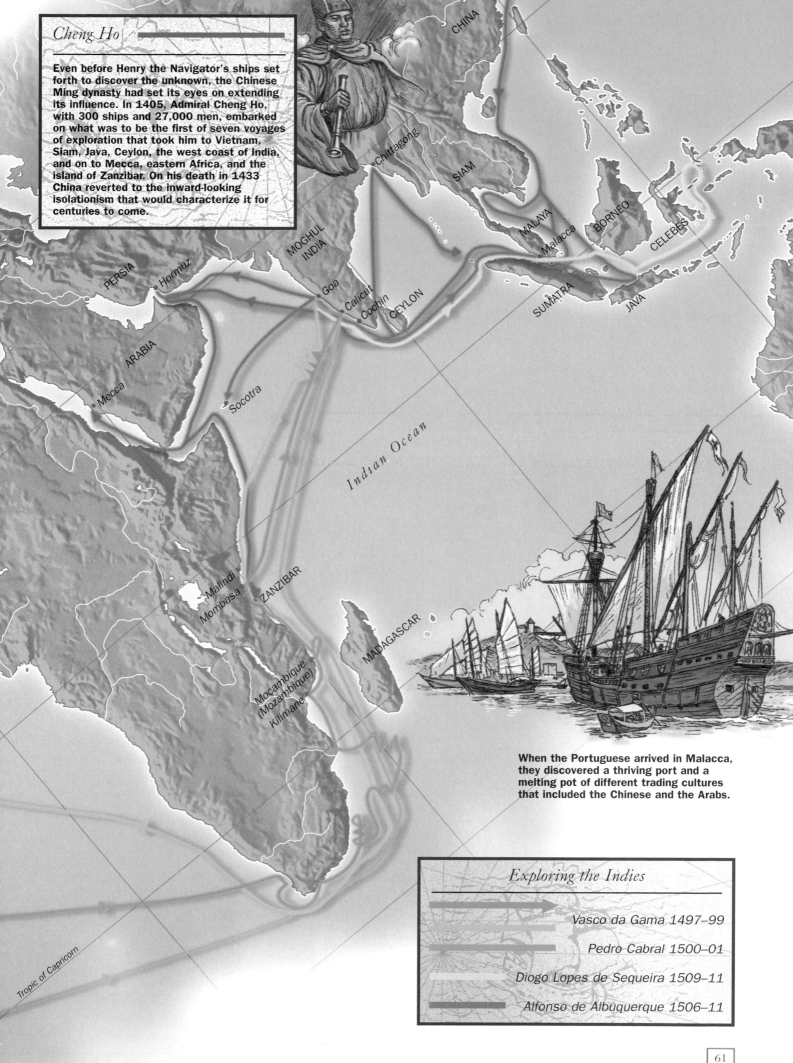

Even before Henry the Navigator's ships set forth to discover the unknown, the Chinese Ming dynasty had set its eyes on extending its influence. In 1405, Admiral Cheng Ho, with 300 ships and 27,000 men, embarked on what was to be the first of seven voyages of exploration that took him to Vietnam, Siam, Java, Ceylon, the west coast of India, and on to Mecca, eastern Africa, and the island of Zanzibar. On his death in 1433 China reverted to the inward-looking isolationism that would characterize it for centuries to come.

CHINA

Chittagong

SIAM

MALAYA

Malacca

BORNEO

CELEBES

MOGHUL INDIA

Goa

Calicut

Cochin

CEYLON

SUMATRA

JAVA

PERSIA

Hormuz

ARABIA

Mecca

Socotra

Indian Ocean

Malindi

Mombasa

ZANZIBAR

MADAGASCAR

Moçambique
(Mozambique)

Kilimane

Tropic of Capricorn

When the Portuguese arrived in Malacca, they discovered a thriving port and a melting pot of different trading cultures that included the Chinese and the Arabs.

Exploring the Indies

Vasco da Gama 1497–99

Pedro Cabral 1500–01

Diogo Lopes de Sequeira 1509–11

Alfonso de Albuquerque 1506–11

VASCO *da* GAMA
c1469 *to* 1524

Vasco da Gama, regarded as the greatest of Portugal's official explorers, used the discoveries of his predecessors as a launch pad for a voyage around Africa and into the Indian Ocean. His return from India's Malabar Coast gave Portugal a monopoly on trade with the wealthy lands of India and the Indies and made her a major European power.

During the last decades of the 15th century, Portugal and Spain were rivals in the field of exploration. Portuguese chronicler Zurara said that Portugal was open to the sea but walled in by Castile. Always the poor neighbor, Portugal had to look toward the sea for economic development.

Right: Vasco da Gama, pictured during his last years when he served as a colonial administrator.

Although Portuguese vessels had a commercial monopoly over the West African coast, increasing numbers of Spanish interlopers threatened to cut off these trade links. Forts were built to protect Portuguese trading stations on the Guinea Coast, and expeditions were sent to explore the African coastline and find new trading partners. Uppermost in everyone's mind was to find a sea trade route to the Orient and easy access to the wealth of the Indian sub-continent.

In 1487 Bartolomeu Dias rounded the Cape of Good Hope (*see pages 34–35*), opening the way for future explorers to enter the Indian Ocean. The same year, King John of Portugal sent Pedro da Covilham to India on an overland route through Egypt. His reports reached Lisbon in 1490, and told of flourishing spice markets in India and on the East African coast. Any exploration and subsequent economic venture was still at risk from Spain, but, unwittingly, Christopher Columbus came to the rescue. When he discovered the islands of the Caribbean in 1492, he thought he had found the sea route to the Orient by sailing west. To avoid war between Portugal and Spain, Pope Alexander VI issued a Papal bull known as the *Inter caestra*, which granted Spain exclusive rights to trade anywhere west of a line running north-south through the mid-Atlantic. King John objected and, in June 1494, after a year of wrangling, a new settlement was reached, known as the Treaty of Tordesillas.

The choice of da Gama

This time, Portugal got the better deal. By its terms the imaginary line was moved almost a thousand miles to the west, running through what is now Brazil, which, in 1494, had yet to be discovered. Everything to the east was an exclusive Portuguese preserve, including all trade with Africa and the sea route into the Indian Ocean around the Cape of Good Hope. Freed from Spanish interference, Portugal was ready to explore her sphere of influence.

When King Manuel I succeeded to the throne of Portugal in 1495, plans were already

underway to launch a voyage of discovery into the Indian Ocean, Portuguese nobleman Vasco da Gama was chosen to lead the expedition. Born in the port of Sines in southern Portugal, da Gama was the youngest son of Estevão da Gama, the city's civil governor. The young da Gama fought against Castile in 1483, but also took time to learn the art of administration from his father, and navigation, mathematics, and astronomy from a Hebrew tutor. His aristocratic background helped his selection, since many of the venture's sponsors were the heads of the country's noble families. Da Gama had piercing eyes, and was described as arrogant, and sometimes cruel. He was, however, also a respected leader of men.

Four vessels were chosen for the expedition and they were fitted out for their long voyage while docked in Lisbon's harbor during the early summer of 1497. As the Captain Major, da Gama was to sail in the nao *São Gabriel*, assisted by her captain, Gonçal Alvarez, while da Gama's brother, Paolo, was given command of a similar vessel, the *São Rafael*. A small caravel, *Berrio*, was included to serve as a scout ship, commanded by Nicolau Coelho, an experienced long-distance mariner. Gonçalo Nunes, a friend of da Gama's, captained a supply ship whose name was not recorded. A total of 170 seamen manned the four ships, which were loaded with trade goods to exchange for spices and gold, along with sufficient rations to last three years.

Above: *Da Gama hands the Samudra of Calicut a letter from the king of Portugal on May 20, 1498. Painting by José Velloso-Salgado.*

A bold sweep

On July 8, 1497, crowds watched the small fleet leave Lisbon. Sailing down the Moroccan coast, the ships passed the Canary Islands and sailed on to the Cape Verdes, where they took on water. Da Gama led the fleet in a bold sweep into the Atlantic, rather than steering along the African coast. Called a *volta* by Portuguese mariners, this curved course took advantage of offshore winds. The fleet sighted land again on November 4, and made landfall only one degree above the Cape of Good Hope. Da Gama's navigational abilities are remembered today—in the British Royal Navy, a navigating officer is nicknamed "Vasco."

The Portuguese named the anchorage St. Helena Bay, and here they encountered local Hottentot tribesmen. Friction between the two peoples forced da Gama to leave and continue south to the cape, then east.

The fleet anchored again in Mossel Bay, almost as far around the cape as Bartolomeu Dias had ventured ten years before. Here, the natives were friendly and traded fresh meat for trinkets. Da Gama abandoned his storeship, which was probably in poor condition, and had it beached and burnt. Passing the last coastal marker erected by Dias, the expedition entered the uncharted waters of the Indian Ocean.

As it was Christmas, they named the coast Natal, then, at the start of the New Year, da Gama made another *volta* to avoid the contrary coastal currents. It failed and the ships were forced onto the coast. Short of water and suffering from scurvy, the seamen spent two weeks recovering.

The expedition pushed on up the coast, reaching the city of Moçambique (Mozambique) during the first week in March 1498. Da Gama's first diplomatic challenge was not a success—he failed to win the support of the local sultan, who was unimpressed by the explorers' cheap trinkets. After a week futilely spent trying to exchange goods, the expedition sailed northward.

Da Gama had a hostile welcome at Mombasa, 800 miles further north, but then his luck changed. At Malindi the local sultan welcomed the Portuguese and offered food, water, and gifts of spices. Da Gama also encountered traders from India—he was close to his goal.

Empty holds, ailing seamen

The Sultan of Malindi offered the services of a local pilot, who helped the fleet to cross the 2,300 miles of Indian Ocean between Malindi and Calicut, India, in just under a month. On May 18, 1498 da Gama and his crew became the first Europeans to reach the Indian subcontinent by sea.

Exploration was only one of da Gama's aims; the establishment of a trade route was also of paramount importance. However, his attempts at trading largely failed, due to a

Below: *Portrait of Vasco da Gama painted by Gregorio Lopes about 1524.*

combination of poor-quality goods and an effective embargo by the Muslim merchants, who refused to deal with the infidels. The Samudra of Calicut, who ruled the city and its hinterland, was unimpressed by the Portuguese and relations quickly soured.

On August 29 da Gama began the return voyage to East Africa, the holds of his ships all but empty. Lacking the local pilot, who had deserted in Calicut, the Portuguese fell foul of contrary winds and calms and took three months to reach Malindi. The crews were decimated by sickness and scurvy, but again the sultan came to their rescue, donating fruit, vegetables, and water.

Deaths from sickness meant that there were insufficient seamen to crew all three vessels, so da Gama abandoned the *São Rafael*, save for her figurehead, which he kept as a memento. The remaining two ships continued south and arrived at the Cape of Good Hope in mid-March 1499. Heading north again, the vessels reached the familiar waters of the West African coast by mid-April, but more men were lost to disease. One of the casualties was Paolo da Gama, who died in the Cape Verde islands.

The expedition arrived back in Lisbon in early August, where the 54 survivors of a once 170-strong crew were given a hero's welcome. Although they had few spices to show for their efforts, they had sailed 27,000 miles and discovered the route to India, something the Spanish had failed to do. Within ten years Portuguese trading bases were established in India and rival Muslim merchants were driven off with a combination of firepower and diplomacy. The government's initiative to carve out a trade route had succeeded beyond every expectation.

Left: This contemporary illustration shows, from top to bottom, Paolo da Gama's vessel São Rafael, *da Gama's flagship the* São Gabriel, *and the small caravel commanded by Nicolau Coelho.*

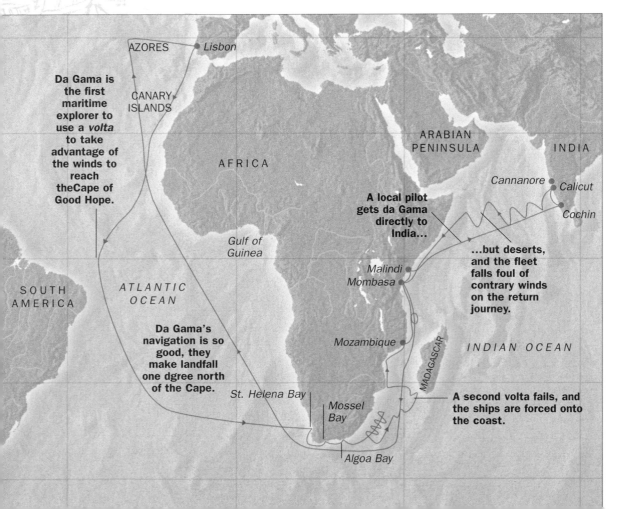

Da Gama is the first maritime explorer to use a *volta* to take advantage of the winds to reach the Cape of Good Hope.

Da Gama's navigation is so good, they make landfall one dgree north of the Cape.

A local pilot gets da Gama directly to India...

...but deserts, and the fleet falls foul of contrary winds on the return journey.

A second volta fails, and the ships are forced onto the coast.

INDIA *in* 1498

When Vasco da Gama sailed into Calicut in 1498, he found a thriving port, richer than anything the Portuguese could imagine. And although he returned almost empty-handed, the few spices he brought back covered the voyage's costs many times over. Da Gama also told tales of the Indian subcontinent to Europeans who had little idea such an exotic land existed.

During the last years of the 15th century, India was a land in turmoil. It was divided spiritually between Hindus and Muslims, and politically fragmented into a patchwork of minor states run by local potentates. The once-powerful Sultanate of Delhi that controlled much of northern India was alarmed at the prospect of an Asian attack from the north, an

Below: An early 16th-century view of the port of Goa, the city that became Portugal's foothold on the Indian subcontinent.

GOA

invasion that would eventually sweep the great Moghul dynasty to power in 1526. The arrival of the Portuguese on the Malabar Coast went unnoticed in Delhi; Europeans had entered India by the back door and would remain in the subcontinent and influence it for another four-and-a-half centuries.

The period from AD 320 until the start of the eighth century is regarded as the classical age of Hindu India. The unification of India by the Gupta dynasty created a stable environment in which religion, the economy, and culture thrived. The empire was based on a levy from the Indian peasantry, and agricultural improvements led to a boom in productivity. Royal patronage resulted in the construction of some of the greatest Hindu temples and Buddhist shrines, and trade links were established with Southeast Asia and the Arabian Peninsula.

In the period following the eighth century, central power devolved into the hands of regional authorities and, although the north remained a highly centralized state, southern India came to be ruled by semi-autonomous warrior dynasties. This classic Hindu era ended after the introduction of Islam during the first decade of the eighth century.

In 711 an Arab invasion entered and quickly conquered the Indian province of Sind. Because the Hindu states were considered too powerful to subdue by conquest, further attacks were avoided, and the two sides coexisted for another three centuries. In the 11th century, Ghaznavid warriors from modern Afghanistan launched repeated raids into India, followed by Turkish invaders, who captured Delhi in 1193. Buddhist monasteries in the north were destroyed and their followers forced to flee into the mountains, and while Hindu resistance had established a new line of defense in central India, the north became a Muslim kingdom.

Trading with Hindus

From 1290, a Delhi-based Muslim dynasty was founded, which would survive as the Sultanate of Delhi until the early 16th century, despite frequent coups, civil wars, and assassinations. When Sultan Mohammed Firuz

1009	1062–1070	1206	1260–1269	c.1300	c.1330	1370	1398
Mahmud of Ghazni, Turkey, conquers northern India.	The kingdom of Chola is dominant in southern India.	Muslims beome established in northern India with the creation of the Delhi Sultanate.	Mongols raid northern India.	The Buddhist faith dies out in northern India.	Peak of the Delhi Sultanate, under Muhammad ibn Tughluk.	Southern India is dominated by the Vijayanagara kingdom.	The Sultanate of Delhi declines following the sack of Delhi by Tamurlane.

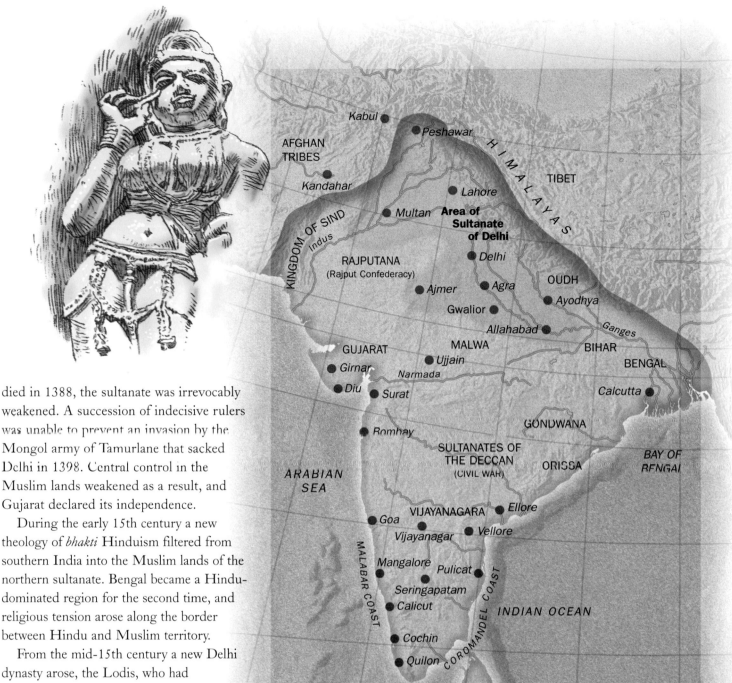

died in 1388, the sultanate was irrevocably weakened. A succession of indecisive rulers was unable to prevent an invasion by the Mongol army of Tamurlane that sacked Delhi in 1398. Central control in the Muslim lands weakened as a result, and Gujarat declared its independence.

During the early 15th century a new theology of *bhakti* Hinduism filtered from southern India into the Muslim lands of the northern sultanate. Bengal became a Hindu-dominated region for the second time, and religious tension arose along the border between Hindu and Muslim territory.

From the mid-15th century a new Delhi dynasty arose, the Lodis, who had previously ruled the Punjab. Sikandar Lodi (1489–1517) has been viewed as the last and most capable of the Sultans of Delhi, largely due to his encouragement of the arts and sciences. For all his virtues, he was unable to control a Hindu resurgence or deflect the threat of another Asiatic invasion.

In the Malabar ports of Calicut and Goa, Hindu rulers allowed Muslim merchants to dominate the marketplaces, where religious principles were considered less important than profit. When the Portuguese first arrived, the local Hindu samudra (ruler) regarded the Europeans as a poor trading prospect, but was as willing to deal with Christians as he was with Muslims. Within a decade the Portuguese had driven off the Arab merchants and established a trading monopoly of their own. To the Hindus, this intrusion was a small price to pay for the potential acquisition of a powerful ally that could defend them from their Muslim enemies.

1469	1498	1500	1510	1519	1524	1530	1539–56
Birth of Guru Nanak, founder of Sikhism.	Vasco da Gama reaches Calicut, India.	Trade links are established between India and Portugal.	Alfonso de Albuquerque captures Goa; the next year he captures Malacca.	Mughals, led by Babur invade India.	Vasco da Gama is made Viceroy of India.	Trading bases are established in Bombay and Sri Lanka by the Portuguese.	The Afghan Sur dynasty force the Mughals from northern India.

PEDRO ÁLVAREZ CABRAL

1467 to 1520

Pedro Cabral has gone down in history as the man who discovered Brazil by accident, during a trading expedition from Portugal to India. His chance discovery provided Portugal with a vital toehold in the Americas; his less publicized achievements include the establishment of faster trade routes from Europe to India and the creation of firm trade agreements between Portuguese and Indian merchants.

Cabral was born into one of the most noble families in Portugal; their land at Belmonte in eastern Portugal's Beira province was both rich and extensive. Pedro became a prominent member of the Portuguese court. He served as a page to King John II, later joined the exclusive Portuguese knightly body, the Order of Christ, and served on King Manuel I's advisory council. This was an exciting period for Portugal—Vasco da Gama had just returned from his remarkable voyage to India.

Under the terms of the Treaty of Tordesillas, while Spain was free to explore the Americas, Portugal could freely concentrate on the trade route around Africa, and da Gama's voyage had proved the potential value of India's markets.

In late 1499, Cabral was appointed as chief captain (admiral) of a fleet of 13 ships and over a thousand seamen and merchants bound for India. Their objective was to build trading settlements on the Malabar coast and to establish the trade route that would bring the first wave of lucrative spice shipments to Portuguese markets. The expedition was commercial rather than exploratory, and its success was of vital importance to Portugal.

Cabral set sail from Lisbon on March 9, 1500. Cabral's pilot and maritime advisor was the seasoned Portuguese explorer Bartolomeu Dias (*see pages 34–35*), but Cabral decided not to follow Dias's favored route, which hugged

Right: Pedro Álvarez Cabral was sent to India to found Portugal's first permanent settlement and on the way accidentally discovered that Portugal also had a claim to a part of the American landmass to the east of the line drawn by the Treaty of Tordesillas.

the African coast. Instead, he swung further out into the South Atlantic from the Cape Verde Islands to take advantage of the mid-ocean winds and currents reported by Vasco da Gama; the maneuver called a *volta*. It was hoped this route would shorten the duration of the voyage.

Land of the True Cross

Cabral passed the Cape Verde Islands as planned, and continued to sail south until his ships reached the trade winds. These near-constant easterly winds are ideal for ships sailing southwest, so Cabral planned to follow that course until he reached the latitude of the Cape of Good Hope, clear of the trade winds, then head east. Bad weather and unforeseen winds had set the ships further to the west than the mariners had anticipated and, unexpectedly, on April 22, 1500 the Portuguese lookouts sighted land to the west. Cabral sailed to investigate.

What they had seen was Mount Pascal, 500 miles north of the modern city of Rio de Janeiro. Cabral landed, claimed the territory for the King of Portugal, and named it Terra da Veracruz (Land of the True Cross). He immediately dispatched a vessel to Portugal with

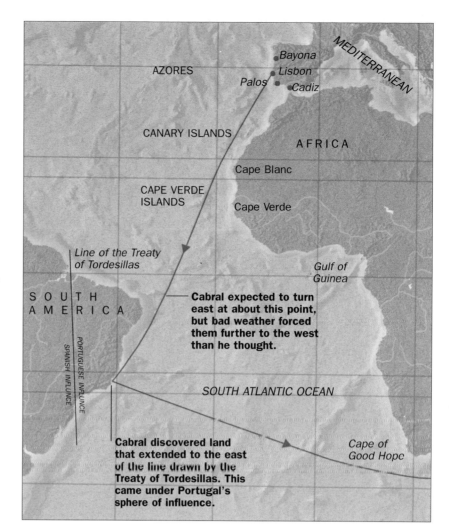

Cabral expected to turn east at about this point, but bad weather forced them further to the west than he thought.

Cabral discovered land that extended to the east of the line drawn by the Treaty of Tordesillas. This came under Portugal's sphere of influence.

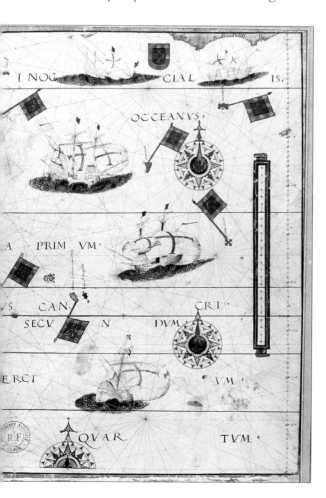

the news, then set about exploring the coast for the following two weeks.

On May 2, 1500, Cabral led his fleet away from their newly discovered coastline, eager to resume the voyage to India. South of the Cape of Good Hope they were overtaken by a severe storm that swamped four vessels and scattered the rest. One of the mariners lost was Bartolomeu Dias. The fleet regrouped off the Mozambique coast, then crossed the Indian Ocean without incident to arrive at Calicut on September 13, 1500. Trouble with Muslim merchants forced Cabral to move south to Cochin, where he established a permanent Portuguese trading settlement. The return voyage was uneventful, and Cabral returned to Lisbon in 1501. Soon after his return, Cabral withdrew from the court to marry and raise a family—he never returned to sea.

Both Vicente Pinzón (*see pages 54–55*) and Amerigo Vespucci (*see pages 92–93*) reached Brazil in the same year, and although it is unclear who found it first, the credit is generally given to Cabral. As brazilwood was discovered in abundance in the new land, the name "Terra da Veracruz" was soon replaced with the less colorful "Terra do Brazil" (Land of Brazil).

Opposite: *A 16th-century map of the Brazil coastline from the Atlas of Diego Homem. Although only a short period after Cabral's discovery, the amount of detail and the number of names along the coast prove that the Portuguese wasted no time in claiming their portion of the Americas.*

DIEGO LOPES *de* SEQUEIRA
1465 to 1520

Right: *On the hill commanding the city, the Fort of St. John housed the Portuguese garrison of Malacca from 1511 until the Dutch took it from them in 1641.*

Little is known about the life of Diego Lopes de Sequeira, but his achievements were more important and their effects longer lasting than many better known explorers of the Age of Discovery. As a Portuguese naval commander, he led the first European expedition to the Spice Islands (now Indonesia), where he discovered a thriving culture and a bustling trading center. His arrival in the Spice Islands marked the beginning of a centuries-long European presence in the region, and allowed Portuguese and, around a hundred years later, Dutch merchants to trade for spices at their source.

In 1504 de Sequeira was made commander of a warship being prepared for a voyage to India, part of a larger Portuguese fleet commanded by Francisco de Almeida. When the fleet sailed in the spring of 1505, Ferdinand Magellan took passage on de Sequeira's ship. The aim of the expedition was to consolidate Portuguese control in the region and guarantee the safety of Portuguese ships trading in spices

It is probable that de Sequeira campaigned

The Portuguese never fully contained the Red Sea and Persian Gulf approaches to the Indian Ocean, but Portugal was the dominant maritime power in the Indian Ocean basin. The next step was to try to obtain a foothold in the Spice Islands themselves.

De Almeida placed de Sequeira in command of a 1509 expedition with orders to sail to the Spice Islands and attempt to establish a base there. Neither man knew anything about the region. This would be a combination of a voyage of discovery and a military conquest, in the best traditions of the later Spanish conquistadors.

The perfect base

De Sequeira sailed from Calicut in the summer of 1509 with a fleet of about a dozen ships. Rounding Ceylon and heading east-southeast across the Bay of Bengal, de Sequeira made landfall on the western end of the island of Sumatra in late August. The locals appeared willing to trade, and the Portuguese established a trade agreement and peace treaty with the Sumatran chiefs.

The Sumatrans also spoke of a great city to the east. This was clearly the fabled city of Malacca, which the Portuguese had heard described by Indian spice merchants. Whatever

Above: *The Mozambique coast of East Africa had been an Arab enclave until the arrival of the Portuguese in the 1500s, who needed to secure it in order to protect their spice trade with the East Indies.*

with Magellan and de Almeida off the east coast of Africa and in defense of Portugal's enclave on India's Malabar Coast. De Almeida's campaigns along the East African coast devastated Muslim trade, and Portuguese power in the region was consolidated by the construction of forts at Sofala in 1505 and Moçambique (Mozambique) in 1507.

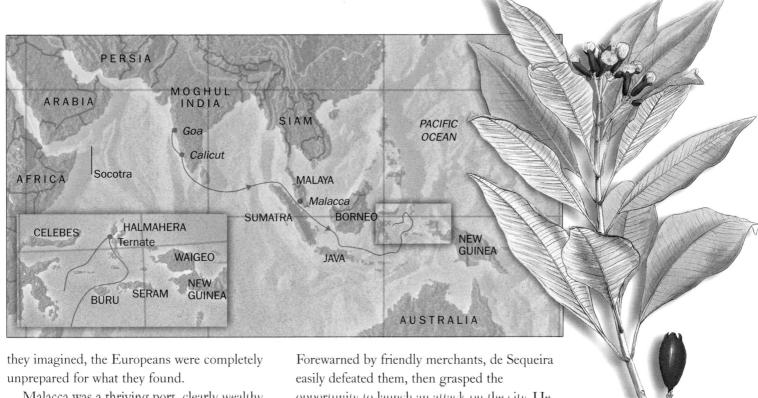

they imagined, the Europeans were completely unprepared for what they found.

Malacca was a thriving port, clearly wealthy and the center of the region's spice trade. Vessels from as far away as China, Arabia, and even Japan crowded the harbor. A Portuguese observer writing in 1515 stated, "no trading port as large as Malacca is known, nor any where they deal in such fine and highly prized merchandise." This was the perfect base for the Portuguese.

The local merchants were wary, but when it became clear that the Europeans only wished to trade, tensions eased, and a Portuguese trading post was established. Local Malay princes were less well disposed and, in mid-1510, they planned an attack on the Portuguese.

Forewarned by friendly merchants, de Sequeira easily defeated them, then grasped the opportunity to launch an attack on the city. He was repulsed, and a tense period ensued during which merchants hired mercenary pirates to fight the Europeans. Reinforcements under the command of Alfonso de Albuquerque (*see pages 72–73*) were sent for, and Malacca finally fell to de Sequeira in 1511.

The Portuguese had captured the richest prize in the Indies and established a firm grip on the spice trade. Diego Lopes de Sequeira went on to explore many of the Spice Islands, reaching as far east as the island of Ternate in the Moluccas. He returned to Portugal in 1512, but declining health prevented him from making further voyages to the Indies.

Above: Of the many spices highly valued by Europeans, the clove was the most prized (see also page 189).

Below: The Strait of Malacca, seen here from the Fort of St. John, became the main highway for the Spice Islands' maritime trade. Sumatra is only 40 miles away on the other side.

ALFONSO *de* ALBUQUERQUE

1453 to 1515

Alfonso de Albuquerque was more of a soldier and administrator than an explorer. His actions helped to consolidate Portuguese power in India and the East Indies, and extended Portuguese influence far beyond the regions explored by Europeans. Born into a prominent Portuguese military family, Albuquerque entered military service as a teenager. He participated in several campaigns in North Africa against the Moors, fighting in Morocco, Tangiers, and in defense of Portuguese trading settlements on the African coast. By the late 1480s Albuquerque had returned home and performed administrative and court duties until 1503, when King Manuel I appointed him commander of a naval force ordered to ensure the security of the new Portuguese trade route from the Cape of Good Hope to India. Hostility toward Portuguese traders was growing among Indians, particularly the Muslims, who felt that their own trading business was being undermined.

Albuquerque sailed to Cochin on the Malabar coast and formed an alliance with the Hindu Raja of Cochin, who allowed the Portuguese to build a fortress to protect their trading settlement. By 1505 the Portuguese had appointed a governor, Dom Francisco de Almeida, who established tight control over the Malabar coast and the island of Ceylon (Sri Lanka).

Albuquerque returned to Lisbon in the

Right: This woodcut shows the coat of arms of King Manuel I of Portugal, flanked by a male and a female Indian, symbolizing the link between Portugal and the Indian subcontinent.

summer of 1504. Two years later he was appointed to lead another naval expedition to disrupt Arab trade with India. He entered the Red Sea and, during 1506 and early 1507, built a fortress on the island of Socotra at the Gulf of Aden. With this route blocked, Arab traders only had the Persian Gulf as an outlet.

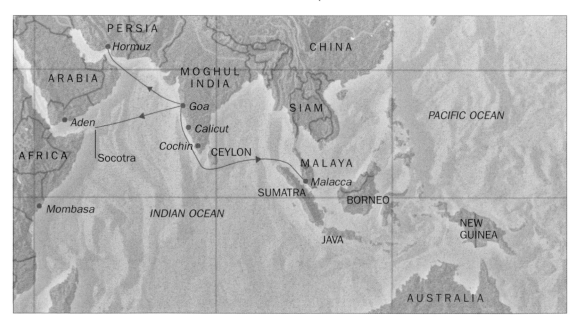

In August 1507, Albuquerque stormed and captured the strategically important port of Hormuz, which guarded the entrance to the Persian Gulf through the Straits of Hormuz. Of the Arab and Persian captives, Albuquerque ordered that all men should have their right hands and their noses cut off, while the women lost their noses and ears. This brutality was partly due to religious differences, but mostly to create a fearsome reputation intended to discourage Arab counterattack or rebellion.

Exploring for victory

During the campaign, Albuquerque sent reconnaissance expeditions deep into both the Red Sea and the Persian Gulf to report on everything that they encountered. His interest lay in military intelligence, not exploration. Nevertheless, the expeditions provided the first detailed accounts of the Arab and Persian communities in these regions since the Middle Ages. Detailed cartographic information was also gathered.

In 1509 Albuquerque was appointed the new Governor of the East Indies, and he quickly decided that Cochin was unsuitable as a major base, since it was difficult to defend and its harbor was too small. Consequently, he led an expedition to capture the Muslim port of Goa, over 400 miles up the Malabar coast. In addition to over 20 Portuguese vessels and 1,500 troops, he employed Hindu mercenaries and a squadron of Malabar pirate craft.

In March 1510 the Portuguese broke through the city defenses after a three-month siege, but were forced out again. The siege continued until November, when the city was finally assaulted and captured. After the male defenders had been massacred, Albuquerque ordered his men to marry the Muslim widows, to ensure the long-term stability of the Portuguese stronghold.

In 1511, Albuquerque was ordered to the East Indies to help Diego Lopes de Sequeira (*see pages 70–71*) capture the port of Malacca, which guarded the strait between Sumatra and the Malay peninsula. Malacca fell the same year, and the Indian Ocean was now a Portuguese sea; but the Arabs made one last attempt to thwart his plans. He returned from Malacca to find that Goa was under siege. In late 1511 he drove off the besiegers, then

pursued the Arab force back into the Red Sea.

For the next few years he continued to defend his fortifications against Arab attacks, but was forced to abandon Socotra in 1514. In late 1515 he fell ill during a campaign in the Strait of Hormuz, and died at sea off Goa in December 1515.

Below: *Alfonso de Albuquerque, shown during his tenure as Governor of the East Indies.*

Discovering the North American Coast

John Cabot	1497
	1498
Gaspar Corte-Real	1500
	1501
Sebastian Cabot	1509
Ponce de León	1513
Giovanni da Verrazano	1525

Hudson Bay

LABRADOR

NOVA SCOTIA

NORTH AMERICA

Gulf of
Mexico

FLORIDA

St. Augustine

Atlantic Ocean

CUBA

Caribbean Sea

HISPANIOLA

PUERTO RICO

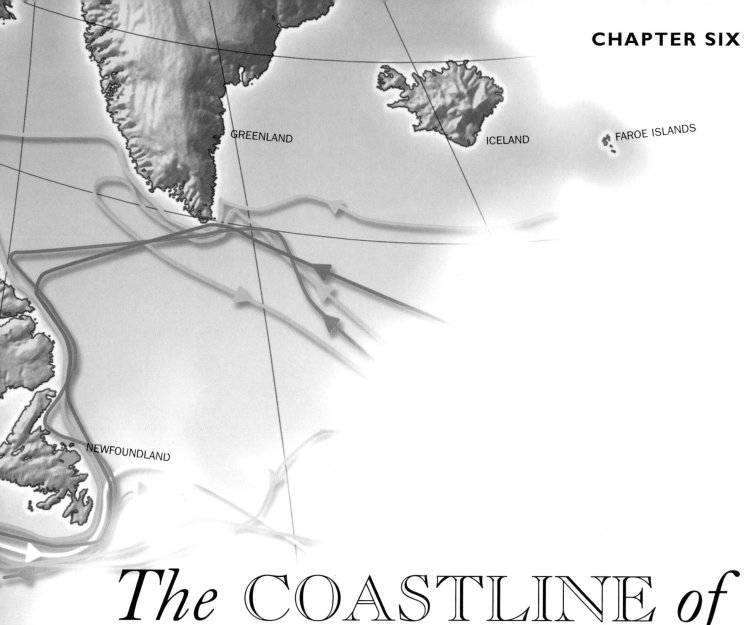

GREENLAND

ICELAND

FAROE ISLANDS

NEWFOUNDLAND

CHAPTER SIX

The COASTLINE *of* NORTH AMERICA

T he Viking Leif Ericson is now known to have landed in Newfoundland five centuries before Christopher Columbus set sail. His discovery was forgotten during the intervening centuries, and the North American continent was abandoned to develop independently from Europe. Although Columbus never saw any part of the continental mainland, his voyage led to other ventures and, within decades, explorers returned to Europe with reports of abundant timber, good soil, and a wealth of wildlife.

The first explorers of the North American coastline, such as John Cabot and Giovanni da Verrazano, treated the local inhabitants with respect, but after them came settlers eager for land, and to the south, Spanish conquistadors tramped inland in search of treasure and territory. The status quo that had existed in the continent for centuries was disrupted forever, and the stage was set for a conflict between Europeans and Native Americans that would last for centuries.

JOHN CABOT

c1450 to c1499

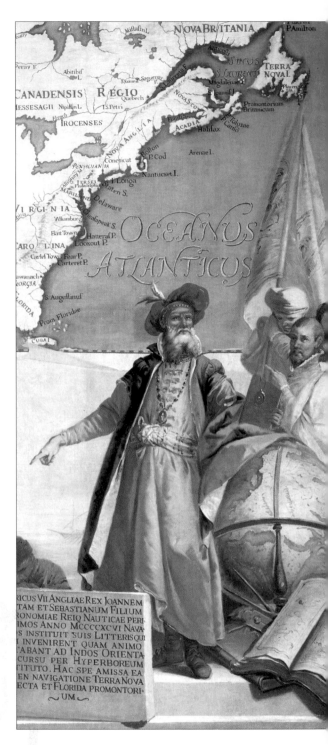

Right: King Henry VII became John Cabot's patron for his voyage to North America. This painting of 1761 by Francesco Griselini, from Doge's Palace, Venice, shows the monarch posed in front of a map of the eastern coast of North America.

The courts of Spain and Portugal rejected John Cabot's proposed voyage to find a northern passage around the landmass of the Americas. The English supported his venture and, although many details of his voyages remain vague, he has been credited as leading the first expedition to set foot in North America since the Vikings.

It is unclear whether John Cabot was born in Genoa or Venice, but in 1476 he became a Venetian citizen and engaged in maritime trade between the city-state and the eastern Mediterranean. He reported that he once traveled as far inland as Mecca, and was well aware of the potential of the Orient before Vasco da Gama reached India in 1497. It is probable that Cabot lived in Spain for at least two years from 1490, and may have been in the country when Columbus returned from his first transatlantic voyage in 1493.

Cabot held the belief that the further north one traveled, the shorter the length of a voyage between Europe and the Orient, due to the earth's curvature. As neither the Spanish nor the Portuguese were prepared to support Cabot and sponsor a voyage to test his theory, he sailed for England. He received a more favorable reception at the court of Henry VII and, in March 1496, Cabot was authorized to sail on behalf of England. Cabot established himself in Bristol, on England's west coast, where sailors from the thriving port had already probed across the Atlantic in search of good fishing grounds. There were even reports of fishermen encountering a landmass in northern waters, which they considered to be the fabled island, "Hy Brazil."

On May 20, 1497, John Cabot sailed from Bristol in a single ship, accompanied by his son Sebastian (*see pages 84–85*) and about 20 sailors. They rounded the southern coast of Ireland and headed west across the Atlantic. Although Cabot's theory about distance and the curvature of the earth had merit, he was unaware that transatlantic voyages in the waters of the North Atlantic would take the same time as ones following more southerly routes because of the contrary flow of the Gulf Stream.

Finding the fishing banks

Cabot sighted land on June 22. It was probably close to St. Anthony on the northern tip of Newfoundland, not far from the landing made by Leif Ericson in AD 1001. Other candidates range as far south as Cape Breton Island in Nova Scotia; although Cabot failed to mention it, the fog, ice, and bad weather that could be encountered in the waters off northern Newfoundland would have made exploration further north quite difficult.

Cabot took possession of the region in the name of the English crown, then raised the

English flag, followed by the flag of Venice. The area surrounding the landing was deserted; it appeared that most of the nearby inhabitants had fled inland, leaving fishing nets and other signs of settlement behind them. Having probably heard tales of the hostile Indians encountered by Columbus, Cabot was concerned about the natives. His crew was too small to risk losing anyone through battle.

Returning to their ship, Cabot and the English explorers sailed southeast, following the northern coast of Newfoundland to reach the eastern side of the Avalon peninsula, an area Cabot thought was an island. He rounded what is now Cape Race on Newfoundland's southeast corner, then continued to the sheltered anchorage of Placentia Bay. Some historians argue that Cabot made a landfall on Cape Breton Island, and instead of reaching as far south as Placentia Bay, he reached the Bay of Fundy, between Nova Scotia and Maine. The confusion arises from the lack of a detailed log or journal, which makes precise identification difficult.

Wherever he reached, Cabot retraced his route north to his original landing place. On the way he noted that the waters were full of fish, which, if taken to be the Newfoundland Banks, supports the theory of a Newfoundland landfall. Either way—Newfoundland or Nova Scotia— he reported that the land was covered with excellent timber.

Cabot returned across the Atlantic to England and arrived in Bristol on August 6, 1497. While Henry VII welcomed his discovery of a northern coast to America, the Bristol ship-owners were delighted with the discovery of an abundant fishing ground. Support for a second voyage of discovery was guaranteed.

Below: John Cabot prepares to sail from Bristol, attended by King Henry VII and senior clerics.

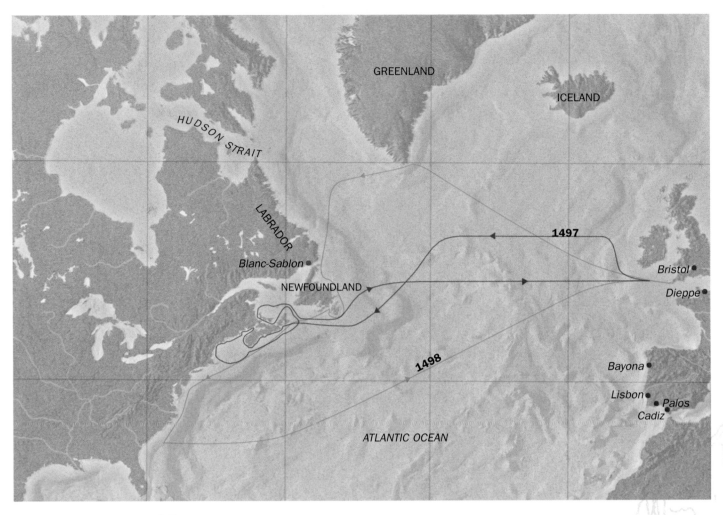

GREENLAND

ICELAND

HUDSON STRAIT

LABRADOR

Blanc-Sablon •

NEWFOUNDLAND

1497

Bristol •

Dieppe •

1498

Bayona •

Lisbon • • Palos
Cadiz •

ATLANTIC OCEAN

Mystery voyage

In February 1498 Henry VII granted John Cabot permission to return to his "Newe Founde Land" and gave him a royal ship and a crew, a gesture matched by the merchants of Bristol, who provided a further four ships. They were keen to establish a route to the Newfoundland fishing grounds, although, like the king, they also wanted to take advantage of any new route to the Indies.

Cabot and his small fleet left Bristol in May 1498 on a voyage that would baffle future historians. One version states that Cabot made a more northerly landfall on the southern tip of Greenland, then sailed up its western coast before heading south past Baffin Island and Labrador to Newfoundland. Cabot then reportedly continued southwest to reach the coast of Nova Scotia, and then explored down the North American coast as far as the Chesapeake Bay. Other versions credit Cabot with sailing north from Newfoundland in search of a northwestern passage around the North American landmass.

One ship returned early to Bristol (the reason

for this has never been explained), and Cabot and the remaining four ships were never heard from again. Accounts that the four vessels returned empty-handed and Cabot retired into obscurity have been refuted by recent historical research into the Bristol shipping records. If the expedition never returned, what happened to it?

Despite the lack of evidence, several clues remain. In September 1498 Cabot's pension from the king was drawn for the last time from the Bristol City authorities. Recent evidence shows that it was drawn by Sebastian Cabot, John Cabot's son. Had the explorer returned, too ill to collect his allowance in person, or was he already missing? Within a year of the return of the surviving ship, Bristol ship owners sent fishing vessels to the Newfoundland Banks, so it seems likely that the vessel brought back further information about the banks' location.

A further clue lies on the map of Juan de la Cosa produced in 1500 (*see pages 122–123*). Although it concentrated on the discoveries made by Spain and Portugal, it depicted the coast of North America as far south as what is now the Carolinas. Its length was marked with

English flags. One historian has gone so far as to postulate that Cabot's expedition was attacked by Spaniards, who killed the English and took the information. Whatever happened to Cabot, historians have generally given him the benefit of the doubt, and have credited him with the post-Viking rediscovery of North America.

Adopting the Cabot legacy

Part of the problem of unraveling the mystery surrounding John Cabot lies with his son. Following the loss of his father, Sebastian Cabot became a successful explorer in his own right. He undertook voyages of discovery to Labrador in search of a northwest passage, and down the coast of South America as far as the River Plate in an attempt to find a southern route around the American landmass. Sebastian, who was much better than his father at publicizing and recording his achievements, appears subsequently to have claimed the credit for several of his father's accomplishments, and he may have deliberately obscured the details of John Cabot's last voyage.

As well as a reputation for able seamanship, John Cabot was widely regarded as one of the most skilled navigators of his day, and as a cartographer he is known to have produced maps and even globes. It seems highly unlikely that he would lose his entire expedition of four ships, unless it was at the hands of some

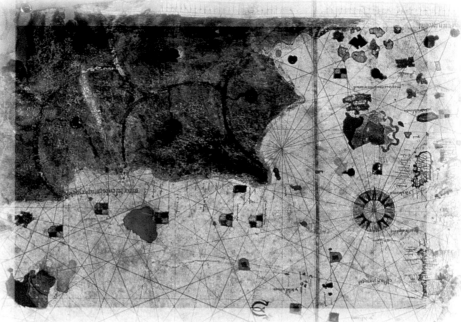

unforeseen natural disaster, such as a hurricane or rapid arctic ice movement, or at the hands of an unknown enemy.

Historians may argue about the explorer's fate, but they agree that Cabot left two legacies. The first was the rediscovery of Newfoundland and its superb fishing grounds. England would stake a greater claim to the territory; indirectly, Cabot's activities paved the way for English (and later British) colonial expansion in North America. His other legacy was the belief that a route existed around North America that would provide a passage from Europe to the Orient. His son was the first of many who searched for this elusive northwest passage.

Above: This detail from Juan de la Cosa's map shows marker flags along the Atlantic coast of North America, which may be a clue to the disappearance of John Cabot's expedition.

Below: The arctic waters surrounding Greenland were visited by several explorers, who used the landmass as a geographical reference point before continuing their voyages

NATIVE CULTURES *of the* ATLANTIC COAST

Above: *A native American village on the eastern seaboard and,* opposite, *a Huron, a member of one of the few tribes that united into large political and administrative confederations.*

While the natives of Central and South America had developed agriculture, sophisticated religion, and simple political systems, those encountered by Juan Ponce de León, Hernando de Soto, and Jacques Cartier further to the north had not advanced beyond the hunter-gatherer stage. Cartier came into contact with the tribes of the Northeast Woodland, a cultural group that extended from the Atlantic coast to the prairies of the Midwest. These people spoke several languages, principally Algonquian, Iroquoian, or Siouan, and shared a common culture based on hunting and gathering. The peoples of the region around the Gulf of St. Lawrence included the Micmac, Algonquin, Abenaki, and Huron peoples, while along the Atlantic coast, Giovanni da Verrazano (*see pages 88–89*) encountered the Massachuset, Narraganset, Susquehanough, and Delaware tribes.

These Iroquoian-speaking societies had lived in the region since the Ice Age and there is archæological evidence that they stemmed from a single parent culture that had existed over 3,000 years earlier. Despite this long development, these tribes lacked the technological impetus found further south and remained hunter-gatherers until they encountered European explorers.

The society of these groups was primarily centered around hunting and fishing, although on the coast they also relied on some agriculture for additional food. Tribes used the slash-and-burn method to clear arable land from the surrounding woodland to grow corn, squash, and beans. Their buildings were primarily bark-covered rectangular longhouses, although wigwams were also found. As warfare was commonplace, their villages were often surrounded by a defensive palisade.

Because some of the villages were large, with up to 4,000 inhabitants, and because this size of community placed a greater emphasis on farming, such centers became the focal point for trade within a tribal region. Cartier encountered substantial Huron settlements during his exploration of the St. Lawrence River and noted the tight organization of urban political and social life. Despite the existence of some agriculture, hunting still made the best use of surrounding woodland. Wild game was abundant in the region, notably deer, bear, and wildfowl, while along the rivers, lakes, and coastline there was extensive fishing with nets, fishing lines, or spears. This natural abundance surprised the first European explorers, who saw the northeastern part of the continent as a garden of plenty.

Cult of the temple mounds

Politically, villages were often loosely bound into tribal confederations, although these had little real power. There were exceptions, especially the Delaware Indians, who maintained a tightly knit confederacy under powerful head chiefs. The Huron tribe also maintained a strong structure, and about the latter half of the 16th century the Iroquois established their five-nation league.

To the south of these, the tribes encountered by the Spanish in what are now Florida, Georgia, and the Deep South were organized in a completely different way. Most of these peoples shared a common language, Muskogean, which in turn was related to the

c.300 BC	c.AD 300	800–900	c.900	c.1000	c.1150	13th century	c.1200
Rise of the Hopewell Indians.	Agricultural societies develop in the deserts of the southwest of North America.	Maize and beans are major food sources in eastern woodlands of North America.	The Hohokam farmers use irrigation systems.	A Norse settlement is established in the northeast (L'Anse aux Meadows).	The Hopewell Indian culture dies out.	The Thule Inuits reach Greenland.	Temple mounds are built at Moundville, Alabama.

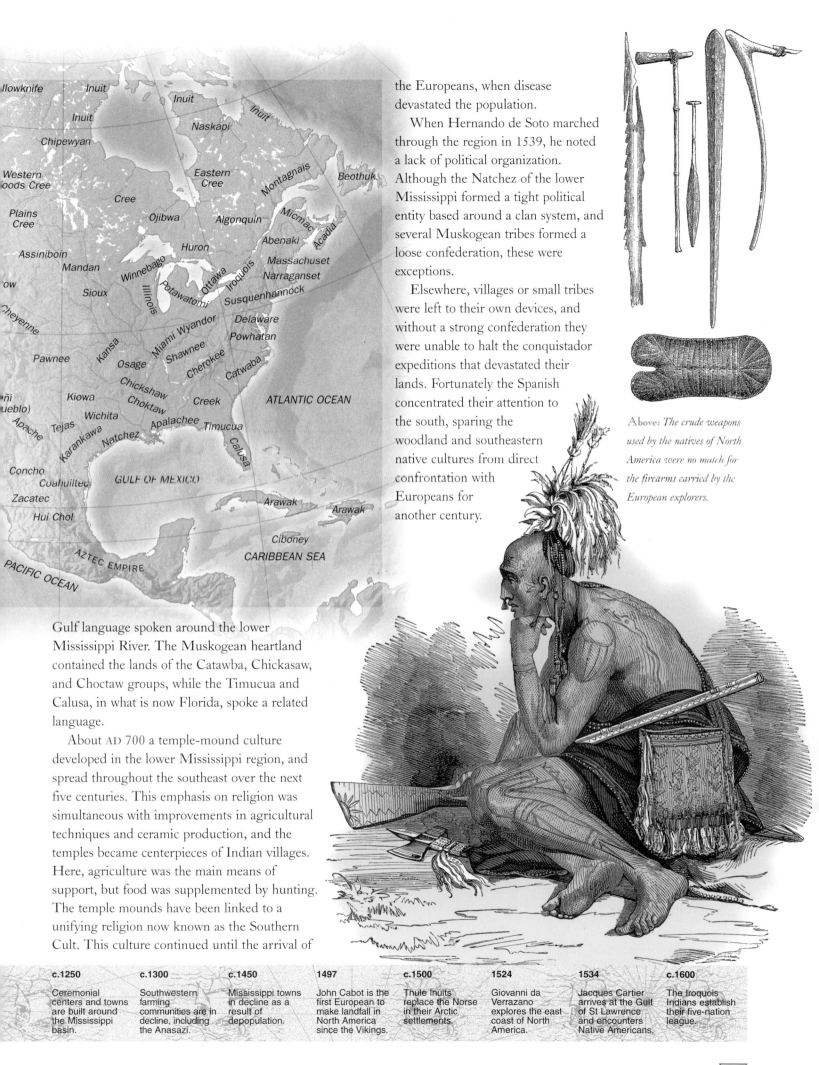

the Europeans, when disease devastated the population.

When Hernando de Soto marched through the region in 1539, he noted a lack of political organization. Although the Natchez of the lower Mississippi formed a tight political entity based around a clan system, and several Muskogean tribes formed a loose confederation, these were exceptions.

Elsewhere, villages or small tribes were left to their own devices, and without a strong confederation they were unable to halt the conquistador expeditions that devastated their lands. Fortunately the Spanish concentrated their attention to the south, sparing the woodland and southeastern native cultures from direct confrontation with Europeans for another century.

Above: *The crude weapons used by the natives of North America were no match for the firearms carried by the European explorers.*

Gulf language spoken around the lower Mississippi River. The Muskogean heartland contained the lands of the Catawba, Chickasaw, and Choctaw groups, while the Timucua and Calusa, in what is now Florida, spoke a related language.

About AD 700 a temple-mound culture developed in the lower Mississippi region, and spread throughout the southeast over the next five centuries. This emphasis on religion was simultaneous with improvements in agricultural techniques and ceramic production, and the temples became centerpieces of Indian villages. Here, agriculture was the main means of support, but food was supplemented by hunting. The temple mounds have been linked to a unifying religion now known as the Southern Cult. This culture continued until the arrival of

c.1250	c.1300	c.1450	1497	c.1500	1524	1534	c.1600
Ceremonial centers and towns are built around the Mississippi basin.	Southwestern farming communities are in decline, including the Anasazi.	Mississippi towns in decline as a result of depopulation.	John Cabot is the first European to make landfall in North America since the Vikings.	Thule Inuits replace the Norse in their Arctic settlements.	Giovanni da Verrazano explores the east coast of North America.	Jacques Cartier arrives at the Gulf of St Lawrence and encounters Native Americans.	The Iroquois Indians establish their five-nation league.

GASPAR *and* MIGUEL CORTE-REAL

c1450
to
1501

c1460
to
1502

The Corte-Real brothers remain unsung heroes of the Age of Exploration, partly because their voyages were conducted under a veil of secrecy and partly because their discoveries mirrored those made by John Cabot two years earlier. In 1500 the Portuguese mariner Gaspar Corte-Real approached King Manuel I of Portugal for permission to undertake a voyage of discovery to the "Newe Founde Land" located by John Cabot in 1498. Cabot's discovery had caused a degree of anxiety in the Spanish and Portuguese courts and, because the location of his landfall lay within Portugal's sphere of influence as defined by the Treaty of Tordesillas, the Portuguese monarch felt justified in claiming the territory for himself. Because this might have threatened the strong political and economic ties between England and Portugal, Manuel ordered that the expedition be planned and executed in secrecy.

Two ships were readied, and they left Lisbon in the summer of 1500. Corte-Real steered on a northwesterly heading and made landfall on the eastern coast of Greenland after a particularly arduous voyage. The expedition turned south and followed the Greenland coast down to its southernmost tip, Cape Farewell, on the latitude of 60°N. Just past this landmark Corte-Real encountered a group of Inuit (Eskimos) on a fishing expedition. Although alarmed by the Europeans, the locals were encouraged to barter with Corte-Real's crew, who tried to discover if the Inuit knew about a passage to the west. The Inuit produced fish but no solid information.

Corte-Real continued northwest along the Greenland coast, to the latitude of about 63°N, before pack ice and weather forced him to abandon his exploration. He returned to Lisbon without finding any trace of Cabot's Newfoundland or of a passage to the Indies.

Corte-Real's failure did not deter King Manuel from his quest, and a second expedition was sponsored in the following year involving three ships and 170 mariners. The Portuguese explorer adopted a different strategy. He knew that his Greenland landfall lay some 600 miles further north than Newfoundland and that if he sailed west from it, he should make a second landfall north of the one made by Cabot. From there, following the coast southward, he hoped to find the entrance to a sea route to the Indies.

Following a disappearance

The expedition sailed in the spring of 1501, and Corte-Real was accompanied by his mariner brother, Miguel. The expedition landed at Cape Farewell, then sailed west as planned. The passage across what would be called the Davis Strait was uneventful and a successful landfall was made on a barren and inhospitable coastline. The Portuguese had reached the coast of Labrador.

Corte-Real followed the coast to the southeast and explored the myriad small inlets and bays along the shores. During this part of the voyage the Portuguese encountered a number of Inuit communities. The locals were questioned about a possible western passage but were unhelpful. When the Inuit looked as though they might turn hostile, Gaspar took hostages.

As soon as they reached the location of modern-day Hamilton Inlet in Labrador, the Portuguese sailed away from the coast as it curved to the south and continued their northeasterly course until they made landfall on the northern coast of Newfoundland. When

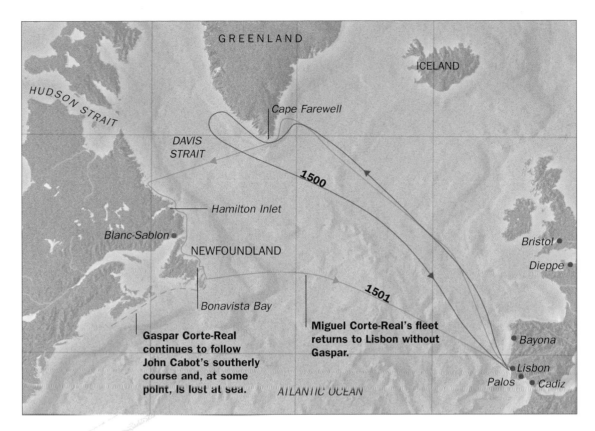

GREENLAND

ICELAND

HUDSON STRAIT

Cape Farewell

DAVIS STRAIT

1500

Hamilton Inlet

Blanc-Sablon

NEWFOUNDLAND

Bristol

Dieppe

Bonavista Bay

Gaspar Corte-Real continues to follow John Cabot's southerly course and, at some point, is lost at sea.

Miguel Corte-Real's fleet returns to Lisbon without Gaspar.

1501

Bayona

Lisbon

Palos   Cadiz

ATLANTIC OCEAN

Opposite and below: The Inuit (Eskimo) cultures encountered by Corte-Real lived in an almost unimaginably harsh environment, yet they found time to make ritual masks like these.

Left below: Even the Arctic summers only provided sparse vegetation unsuited to grazing, so Inuit communities were invariably hunters and fishermen, quick to take offense and turn hostile toward the European explorers.

they reached Bonavista Bay the explorers found that the land was far more hospitable, and they noted an abundance of fish.

The expedition continued south, down the eastern coast of Newfoundland, for some distance before the brothers decided to go their separate ways. While Gaspar Corte-Real continued his voyage to the southeast, following the course of Cabot's 1497 voyage, Miguel was to return to Lisbon with the remaining two ships, taking the Inuit hostages with him.

Miguel reached Portugal in late 1501, but Gaspar and his crew were never seen again. It is considered likely that Gaspar's ship foundered during its return voyage. In May 1502 Miguel Corte-Real set out in search of his missing brother in a single ship, but he too disappeared without trace. The fate of the Corte-Real brothers remains one of the great mysteries of the Age of Discovery.

SEBASTIAN CABOT

c1476 to 1557

Below: *Sebastian Cabot was one of the first men who tried unsuccessfully to find the northwest passage around America to the Orient.*

E merging from the shadow of his father, Sebastian Cabot became one of the most active explorers of the Age of Discovery. He undertook voyages for both England and Spain as he pursued his two passions: finding a northwest passage and updating cartographic knowledge. Cabot was born in Venice about 1476, and of his early life we only know that he spent some time in Spain and then accompanied his father, John Cabot (*see pages 76–79*), to Bristol in England about 1490. Controversy surrounds the Cabots; John because he vanished in 1498, and his son for allegedly being a self-publicist who claimed greater achievements than he should.

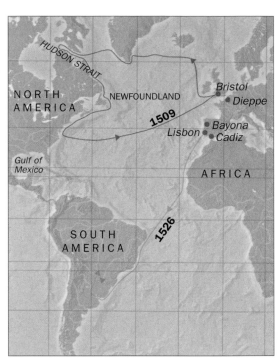

What is certain is that Sebastian Cabot accompanied his father on the 1497 Newfoundland voyage and that he remained in Bristol when John sailed the following year, never to return. It is unclear when Sebastian Cabot led his first voyage, but the general view is that it was in 1508, on behalf of English King Henry VII to look for the northwest passage.

He made landfall on the northern coast of Newfoundland, then continued north along the coast of Labrador. After almost 800 miles he entered a wide strait, which Cabot felt sure was the entrance to the fabled passage. It was what would be called the Hudson Strait. Passing between Labrador and Baffin Island, Cabot continued up the strait and sailed around the Ungeva Peninsula to enter a vast inland sea that he was certain would lead to the Pacific. It is thought that Cabot reached as far west as the Foxe Channel before being forced back by advancing winter ice. The expedition returned to Bristol in early 1509.

Seduced by dreams of wealth

Although he had found a passage that might lead through the Arctic to the Orient, he returned with nothing to interest his mercantile backers. Since Henry VII had died while he was away and his son Henry VIII had little interest in exploration, Sebastian Cabot was unable to raise the funds or support necessary to launch a return journey.

In late 1509 Cabot entered the English royal service as a cartographer, where his skills were put to use in the compilation of maps that might aid Henry VIII's military campaigns. Cabot also served Ferdinand of Aragon and Spain—then England's ally against France—as a maritime cartographer to record the details necessary for Spain to understand the full extent of her New World empire.

Cabot served the Spanish crown for the next 30 years and rose to be a maritime advisor to the Council of the Indies in 1518, the body established by Emperor Charles I to oversee the shipping between Europe and the Spanish Main (Spain's colonies in the Caribbean basin). From the 1520s this included overseeing the treasure fleets that carried to Spain the silver and gold recovered in the Americas.

In 1522 the survivors of Magellan's circumnavigation voyage (*see pages 126–131*) returned to Spain having discovered the route around the Americas into the Pacific Ocean. Five years later Cabot was placed in charge of an expedition to look for an alternative, shorter route, which he expected to find somewhere along the coastline of South America.

The expedition sailed from Sanlúcar de Barrameda on April 3, 1526, and Cabot, leading his four ships southwest from the Cape Verde Islands, reached the easternmost point in Brazil in late September. He sailed south until he arrived at what is now the southern border of Brazil, where he rescued two Spanish castaways. They reported that a wealthy kingdom lay inland, so Cabot ignored his mission and began to search. He sailed up the Rio de la Plata—named by Cabot after the

silver looted from settlements along the shore—and ventured as far as 600 miles inland through what is now modern Paraguay, before he was forced to retire due to Indian attacks. He returned to Spain empty-handed in November 1529, and was exiled for disobeying his orders.

By 1547, he had been restored to favor, but he chose to return to England, where he mounted two more unsuccessful expeditions to

find the northwest pPassage, and a third that attempted to sail around Norway and Russia, the northeast passage. In this last voyage, he at least helped to establish trade links with Muscovy (Russia), and this went a long way to boost his image as the "elder statesman of the Age of Discovery."

Above: *Sebastian Cabot explored the coast of South America as far as the River Plate, where he sailed deep into the hinterland of the continent.*

JUAN PONCE *de* LEÓN

c1460 *to* 1521

Opposite top: *A 19th-century impression of de León greeting the Florida Indians.*

Below: *Juan Ponce de León, the discoverer of Florida.*

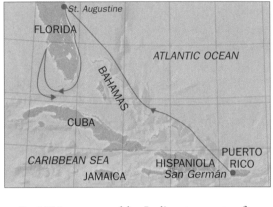

Juan Ponce de León is perhaps best remembered as the Quixotic figure who searched for the mythical fountain of eternal youth he believed to exist in La Florida. Although he really believed in the fountain, de León was not a whimsical man, in fact he was a practical colonizer who helped to reinforce Spain's claim to North America. De León served in the court of Castile before he accompanied Columbus on his second voyage to the Americas in 1493 (*see page 48*). In 1502 he volunteered to participate in Nicolás Ovando's expedition to Hispaniola (now Haiti and the Dominican Republic). He was made the governor of the west of the island, and his administration was marked by a lack of friction between Spaniard and native.

In 1508, prompted by Indian accounts of a rich island to the east, he launched an expedition to explore and colonize Puerto Rico. He founded a colony at San Germán and was appointed the island's governor by the Spanish king. In 1511, he applied for a grant to settle the islands of the Bahamas (Bimini).

He sailed from Puerto Rico in March 1513 with three ships and headed northwest along the outer fringe of the Bahamas. At the northern end of the island chain, he inexplicably continued on the same course and sighted a low eastern coastline on March 27. Indians had told the Spanish that somewhere to the west lay a land that contained the fountain of youth, and anyone who drank from it would recover their youthful looks. The coast he was looking at seemed to fit the description, and de León landed six days later, on April 2. He was the first Spaniard to set foot on the continent of North America. The landfall was a few miles north of the modern city of St. Augustine, on a long desolate stretch of beach with sand dunes. De León named the region Tierra La Florida (the land of flowers) in honor of Easter Sunday (called *Pascua Florida* in Spanish).

Mapping Florida

Returning to their ships, the Spanish sailed south and hugged the flat and featureless coast. Then they discovered the channel between Florida and the Bahamas (the Bahamas Channel), which offered the possibility of a new shipping route for the Spanish returning home from their New World settlements. They continued to the southwest, skirted the islands

of the Florida Keys, which de León named Los Martyres (Martyrs), and then, by turning north, discovered that Florida was a peninsula.

De León probably reached as far north as what is now Pensacola Bay before turning his fleet around to retrace the path southward. Despite searching, the legendary fountain of youth remained a myth, and de León turned his mind to more practical matters. Skirting Los Martyres again, he reached the islands he named Tortugas (Turtles), now the Dry Tortugas, and then swung south into the Straits of Florida, which he crossed to reach the Cuban shore. From there, he traveled along the coasts of Cuba and Hispaniola until he reached Puerto Rico in September 1513.

Ponce de León returned to Spain in 1514, where he was knighted by his king, and granted the right to colonize Bimini and La Florida. Another seven years passed before he would take advantage of this opportunity. In February 1521 he sailed from Puerto Rico and landed in western Florida, probably near Sanibel Island, where he tried to establish a colony. The native Indians proved hostile, and Ponce de León was mortally wounded in a skirmish. The expedition withdrew to Havana, where the explorer died in July 1521. Unlike many of his fellow Spaniards, Ponce de León favored a friendly relationship with the natives he encountered, and it is ironic that he should die at their hands.

Below: *Florida Indians hunting alligators in a late 16th-century engraving by Theodore de Bry.*

GIOVANNI *da* VERRAZANO

c1485 *to* c1528

An Italian, Giovanni da Verrazano explored the American coast from the Carolinas to Maine for the French crown. Earlier explorers had covered the same area, but he brought back the most detailed descriptions of North America yet and also reinforced France's claim to some of the New World. Giovanni da Verrazano's aristocratic family held estates to the south of Florence. Despite his wealthy background and good education, he moved to Dieppe in France about 1506 in order to go to sea.

He had sailed on several commercial voyages before he entered royal service, where he quickly rose to command a French warship engaged in protecting French commerce in the Mediterranean. France and Spain were at war, and da Verrazano proved his naval skills by capturing a number of prizes.

In 1524, the French king, Francis I (*pictured on page 19*), commissioned da Verrazano to explore the Americas, with the joint aims of selecting an area suitable for French settlement and locating a northern passage to the Indies

Below: Following the catastrophic French defeat at the Battle of Pavia (1525), Francis I was more interested in recovering his lost influence in Europe than sponsoring voyages of exploration.

clear of areas held by the Portuguese and Spanish. In January 1525 da Verrazano set sail in four ships, accompanied by his cartographer brother, Girolomo. Two ships were lost at sea on the transatlantic voyage, and the surviving vessels made landfall at what is now Cape Fear, North Carolina.

He sailed south in search of a suitable anchorage, but turned around too soon—had he continued to the south, he would have sighted the natural harbor where today Charleston stands. However, he did reach Chesapeake Bay. Thinking that it marked the entrance to a channel to the Pacific Ocean, he eponymously named it the Verrazano Sea. (A *mappa mundi* [world map] produced by Girolomo da Verrazano in 1529 marked the bay as the mouth of a possible passage through North America.) He continued northward in search of the main objective: a suitable site to found a French colony.

Da Verrazano followed what are now the Delaware and New Jersey coasts until he found a well-protected anchorage, sheltered by a long

island. He named the area Francesca, in honor of his king. On April 17, 1525, he anchored in a passage that became the Verrazano Narrows, the channel in modern-day New York harbor between Brooklyn and Staten Island. He named the bay to the north of it Santa Margarita, and described it as "a pleasant lake."

Land of the bad people

From Francesca he continued north, probing well into every bay or inlet he encountered, until he was driven into modern Narragansett Bay by a bad storm. The Indians he encountered proved to be friendly, and even guided da Verrazano to a sheltered anchorage off what is now Newport, Rhode Island. He remained in the bay for two weeks and sent scouting parties into the hinterland, and gathered water and provisions. The scouts reported that the soil was fertile, even far inland, that there was an abundance of timber, and that all the Indian villages were friendly.

On May 5, da Verrazano left the bay and continued north. He passed through what is now Nantucket Sound and rounded Cape Cod to reach Maine at Casco Bay. Less impressed with the Indians he encountered here (Abinaki), he named the region the "Land of the Bad People," but in detailed descriptions of the coast, he described the sea as turquoise and the inlets and islands "pleasant to the view." He continued north around Nova Scotia and Newfoundland, both of which were becoming popular destinations for European fishermen, particularly Basque whalers from the north of Spain. From there he returned across the Atlantic and arrived in Dieppe in July 1525.

The French defeat at the Battle of Pavia (1525) had plunged France into turmoil, and, since Francis I had been captured on the battlefield by the Spanish, da Verrazano had to wait until the king was released before obtaining royal patronage for a second voyage. This time he made landfall in Florida, then sailed down the chain of the Leeward Islands. The explorers anchored off one of the islands, probably Guadeloupe, and da Verrazano went ashore with a small party. They were attacked and killed by cannibals before their comrades aboard the ships could rescue them. It was a horrific end to a talented explorer who greatly expanded his contemporaries' knowledge of the Americas.

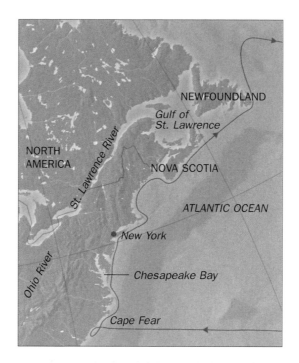

Below: *Giovanni de Verrazano helped lay the groundwork for French settlement in the Americas.*

CHAPTER SEVEN

The DISCOVERY *of* SOUTH AMERICA

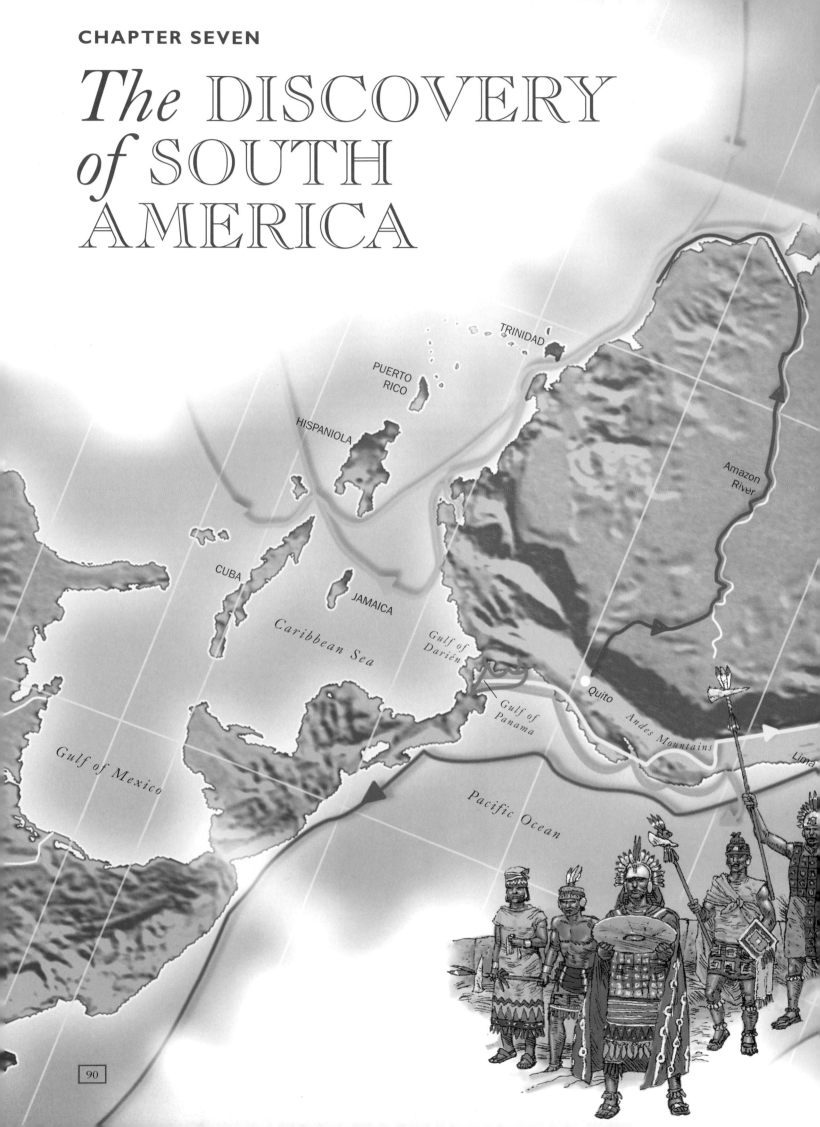

TRINIDAD

PUERTO
RICO

HISPANIOLA

CUBA

JAMAICA

Caribbean Sea

Gulf of
Dariën

Gulf of
Panama

*Amazon
River*

Quito

Andes Mountains

Lima

Gulf of Mexico

Pacific Ocean

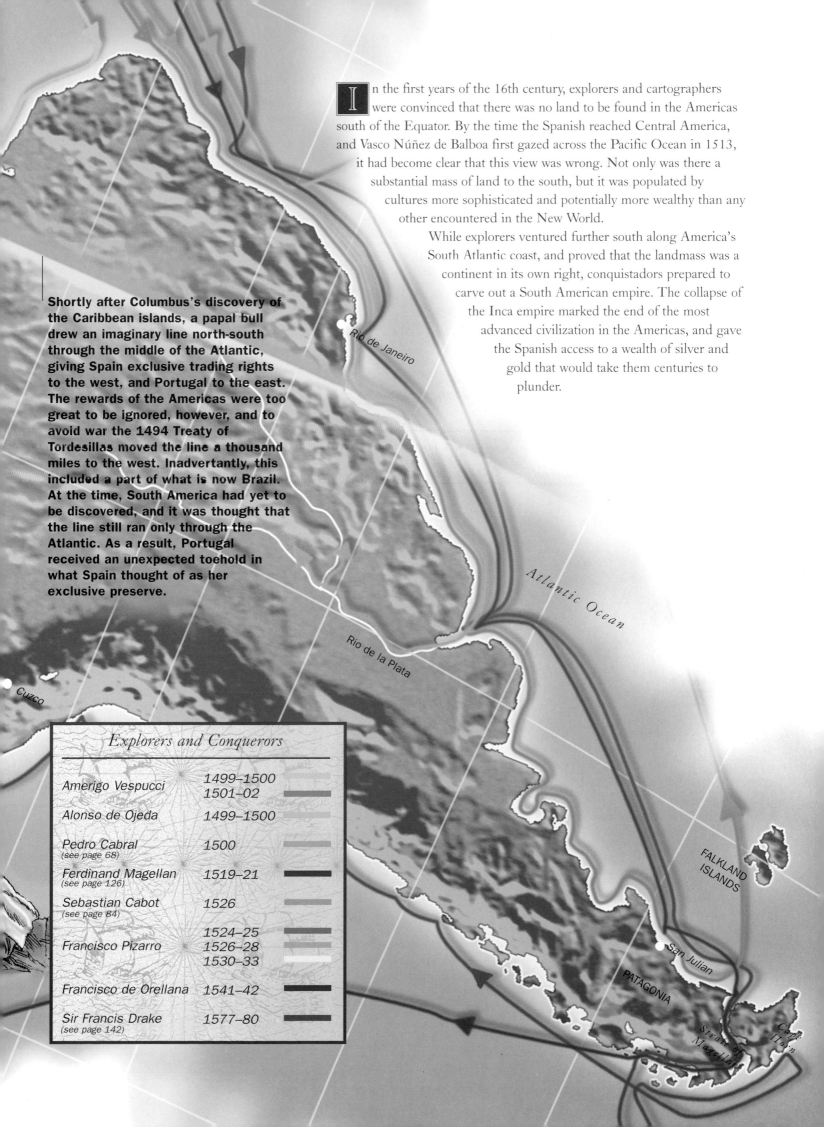

In the first years of the 16th century, explorers and cartographers were convinced that there was no land to be found in the Americas south of the Equator. By the time the Spanish reached Central America, and Vasco Núñez de Balboa first gazed across the Pacific Ocean in 1513, it had become clear that this view was wrong. Not only was there a substantial mass of land to the south, but it was populated by cultures more sophisticated and potentially more wealthy than any other encountered in the New World.

While explorers ventured further south along America's South Atlantic coast, and proved that the landmass was a continent in its own right, conquistadors prepared to carve out a South American empire. The collapse of the Inca empire marked the end of the most advanced civilization in the Americas, and gave the Spanish access to a wealth of silver and gold that would take them centuries to plunder.

Shortly after Columbus's discovery of the Caribbean islands, a papal bull drew an imaginary line north-south through the middle of the Atlantic, giving Spain exclusive trading rights to the west, and Portugal to the east. The rewards of the Americas were too great to be ignored, however, and to avoid war the 1494 Treaty of Tordesillas moved the line a thousand miles to the west. Inadvertantly, this included a part of what is now Brazil. At the time, South America had yet to be discovered, and it was thought that the line still ran only through the Atlantic. As a result, Portugal received an unexpected toehold in what Spain thought of as her exclusive preserve.

Río de Janeiro

Atlantic Ocean

Río de la Plata

Cuzco

Explorers and Conquerors

Amerigo Vespucci	1499–1500 1501–02
Alonso de Ojeda	1499–1500
Pedro Cabral (see page 68)	1500
Ferdinand Magellan (see page 126)	1519–21
Sebastian Cabot (see page 84)	1526
Francisco Pizarro	1524–25 1526–28 1530–33
Francisco de Orellana	1541–42
Sir Francis Drake (see page 142)	1577–80

FALKLAND ISLANDS

San Julián

PATAGONIA

Strait of Magellan

Cape Horn

AMERIGO VESPUCCI

1451 to 1512

Below: *Amerigo Vespucci in his later years and,* opposite top, *amid the sea nymphs and strange creatures supposedly found in the New World.*

The man who gave his name to two continents was a controversial figure. He was accused of self-aggrandizement and of stealing the glory from other, more worthy explorers, and yet his achievements for Spain and Portugal were highly significant, and make him worthy of the honor bestowed on him. Amerigo Vespucci was born into a mercantile family in Florence at the height of the Italian renaissance. A gifted man, his talents extended to poetry and cosmography, as well as commerce and banking. In his 20s he served as an ambassador for Lorenzo de Medici in France, but he left his siblings in 1492 and moved to Spain, where he opened a ship brokerage business in Seville. In the wake of Columbus's discoveries, he supplied the ships, loans, and supplies needed by the new band of transatlantic explorers and the settlers who followed them. It was inevitable that Vespucci would want to see these new lands for himself.

It is unclear when Vespucci made his first voyage, but the consensus rejects the evidence of a letter he wrote in 1504 that indicates he participated in four expeditions, the first in 1497. Correspondence written to the de Medici family in Florence described two voyages, which is considered the more likely number.

The first of these was in 1499, when Vespucci participated in the expedition of Alonso de Ojeda (*see pages 94–95*). Although Vespucci was the commercial advisor, when the expedition reached the Cape Verde Islands he was allowed to explore on his own. The South American coast was divided into two parts, based on the landfall made by Columbus the previous year in the vicinity of Trinidad and the Orinoco River. Vespucci was dispatched to explore the coast to the south of this line.

He made landfall near the modern town of Fortaleza, to the northwest of Cape São Roque, the easternmost point of what is now Brazil. This made him the first person to explore the Americas south of the equator. Vespucci explored the coast, sailing northwest for 700 miles, noting the mouths of several rivers.

Defining the Americas

Vespucci reached the mouth of a wide gulf or estuary, which he named the Gulf of Santa Maria, and noted the fresh water that was present for miles out to sea. He remained unaware that this was the mouth of the Amazon River. Continuing north, he discovered the mouth of the Orinoco, a delta noted but not explored by Columbus the previous year. He had reached the limit of his exploring brief, and continued up the coast of Venezuela before heading across the Caribbean Sea for his planned rendezvous with de Ojeda at Hispaniola.

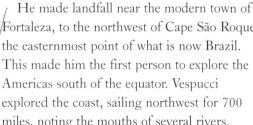

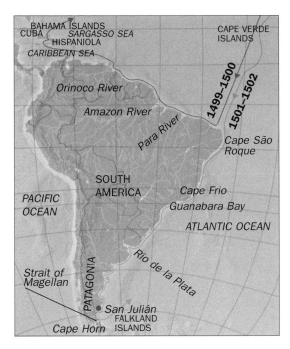

Back in Spain, Vespucci found that other explorers received preference in the Spanish court; he would have to look elsewhere for patronage. He noticed that his landfall in Brazil lay well to the east of the line of demarcation between Portugal and Spain, as defined in the Treaty of Tordesillas (1494). Consequently, he approached the Portuguese court, and King Manuel I was intrigued by the possibilities of this territory, which was unknown to him (the Portuguese explorer Pedro Álvarez Cabral [*see pages 68–69*] had already discovered it but had not yet returned to report his findings). Vespucci was told to investigate further.

On May 13, 1501, he left Lisbon and sailed for the Cape Verde Islands. By luck, he encountered Cabral returning to Portugal, and the men exchanged information. Landfall was made at Cape São Roque, then Vespucci sailed on a southwesterly course. There is some dispute about how far he traveled, but it is probable that he reached the mouth of the Rio de la Plata, while Vespucci claimed that he reached Patagonia. He named his southernmost discovery San Giuliano (now San Julián in Argentina).

He returned to Lisbon in July 1502 with evidence that Portugal had extensive South American lands on its side of the Tordesillas line. It was also clear that the Americas were more extensive that had previously been thought, and could not be part of the Orient, as Columbus believed.

The popularity of his published account of

his "New World" discoveries prompted the German cartographer Martin Waldseemüller to name South America "the land of Amerigo" in 1508. By 1538 both landmasses had become "America," in honor of the man who proved they were indeed continents in their own right.

Below: Vespucci navigating with the help of the Southern Cross.

ALONSO *de* OJEDA
1466 *to* 1515

Alonso de Ojeda began his career in the New World as a captain on Columbus's second voyage, and went on to found the first European settlement in South America. At heart he was more a pillager than a settler or explorer, and his quest for wealth was the driving force behind his expeditions in the Americas.

Although his date of birth is a mystery, it is known that in his 20s de Ojeda fought against the Moors in southern Spain under the Duke of Medina Celi. Following the conquest of Granada in 1492, de Ojeda looked elsewhere to advance his career and joined Columbus's second voyage in 1493. He commanded a ship—the Spanish frequently appointed a soldier as titular captain, while a ship's master handled the ship. On Hispaniola he earned a reputation by exploring the interior of the island, fighting Indians, and searching for plunder.

When de Ojeda returned to Spain in 1495, he was considered one of the first veterans of the New World, and the king chose him to lead an expedition to find sources of wealth in the Americas. The 1498 landfall made by Columbus in modern Venezuela would be the starting point. On May 16, 1499, de Ojeda sailed from Cadiz, along with Amerigo Vespucci (*see pages 92–93*) and the cartographer Juan de la Cosa (*see pages 122–123*).

Below: A 16th-century view of Spanish conquistadors under attack by South American Indians.

At the Cape Verde Islands off West Africa, the expedition split in two; de Ojeda to concentrate on the coast north of the Orinoco River, Vespucci to explore the lands to its south. He made his landfall on the island of Trinidad, then explored the almost landlocked body of water behind it, the Gulf of Paria. Next, he followed the coast to the west, where he explored the island of Curaçao, then rounded the northward projection of the Paraguaná peninsula into the Gulf of Venezuela.

Exploring southward to the mouth of the Gulf, de Ojeda found the entrance to a large lagoon, now known as the Lake of Maracaibo. He named the immediate area surrounding the lake Coquibacoa. The locals he encountered were mostly fishermen who lived on houses built on stilts over the water, which inspired de Ojeda to name the whole region Venezuela (Little Venice). He described the native Indians he met as "Caribs" or "cannibals" and friendly to the Spanish, but this did not prevent him capturing hundreds as slaves, and looting the pearl fisheries he encountered along the coast.

Violent and greedy actions

Heading north out of the lake, he rounded Cape Gallinas and continued to sail southwest, skirting the coast of modern Colombia for a time before heading north for his arranged rendezvous with Vespucci on Hispaniola. The Spanish crown was delighted and de Ojeda was named Governor (adelantado) of Coquibacoa, and granted land licenses in Hispaniola as a reward.

De Ojeda led another expedition to the region in 1502. After a landfall near Trinidad again, he sailed up what he named the Pearl Coast, trading with the Indians for pearls, and attacking any who refused to deal with him. By the time of his return to Hispaniola, he had amassed a fortune, but found himself accused of

cheating the king out of his share of the profits. He returned to Spain to clear his name in 1503, and then undertook a third financially successful voyage in 1505. De Ojeda's immense wealth funded his own expedition in 1508 and he chose

to explore what is now the Colombian coast.

This expedition reached Venezuela close to Cape Gallinas, and then sailed along the Colombian coast until it reached the site where Cartagena would be built. De Ojeda attacked and enslaved the Indian settlement he found there, an act that enraged the Indians in the vicinity. The Spanish camp came under counterattack and the invaders succumbed to the hail of arrows and poisoned darts. Only de Ojeda and a handful of the expedition escaped with their lives.

Undeterred, de Ojeda returned in 1510 with more settlers and established the colony of San Sebastián on the Gulf of Urabá. Because it was subject to almost constant Indian attack, he went to Hispaniola for reinforcements, but during his absence the colony was wiped out. Alonso de Ojeda had now lost all his capital, and he died in poverty on Hispaniola in about 1515.

Above: The coastline of Venezuela offered great opportunities for settlement, but also housed some of the fiercest Native American tribes.

The CONQUISTADORS: WINNING *an* EMPIRE

The initial Spanish settlement of the Caribbean was accomplished after a series of minor military struggles against the local Arawak and Carib populations. Many settlers had already seen military service during Spain's crusade against the Moors, and were trained soldiers. They grouped into miniature armies led by young Spanish noblemen, and were sent

Below: Cortez and his conquistadors fighting in the streets of Tenochtitlán, from a 16th-century Spanish work by an unknown artist.

to take on the might of the Americas' great native empires. These soldiers became known as Los Conquistadores (the conquerors) after they rapidly quashed all opposition to Spanish rule in

the Americas. Today, the term "conquistador" combines the notion of brutality with immense bravery and skill, characteristics that gave them a vital role to play in the Age of Discovery.

When Ferdinand and Isabela retook the Moorish province of Granada for Spain in 1492, they did so at the head of a battle-hardened army. Their military structure was based around a core of feudal knights augmented by other more innovative types of troops. The light cavalry, known as *Ginetes*, were copied directly from the Arabs, and these supported the slower-moving bodies of knights. During the century firearms had begun to be employed, and while few were available in 1492, they would become increasingly common during the 16th century. In 1492, missile fire was still provided by the crossbow, a weapon that was slow to reload but had a long range and a devastating penetrative power. By the 1520s, the crossbow had been largely replaced by the firearm as the primary missile weapon, although crossbows were still widely used in the Americas where powder stocks were harder to replace.

The reintroduction of the pike into warfare during the 15th century gave infantry the ability to repulse cavalry. A particularly Spanish addition was the use of sword and bucklermen; armored swordsmen who carried round shields (bucklers). Apart from knights, armor was generally limited to the wearing of a helmet, and possibly a reinforced jacket or a back-and-breast plate. The advent of firearms made anything else impractical and ineffective. Artillery was also becoming increasingly common, both in the siege of fortifications and also on the battlefield. Armies had to develop tactics to suit new troops and technologies, and the conquistadors did this better than anyone. Their armies were miniature versions of the domestic Spanish armies, although they possessed significant military advantages. Horses were unknown in the Americas, as were hunting dogs, and both provided the Spanish with a psychological advantage. In several instances, Inca and Aztec

troops simply melted away in the face of a determined cavalry charge. This was used to powerful effect, as were the devastating effects of firepower at long range.

A new theater of war

The Spanish army was partly disbanded when the Moorish-Spanish war concluded with the recapture of Granada, so many soldiers departed for the New World to take advantage of the military and financial opportunities there. A number of settlers were *hidalgos*, young men of noble but impoverished backgrounds, many of whom had undergone military service. The opportunity to go to war again, this time not only as part of a national and religious crusade but also to win personal glory and status independent of a feudal master, was seductive.

Some of the greatest conquistador leaders, such as Hernán Cortéz (*see pages 118–121*) and Francisco Pizarro (*see pages 98–101*), actually came to the New World as farmers, not as soldiers, but the region presented opportunities too great to ignore. A later wave went purely to fight for land. The conquistador Bernal Diaz claimed that he came to the New World "to serve God and His Majesty, to give light to those who were in darkness, and to grow rich, as all men desire to do."

These men furnished expeditions, either at their own expense or with money borrowed from provincial governors or moneylenders, and risked everything they had, including their lives. Consequently, they expected to be heavily rewarded for the risks they took. It is estimated that Cortéz and Pizarro acquired personal fortunes that today would be valued in tens of millions of US dollars. Their private armies, often only a hundred men, were able to rout forces many times their number through a combination of superior technology, military prowess, cunning diplomacy, and an overwhelming will to win. In a period of less than 30 years, the conquistadors overran much of two continents and placed the flags of Spain and the Catholic Church firmly in the Americas.

Above: *The conquistadors fight Indians, assisted by Central American allies. From a 16th-century Mexican Codex.*

FRANCISCO PIZARRO

1475 to 1541

Below: *Francisco Pizarro shown wearing the robes of a knight of the Order of Santiago.*

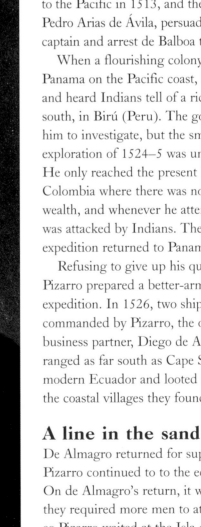

The name Pizarro has become synonymous with the Spanish term "conquistador." Ruthless, fearless, cruel, and enterprising, Pizarro was the ideal man to take on the most developed native people in the Americas. He started life less gloriously. The illegitimate son of a soldier, Francisco Pizarro had no hope of advancement in Spain, so in 1502 he sailed to Hispaniola in a fleet under the command of Nicolás de Ovando. In 1509 he joined Alonso de Ojeda's expedition (*see pages 94–95*) and was left in charge of the San Sebastián colony when de Ojeda sailed away for supplies. In the subsequent Indian attack, Pizarro and a few survivors withdrew to their ship and watched the settlement burn.

Up the Venezuelan coast they encountered a supply ship bound for San Sebastián and, as they returned in consort, the ship was wrecked. Among the rescued crew was Vasco Nunéz de Balboa (*see pages 114–115*), who suggested they attack an Indian village at Darién and settle there. Pizarro led the attack, but once the settlement was made, he turned to farming and trading. He accompanied de Balboa's expedition to the Pacific in 1513, and the new governor, Pedro Arias de Ávila, persuaded him to act as his captain and arrest de Balboa the following year.

When a flourishing colony was established at Panama on the Pacific coast, he moved there and heard Indians tell of a rich empire to the south, in Birú (Peru). The governor permitted him to investigate, but the small coastal exploration of 1524–5 was unsuccessful. He only reached the present border of Colombia where there was no sign of any wealth, and whenever he attempted to land he was attacked by Indians. The badly reduced expedition returned to Panama.

Refusing to give up his quest for Peru, Pizarro prepared a better-armed second expedition. In 1526, two ships set out, one commanded by Pizarro, the other by his business partner, Diego de Almagro. They ranged as far south as Cape San Francisco in modern Ecuador and looted a little gold from the coastal villages they found.

A line in the sand

De Almagro returned for supplies, while Pizarro continued to to the edge of Peru. On de Almagro's return, it was decided that they required more men to attempt a conquest, so Pizarro waited at the Isla del Gallo off the Colombian coast while de Almagro returned to raise troops. Back in Panama, the new governor halted the expedition, and even sent ships to order Pizarro home. Pizarro reportedly drew a line in the sand—anyone who crossed it would join him in defiance of the governor. Twelve men crossed the line and stayed on the island, the remainder sailed back to Panama.

De Almagro had arranged to return with another ship, but it was seven months before it arrived. The small force made any invasion impossible, but they sailed as far south along the Peruvian coast as the Gulf of Guayaquil and to

the Inca city of Tumbes, where Alonzo de Molina was left as an envoy. It was clear that the Inca Empire was large, wealthy, and well organized.

Pizarro returned to Spain to lobby for approval for an expedition of conquest. As evidence of Inca wealth he offered the king gold, rich fabrics, and a captured llama. As a result he was named Captain General of Peru in July 1529, and given full authority to conquer the region in the name of Spain.

Pizarro, at the head of a small army, set sail from Panama on December 27, 1530, bound for the Gulf of Guayaquil, but contrary winds forced him to land his force over 300 miles to the north, at San Mateo Bay. After marching for months through jungle, the army arrived at Tumbes to find the city in ruins following a civil war. The weary conquistadors occupied the city and waited for reinforcements. Over the

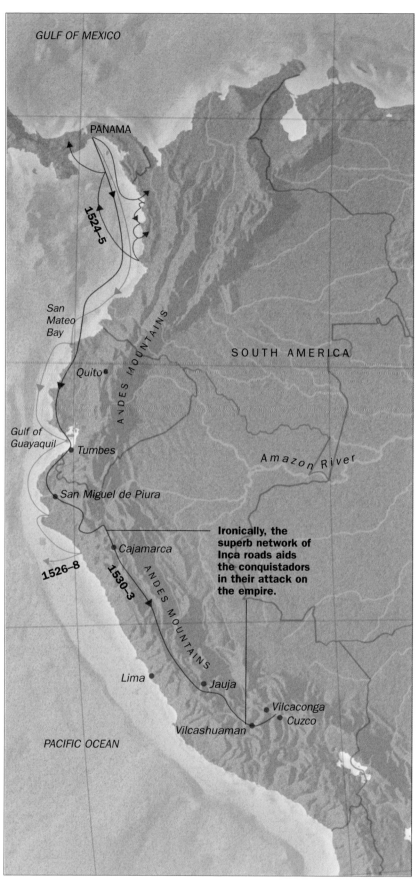

GULF OF MEXICO

PANAMA

1524–5

San Mateo Bay

Quito

ANDES MOUNTAINS

SOUTH AMERICA

Gulf of Guayaquil

Tumbes

Amazon River

San Miguel de Piura

Cajamarca

Ironically, the superb network of Inca roads aids the conquistadors in their attack on the empire.

1526–8

1530–3

ANDES MOUNTAINS

Lima

Jauja

Vilcaconga

Cuzco

Vilcashuaman

PACIFIC OCEAN

following year, more than 130 men, including Hernando de Soto (*see pages 160–163*), munitions, and supplies were brought to Tumbes. By spring 1532, Pizarro was ready to launch his full-scale invasion of the Inca Empire.

Above left: Pizarro in his conquistador's armor.

Conquistador treachery

In May 1532 Pizarro led his small force south from Tumbes and crossed the Chira River, where he received his first reliable information about the Inca civil war. The old ruler Huayna Capac had died, as had his heir. The empire had been split between the emperor's younger sons—Huascar, who was based in the southern city of Cuzco, and Atahualpa, whose

Below: Atahualpa, the Inca leader captured and held to ransom by Pizarro.

ATHABALIBA
ultimus Rex Peruanorum

headquarters was at Quito in the north. This situation was highly advantageous to the Spanish, who were able to pursue a policy of divide and conquer.

On the Piura River, Pizarro established a Spanish colony that he named San Miguel de Piura, and left a garrison to help make it a secure Spanish base. He pressed on with a tiny force of less than 200 conquistadors, both infantry and cavalry. The superb Inca road network speeded Pizarro's advance, and the Spanish reached the important city of Cajamarca in good time. They found Atahualpa and most of his army camped outside the city.

Vastly outnumbered, a military attack was out of the question, so the Spanish used cunning to further their aims. Envoys traded messages between the two groups, and a friendly meeting was arranged between Pizarro and Atahualpa inside the city. The conquistador planned an ambush, and hid soldiers in Cajamarca's buildings. Atahualpa and his entourage appeared, the emperor carried in a litter lavishly decorated with parrot feathers and flanked by guards dressed in gold.

Pizarro gave the code word "St. James" and his soldiers rose up and fired into the crowd of bodyguards. Pizarro grabbed Atahualpa and threw him from the litter so that the Spanish could bind him and drag him away. When the smoke cleared, the square was empty of courtiers, Atahualpa was a prisoner, and Pizarro controlled half of a kingdom. A truce was declared between the Inca and the Spanish.

Choosing blade over fire

Atahualpa was held for a ransom of a large room filled with gold and silver. One-fifth would be reserved for the Spanish king, while the remainder would be divided among the conquistadors. The treasure came in throughout June 1532, and the soldiers realized they were rich beyond all expectation. But Pizarro was still in a precarious situation, since he had only conquered half of the Inca Empire.

News reached Cajamarca that Atahualpa's brother, Huascar, had been poisoned, presumably by supporters of his captive rival. With a leaderless army drifting home from Cajamarca, one leader imprisoned, and his rival dead, the empire was plunged into chaos. Spanish reinforcements arrived, and Pizarro's position became more secure. He had to act swiftly to take advantage of the chaos, and to react to rumors that Inca generals were gathering a force to rescue their surviving emperor, thereby breaking the truce. The rumors and the murder of a potential ally were all the excuses Pizarro needed. Atahualpa was condemned to burn at the stake as a heretic, a fate abhorrent to the Inca. Atahualpa agreed to convert to Catholicism, if the mode of death could be decapitation. He was executed in mid-July 1533 and Pizarro was free to complete his conquest.

Pizarro marched on Cuzco at the head of 100 horsemen and 30 infantry along the Royal Inca Highway, a road that crossed the otherwise impenetrable Andes range. The city lay almost 700 miles away and Pizarro had to fight through Inca resistance to reach it. In the toughest battle, at Jauja, the Spanish cavalry routed vastly superior numbers of Inca infantry. Three further battles were fought, including a last-ditch attempt in the pass in front of Cuzco. At last Pizarro marched into the Inca city and his conquest was all but complete. Pockets of resistance continued in remote areas until 1572, but Spanish control was never threatened.

Pizarro consolidated his grip by establishing his capital city of Lima in January 1535. Within a year a quarrel between Pizarro and his old ally Diego de Almagro degenerated into civil war. After crushing de Almagro, Pizarro sent rival subordinates on far-flung expeditions, to keep intrigue to a minimum. It was to little avail. On July 26, 1541, Francisco Pizarro was murdered in Lima by de Almagro's illegitimate son; a brutal end for a brutal conqueror.

Above: *Pizarro and his soldiers, from a mosaic on his tomb at Lima Cathedral.*

Left: *Francisco Pareja teaching Christianity to the Indians.*

SOUTH AMERICAN CULTURE
in the 16th CENTURY

S outh America contained an array of different cultural groups, from the highly advanced Inca civilization to the cannibalistic tribes of the Amazon rainforest. During the early 16th century, many of these peoples came into contact with Spanish conquistadors and Portuguese settlers. The Europeans conquered, enslaved, and converted wherever they could, creating a Latin-American cultural assimilation that has continued to the present day.

Below: A Peruvian jar portrait.

The cultures of the northern coasts of modern Venezuela and Colombia retained links with the peoples of Central America and the Caribbean Islands. These disparate cultures, grouped under the anthropological umbrella of Circum-Caribbean people, shared vague linguistic, social, and cultural traits. To the west of the landmass, the mountains of the Andes and the coastal strip beyond combined two pre-Inca cultural groups with separate cultural and linguistic traditions, who had no link to the people found east of the mountain range. To the south, nomadic hunter-gatherers lived in the vast open lands of modern Paraguay and Argentina in a manner similar to the plains Indians of North America. With the exception of a small coastal population subsisting on fishing, the rest were farmers, grouped into village clearings amid the tropical rainforests of the Amazon basin.

The nomadic people of the south, the region Magellan named Patagonia, have generally been portrayed as culturally inferior to those of the Andes. Evidence of hunting in the region extends back 12,000 years, yet by AD 1400 this society showed signs of evolving, with communities based on ranching and farming becoming established in what is now northern Argentina.

To the north, the Atacameño and Diaguita people established arable areas around rivers and oases, but hunting remained the principal focus of their communities. Their stone, fortress-like structures have

Map labels

ATLANTIC OCEAN
PACIFIC OCEAN

Area of Inca Empire

Guajiro, Cuna, Choco, Quahibo, Paez, Warau, Yanomamo, Carib, Arawak, Tucano, Macú, Witoto, Tumbes, Trio, Waiwai, Chimu, Yagua, Jivaro, Omagua, Cawahib, Munduruçu, Teremembe, Tenetehara, Timbira, Shipibo, Piro, Cayapo, Shavante, Tupinamba, Campa, Nambicuara, Quechua, Bororo, Caraja, Nazca, Aymara, Mojos, Guato, Siriono, Caigua, Botocudo, Atacameños, Mataco, Diaguita, Abipon, Guarini, Tupinamba, Kaingang, Chiriguano, Araucania, Puelche, Muchic, Huilliche, Magellan

Timeline

c.AD 500	c.900	c.1000	c.1200	1370	1470	1498	1500
The Huari Empire is founded in the Peruvian highlands.	The Lambayeque valley is established as the center of the Sicán state.	The Huari and Tiahuanaco empires are in decline.	The Chimú state begins to expand.	The Chimú people conquer the state of Sicán.	The Chimú Empire on the coast of Peru is conquered by the Incas.	Christopher Columbus discovers South America.	Pedro Cabral discovers Brazil.

been likened to the Pueblo cultures of the southwestern United States. They also retained cultural links with the people of the Andes, and ceramic finds indicate that the two cultures traded with each other.

Further to the south, the Aruacanians were a farming people, scattered in small hamlets and lacking any tribal unity. This made them particularly susceptible to Spanish attack. Staple diets for these farmers were corn in the north, and potatoes in the south, supplemented by meat supplied from the ranching of domestic animals. Following the Spanish colonization of Patagonia, most of these farming and ranching communities were rapidly conquered by the invaders.

The exception was the Indians of southern Patagonia, a tribe known as the Huilliche. Like the Apache of North America, they united under military leaderships, stole horses from the Spanish, and developed hit and run tactics to keep their enemy at bay. The Huilliche were successful, and continued as one of the few culturally independent tribes of South America until the 19th century.

Tribes of the rainforest

Apart from the technologically advanced Inca Empire in western South America, the tribes that lived in the tropical rainforest dominated the remainder of the region. For the most part these were simple village societies based on kinship, the settlements concentrated along the coast or on rivers. The nature of the forest itself made these communities semi-nomadic, moving on every few years in search of fresh and fertile soil. The jungle also limited the size of these communities, since they rarely produced more than the minimum quantity of food required to survive. Although there was little linguistic unity, the tribes have been grouped by anthropologists into larger cultural units. The Arawaks and Caribs of the coast were linguistically tied to the other Circum-Caribbean peoples of Venezuela, while the remainder spoke variants of an Andean-Equatorial language (the Ge language group).

It is easiest to envisage these peoples as a patchwork of independent village settlements sharing certain social and cultural roots rather than as a collection of tribes displaying any political unity. Any Spaniards who encountered the people of the Amazon Delta noted that most were cannibals, warlike, and brutal. The semi-nomadic existence of many of these peoples made the establishment of religious centers or townships difficult. Some groups such as the Chiriguanos (part of the Guariní culture) even became nomads, migrating across the center of the continent until stopped by the line of Inca outposts in the Andes. The exception to the semi-nomads were the Tupinambá people of the Brazilian coast, who maintained permanent fishing communities containing up to 1,500 inhabitants. Most of these peoples had no contact with Europeans during the 16th century. Apart from the settlements along the Brazilian and Patagonian coasts, most South American native communities were too remote and their land too poor to be of interest to European invaders.

Above: A gold monkey-head bead, part of funerary goods buried with Muchic nobility found on the north coast of Peru.

Below: This elaborately crafted golden bird is typical of the Inca treasure the conquistadors were searching for in Peru.

1520	c.1525	1533	1534	1535	1536	1542	1545
Ferdinand Magellan reaches San Julian, Argentina.	The potato is introduced to Europe from South America.	Sebastian de Belalcazar conquers Ecuador.	Slaves from Africa arrive in Brazil.	Francisco Pizarro founds Lima.	Pedro de Mendoza founds Buenos Aires and explores Rio de la Plata.	Francisco de Orellana reaches the mouth of the Amazon river.	Silver mines in Potosí, Peru, are worked for the Spanish.

The INCA EMPIRE

The great Inca Empire that the Spanish destroyed was the last of a series of Indian civilizations that flourished west of the Andes, a culmination of 6,000 years of development. Francisco Pizarro and less than a hundred men brought the whole empire to its knees—the Inca culture was not as perfect as it had seemed.

Like the Aztec of Central America, the Inca boasted an advanced civilization whose emperor ruled millions of subjects through a highly developed civil service, supported by a powerful army, an extensive logistical infrastructure, and considerable economic resources.

Coastal deserts and impassable mountains made the geography of the region less than ideal for settlement, particularly as less than two percent of the available land in the empire was fit for agriculture. Nevertheless, the Inca harnessed the terrain and, with terraces and irrigation systems, created farmland on the mountainous slopes. The mountains contained a wealth of mineral resources—gold, silver, copper, and other metals that were used for trade. As a result, the local population became skilled metallurgists.

The first Peruvian peoples date from about 13,000 years ago, while the first permanent village settlements date from c.1500 BC. Religious centers developed from about 500 BC, as did other indications of urban life, such as large ceramics warehouses, corn storehouses, and metallurgical centers.

During the first millennium AD, a cultural and technological transformation of the region took place as agricultural techniques improved. During the same period the city-states of northern Peru developed a warrior elite, similar to the feudal structure of medieval Europe.

While northern territories, such as Ecuador and southern regions of what is now Chile, avoided this militaristic emphasis, the central regions thrived on it, with a small caste of warriors engaged in almost permanent warfare. Conflict, which was stylized, had little effect on the general populace, who created the economic base for such a system to operate. Military conquest by one city-state over another led to a gradual amalgam of many of these urban societies into a larger political unit.

Farming for the empire

The first of these states was a religious warrior group based at Wari, in southern Peru. Wari society exhibited proto-Inca styles of religion, architecture, and social structure, as did the Tiahuanaco society in the southern Andes. Defensive influences were visible in settlements, while roads linked cities for purposes of military

Opposite: The Inca mountain city and stronghold of Machu Picchu is still one of the wonders of the Americas.

Below: This functional drinking vessel shows an Inca priest or ruler.

Quito
Cuenca
Tumbes
Chan Chan
Cajamarca
Pachacamac
Huamachuco
Bombón
Machu Picchu
Incahuási
Ollantaytambo
Vilcashuamán
Cuzco
Limatambo
Lake Titicaca
Tiahuanaco
Lake Poopo
Amazon
ANDES
ANDES

Inca Roads

PACIFIC OCEAN

Area of Inca Empire in 1525

c.AD 400	c.1200–1230	1470	1524	1525	1527	1529	1532
Moche culture extends from the Andes to the Pacific.	Manco Capac founds the Inca state at Cuzco.	The Incas conquer the Chimú Empire in coastal Peru.	A Spanish expedition from Panama, led by Pizarro, explores Peru.	Death of Huayna Capac at height of Inca Empire.	Atahualpa becomes ruler of the Inca Empire, succeeding Huayna Capac.	Pizarro's forces invade.	Atahualpa seized by Pizarro, held for ransom, but eventually murdered.

maneuverability and trade. All these factors have been deemed Inca but preceded Inca society by several centuries.

One of these feuding city-states was based in the Cuzco basin of the Andes foothills. From the 11th century onward they began to expand by subduing neighboring urban states until, by the early 15th century, they had established a substantial central Peruvian Inca kingdom. During the next century Inca conquests would turn this kingdom into an empire extending as far north as Ecuador and south for a thousand miles beyond Lake Titicaca.

By 1525, on the eve of Pizarro's invasion, ruler Huayna Capac consolidated the last areas that held out, to create an empire of seven million people, dozens of highly structured cities, and a network of trade routes and highways. The Inca Empire therefore came into being as a political entity only a few scant years before it was destroyed.

In uniting this disparate collection of city-states, the Inca incorporated the local rulers by making them provincial administrators, when appropriate, and by removing them when not. The empire, based on absolutism, was a feudal hierarchy that encompassed the entire society.

Warriors were the Inca noblemen, but the structure extended down to the urban and the household unit. A typical farmer labored on temple land, followed by state land, and then his own, since every piece of property, land, or business was, in theory, controlled by an emperor who was both a secular and spiritual leader.

This structure was part of the empire's strength as well as a reason for its final demise. The civil war that split the people, the state, and the priesthood allowed the conquistadors to carve up the empire with ease. Military superiority, together with an almost supernatural aura surrounding the Spanish invaders, made resistance ineffective, and the Inca Empire disintegrated within months.

Below: By 1600, the absorption of the Inca Empire into the Spanish was complete. This unique vase c.1650 depicts an Inca dignitary, a white man playing a trumpet and a black man playing a drum.

1533	1535–6	1537	1541	1572	1591	1783	1821
Pizarro's forces move on Cuzco, ultimately taking the city and the Inca Empire.	Inca revolt in Peru is defeated by Spanish occupation forces.	Manco Capac II recaptures Cuzco and establishes a new Inca state at Vilcabamba.	Pizarro is assassinated in Lima.	Tupac Amaru, the last of the independent Inca rulers, is executed.	Spain passes a law integrating the former Inca Empire into the Spanish Empire.	Tupac Amaru II and his family are tortured and executed by the Spanish.	Peru declares its independence from Spain.

FRANCISCO *de* ORELLANA
1511 *to* 1546

Francisco de Orellana was a true conquistador. He participated in the pacification of Peru, searched for lost cities, and crossed the Andes, but his greatest achievement—an expedition that traveled the length of the Amazon—came by accident.

A kinsman of Francisco Pizarro, de Orellana reached the New World in his late teens, most probably in 1527. He first settled in the colony at Darién, having reached the region while Pizarro was away on his second expedition. When Pizarro launched his conquest of Peru, de Orellana accompanied him, served with distinction, and lost an eye during the advance on Cuzco in 1533.

After the conquest, de Orellana settled in Portoviejo, near the northern border of Inca territory in what is now Ecuador. He helped to repulse Indian attacks on the region and, during the civil war between Pizarro and Diego de Almagro (*see page 101*), he sided with his kinsman and old commander.

After the death of de Almagro, Pizarro became concerned about the number of conquistadors within his territory who now had little to do. Rather than have them foment another rebellion, he sent many of them to undertake new expeditions. De Orellana was ordered to conquer the hinterland of Ecuador, which still contained hostile Indian groups. He achieved this by 1537, and reestablished a settlement on the site of the modern city of Guayaquil, a Spanish settlement to rival the ruined Inca city of Tumbes.

In 1541 he agreed to join Francisco Pizarro's half-brother Gonzalo in an expedition beyond the Andes to search for cinnamon forests and the fabled land of El Dorado, a lakeside surrounded by gold. De Orellana and his small force were left behind by Gonzalo Pizarro's main force, and only caught up with them beyond the Andes in December 1541, after a demoralizing forced march.

The lure of the Amazon

On his arrival, de Orellana found that Pizarro's party was reduced to eating grass and nuts. De Orellana was duly sent down the Coca and Napo rivers to gather provisions, with 57 men in a small barge and a handful of canoes.

Above: Sent by Pizarro to find fabled El Dorado, the city said to be surrounded by gold, de Orellana discovered the mighty Amazon instead.

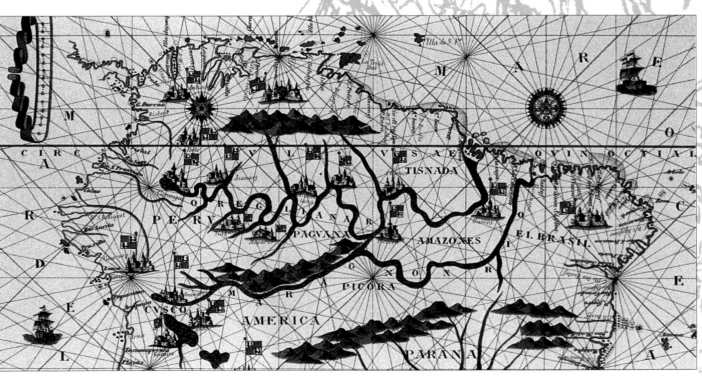

The conquistadors followed the rivers for nearly 700 miles, but found no sources of food, and far from helping feed Pizarro, de Orellana's men faced starvation themselves.

Finally, on January 9, 1542, they came upon a village whose inhabitants were willing to barter for food. At that point, probably because the swollen winter rivers prevented a return upstream toward Pizarro, de Orellana decided to follow the river down to the Northern Ocean (Atlantic). His chronicler reported that de Orellana "found the currents of such force… considering what way he had made in three days, he found that in a whole year it was not possible to return that way again." He had no choice but to continue. Meanwhile, Pizarro and his expedition's survivors returned to the coast after a year in the jungle, blaming their failure on de Orellana.

After building a larger barge, de Orellana and his men headed south again on April 24 and followed the river downstream. Most Indians they encountered were curious rather than hostile. On June 3 they reached the confluence where the Amazon and Negro rivers created a vast waterway.

The Spanish also heard rumors of a tribe of warrior women. Friar Gaspar de Carvajal, the chronicler of the expedition, reported that they encountered some of these warriors, and that de Orellana named them "Amazons," after the female warriors of Greek legend. The name soon became associated with the river itself. As the river widened they learned to keep to its center, out of bow and dart range of the hostile natives now lining the banks.

Finally, on August 26, 1542, de Orellana reached the sea, where he successfully negotiated the tidal surges and navigational hazards found in the Amazon delta. He followed the South American coast to the northwest, and his two remaining boats eventually reached safety at the Spanish settlement of Cubagua Island, off Venezuela. Back in Spain, de Orellana shrugged off Pizarro's accusations of desertion, gained royal funding for a new expedition to the Amazon in 1545, but died soon after his arrival at the river's mouth.

Above: The Amazon near Iquitos, Peru: the narrow oxbows and impenatrable jungle almost defeated de Orellana.

Opposite below: A Spanish map of 1582 shows the winding course of the Amazon River from the Andes to the Atlantic.

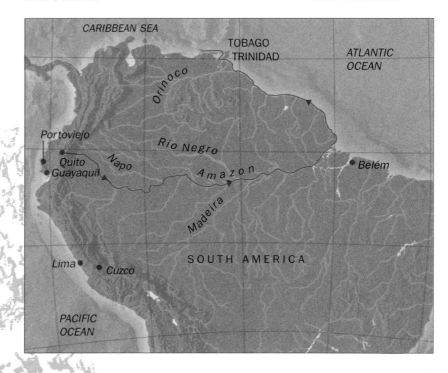

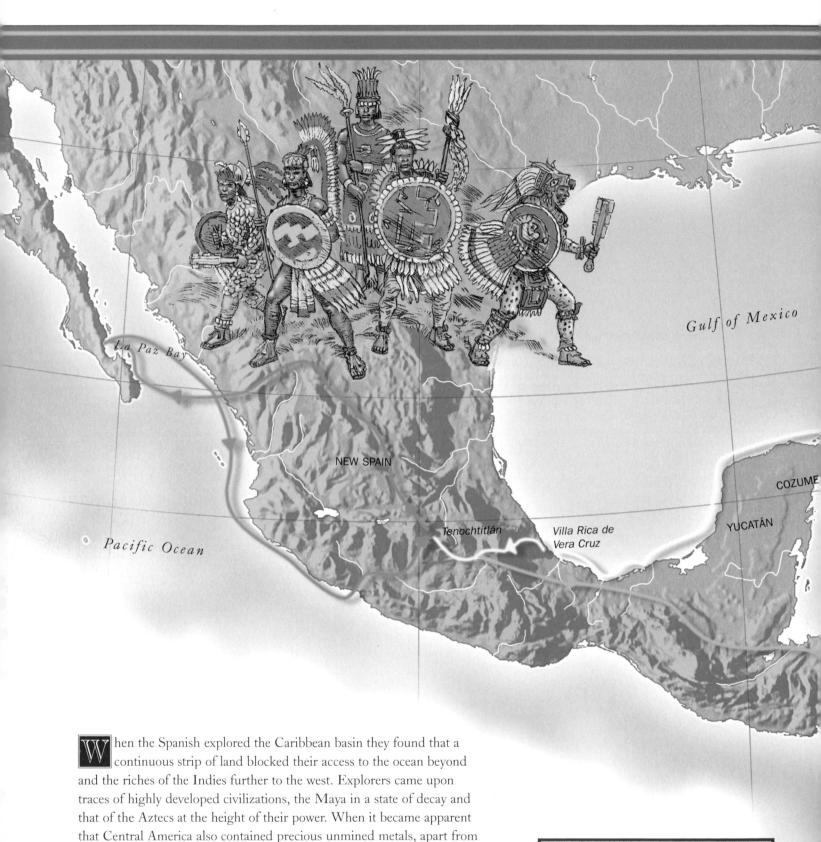

Gulf of Mexico

La Paz Bay

NEW SPAIN

Pacific Ocean

COZUME

YUCATÁN

Tenochtitlán   Villa Rica de
                   Vera Cruz

When the Spanish explored the Caribbean basin they found that a continuous strip of land blocked their access to the ocean beyond and the riches of the Indies further to the west. Explorers came upon traces of highly developed civilizations, the Maya in a state of decay and that of the Aztecs at the height of their power. When it became apparent that Central America also contained precious unmined metals, apart from the fabulous adornments of the Indians, the region's fate was sealed.

While settlers and conquistadors carved out a foothold in the narrows of Panama and explorers mapped the coastline to the north, plans were laid to conquer these powerful civilizations and grab whatever wealth could be found. The conquest of New Spain (Mexico) by a small conquistador army was one of the most decisive military campaigns in history, and subsequent expeditions of exploration and conquest ensured that the whole region would become part of Spain's New World Empire.

Treks of Discovery		
Juan de la Cosa	1499	
	1504–06	
	1519	
Hernán Cortéz	1524–26	
	1535–36	

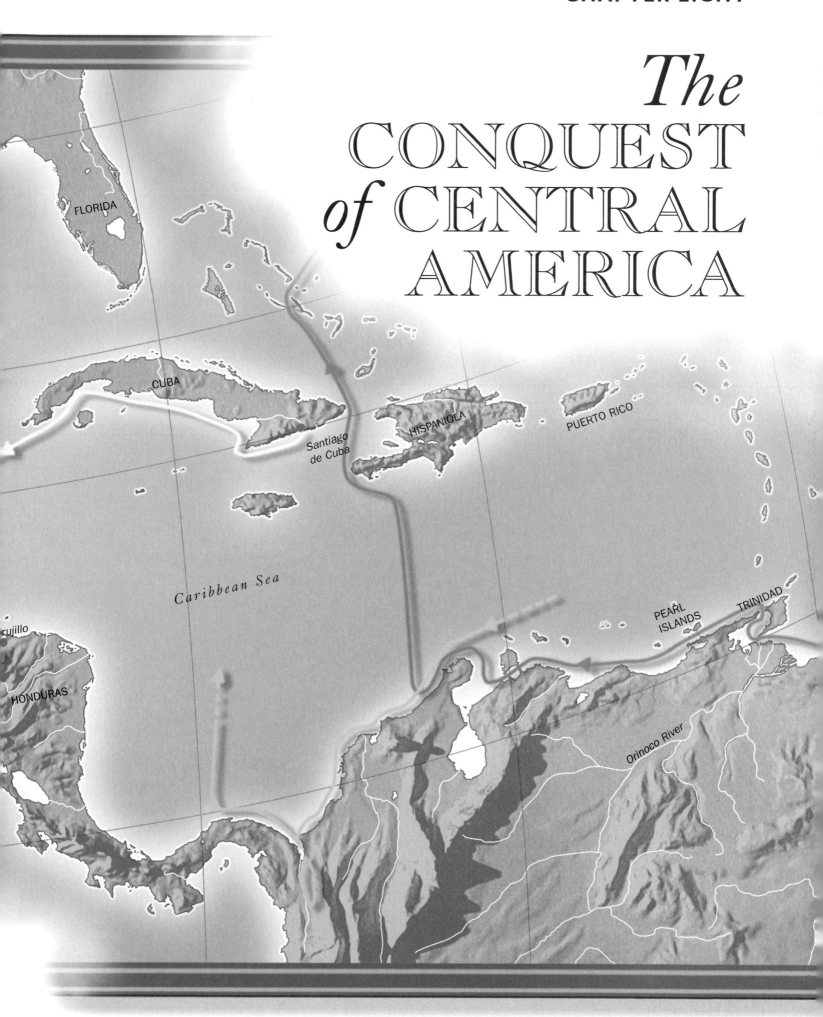

FLORIDA

CUBA

Santiago
de Cuba

HISPANIOLA

PUERTO RICO

Caribbean Sea

rujillo

HONDURAS

PEARL
ISLANDS

TRINIDAD

Orinoco River

CHAPTER EIGHT

The CONQUEST *of* CENTRAL AMERICA

The MAYA CULTURE

As their first contact with Native Americans had involved the unsophisticated Arawak culture, the Spaniards were dumbfounded to discover traces of a much more advanced civilization on the Central American mainland. The Maya's ceremonial civilization was centered on great temple cities that were the wonder of the Americas.

Maya territory extended from the highlands of Guatemala and the Pacific Coast northeast into a central region in what is now Honduras and a northern region encompassing the Yucatán Peninsula. Agriculture in the southern area created a food surplus that allowed large cities to be established in the less fertile regions of the flat Yucatán with its limestone bedrock.

The Maya, clearly related to other Central American cultures, shared nomadic roots that stretched back to at least 8000 BC. Village cultures in the region date from about 1600 BC, and by 300 BC towns and even cities were being supported by an agricultural economy. Izapa, near the Pacific coast, is seen as a proto-Mayan civilization, and its people may have passed on their social forms to later generations that spread their influence throughout what would become the Maya region.

The Maya are therefore seen as the inheritors of previous Middle American cultures, although they built on the legacy to create one of the greatest of American civilizations.

Although most of the Maya land was covered by rainforest and the land contained few natural resources, substantial settlements developed from the fourth century AD onward—ceremonial religious centers, whose populations of priests, nobles, and artisans were supported by agricultural settlements in the surrounding area. Crude villages of wooden huts were set amid circles of land cleared from the jungle. If the soil became unproductive, the village was moved elsewhere until the soil quality recovered.

The cities combined the functions of regional capitals, trading centers, military barracks, and, above all, religious sites. The Maya nobility controlled trade within these cities, although a professional mercantile class transported products overland and shipped goods along the coast by canoe. Archæological evidence suggests that the Maya maintained trading links with the Mexican cultures to the north and the Cuna of the Panama isthmus further south.

Religion and astronomy

Much of the nature of Maya society during its classic period (AD 300–900) can be traced through surviving carved stone columns (stelae), which indicate an autocratic society, dominated by an elite caste. This mixture of a caste system and a feudal structure created the need for substantial dwelling places, along with the religious edifices that dominated Maya cities. As a result, the Maya developed a distinctive architectural style, and their ceremonial structures could be extensive, including religious platforms, pyramids, palaces, monasteries, astronomical observatories, and even sporting grounds for the ritual ball game.

The stelae also show that the Maya had an advanced understanding of astronomy, and their calendar, based on astronomical observations, affected all aspects of their lives. Every facet of their civilization, from crop growing, trading, warfare, marriage, even birth and death, were ruled by their priests through calendric charts. Other linked religious totems were the sun, moon, and rain, the last being of vital importance in a region containing few rivers. Rain was collected in massive wells (cenotes),

Below: *This jade mask found at Palenque dates from the Classic Maya period. Composed of seven parts, it was used in burial rituals.*

c.350–300 BC	c.200 BC	AD 36	c.300–600	c.300
The earliest Maya city states appear.	The earliest examples of Maya writing date from this time.	The first Maya calendrical inscriptions are made.	Teotichuacán becomes an influence on the Maya.	Corbeled arches and vaults first appear in Maya architecture.

where water collection was combined with sacrificial religious ceremonies.

The last dated stele was erected in AD 928, and probably marks the decline of the classic period of Maya civilization. The end was sudden, as unfinished building projects testify. Several causes for this decline have been suggested: lowered water tables, soil exhaustion, epidemic disease similar to the Black Death in Europe, and invasion. These theories may explain what happened in some regions, but not all over, for the land was still well populated when the Spanish arrived.

The most popular hypothesis is that a revolution spread throughout the region, overthrowing the elitist caste system and its attendant religion. As the Maya civilization lacked political unity beyond the level of individual cities, a revolution would be a relatively simple process. The cities were abandoned to the jungle, leaving an enigmatic trace of their former greatness to baffle

European explorers. By that time, the region had become a satellite of the new power in Central America, the Aztec.

Above: *A stele with glyphs representing dates in the Maya calendar.*

Left: *Rising like a mountain from the Yucatán jungle, the Pyramid of the Magician towers above the city of Uxmal. When the Spanish arrived, it was already abandoned, probably because the water table had become lowered, making it uninhabitable for the Maya.*

562	695	799	800	c.900	928	1524	1546
The Maya state of Tikal is defeated by the state of Caracol.	King Jaguar Paw of Calakmul is captured and sacrificed by Ah Cacau of Tikal.	The last momuments are erected at Palenque.	The calendar falls into disuse.	Chichén Itzá becomes the dominant Maya center.	The classic period of Maya civilization comes to an end.	Spanish conquest of the Maya.	Spanish occupying forces put down a Maya insurrection.

CONQUEST OF CENTRAL AMERICA

The AZTEC

Right: An Aztec pendant of gold representing the sun. Artifacts like this were what the conquistadors wanted most from their captives.

The conquest and domination of earlier Indian cultures created the Aztec Empire. In their turn, the Aztec were subjugated by Spanish conquistadors, but more than any other American people, the brutal civilization they created has been a source of fascination for centuries.

When Hernán Cortéz discovered the Aztec civilization, his soldiers were in awe: "so large a market place and so full of people, so well regulated and arranged, they had never beheld before." The culture of the Aztec reflected the Middle American civilizations that had preceded it. From his capital city of Tenochtitlán (now Mexico City), with a pre-Spanish population of about 60,000, the Aztec emperor ruled five million subjects and allies, a political unity rivaled only by the great Inca Empire of South America.

The Aztec Empire was a loose one, with most cities and regions maintaining a high level of autonomy. Domination of the trading markets within its borders and the extraction of tribute from subject cities ensured the empire's rule. The foundation of this empire and warrior

Below: A detail from the Codex Cospi that shows Venus (Tlauixcalpantecuhtli) attacking jaguar warriors. The god's spear has pierced the jaguar's heart.

culture was brought on by economic necessity. The Aztec were the last of successive groups who settled Mexico's central valley, and they are noted as a distinctive culture from the 13th century onward. As these cities grew, the surrounding land became insufficient to sustain it. The Aztec solution to the problem was to annex their neighbors.

From about 1425, the island settlement of Tenochtitlán became the center of a group of Aztec lakeside settlements known as the Triple Alliance. Their influence was extended by conquest, and soon the Aztec (or Tenochca, the dwellers of Tenochtitlán) became the dominant power in the region. As Aztec power grew, Tenochtitlán grew into a substantial city, with temples, markets, barracks, and schools. Lakeside arable land was augmented by floating islands of grass, known as *chinampas*, whose use revolutionized agriculture in the lake region, and allowed the city to grow into one of the largest settlements in the Americas.

Wars on all sides

From the reign of Montezuma I (1440–68) onward, Aztec rulers established a confederation of subservient allies, most notably the Mixtec and Zapotec peoples to the south. In effect, the Aztec acted as predators, demanding tribute from their neighbors in return for peace. In this manner, Aztec influence extended as far south as Guatemala, west to the Pacific Ocean, and east

c. AD 100	c.1325	1345	1428–1430	1434	1440–1468	1455	1468–1481
The first pyramids are constructed in what is now Mexico.	Aztec people settle around Lake Texcoco and found Tenochtitlán.	Tenochtitlán is made the capital.	Aztec forces defeat the Tepanaca, earlier settlers of the Valley of Mexico.	Triple alliance formed between Tenochtitlán, Texcoco, and Tlacopan.	Under Montezuma I the Aztec Empire expands south of Mexico City.	A four year drought precipitates a major famine.	Under Axayactl the Aztec Empire expands to the Gulf of Mexico and the Pacific.

to the Caribbean Sea during the last half of the 15th century.

By this time Aztec groups had also settled to the south and east of Tenochtitlán, becoming the Toltec or Aztec Chichimeca. Their cities of Tlaxcala, Cholula, and Huexotzingo remained in an almost continual state of warfare with the Aztec of Tenochtitlán throughout the late 15th and early 16th centuries. As the Aztec were either engaged in civil war or fighting rebellious allied cities for most of the century before 1519, the army played a major role in Aztec society.

Information about Aztec warfare is contained in their hieroglyphic *codices*. The troops were divided into *calpulli* (corps) corresponding to city districts or clans. *Xiquipilli* (regiments) of foot soldiers were organized as full-time units, and bravery was encouraged by the opportunity for social advancement. Armies could amount to as many as 300,000 warriors if allied contingents were added, and, although technologically far inferior to the Spanish conquistadors they encountered, sheer weight of numbers meant that Hernán Cortéz (*see pages 118–121*) could not conquer the Aztec Empire by military means alone.

Religion and the military dominated Aztec society and the two were closely linked because the economy was based on tribute plus a steady stream of prisoners for religious sacrifice. Under Aztec influence, sacrificial cults

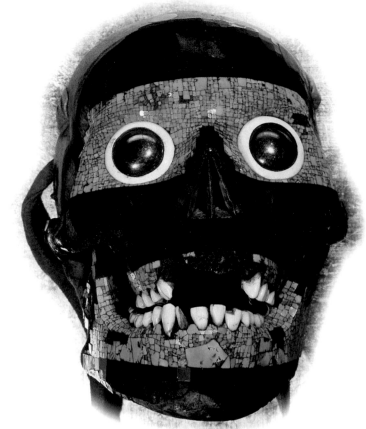

dominated Central America, a form of ritual massacre on a colossal scale that was seen as barbaric by the Spanish invaders.

The Aztec Empire's obsession with religion in the early 16th century can be partly explained by economic factors. Although central Mexico was still a relatively fertile region, the Spaniards noticed the soil exhaustion and erosion. It was increasingly difficult for the land to sustain the levels expected of it by the Aztec. In 1519, it was already a civilization in decline.

Above: Known as "The Smoking Mirror," this mask of Tezcatlipoca is made from a mosaic of turquoise and lignite formed over a human skull.

GULF OF MEXICO

Azcapotzalco | Tula
Tamuín
Tenochtitlán
Capital of
Aztec Empire
Tiayo
El Tajín
BAY OF CAMPECHE
Tzintzuntzán
Texcoco
Cempoala
Ortices
Tlacopán
Tlaxcala
Cholula
Xochicalco
Teotitlan
Mitla
Guiengola
PACIFIC OCEAN

Mayapán
Chichén Itzá
Cozumel Island
Uxmal
Tulum
CARIBBEAN SEA
YUCATÁN PENINSULA
Ichpaatun
Maya lands
Palenque
Lamanai
Tikal
Zaculeu
Iximché
Xoconusco
Dominated by Aztecs
under Ahuitzotl and
Montezuma II between
1486 and 1520

Aztec lands

1473	1487	1502	1519	1520–1	1522	1524	1545
Tenochtitlán and Tlatilulco fight a bitter civil war. Tlatilulco is crushed.	The Aztecs sacrifice 20,000 at Tenochtitlán by ripping their hearts out.	Montezuma II becomes the Aztec ruler and continues Aztec expansion.	Hernán Cortéz' forces attack the Aztec Empire.	Spanish forces crush an Aztec uprising and take the whole Aztec Empire.	The Spanish found Mexico City on the ruins of Tenochtitlán.	Cuauhtemoc, the last Aztec king, is hanged by the Spanish.	Indigenous Mexican populations are devastated by smallpox.

VASCO NÚÑEZ *de* BALBOA

1475 to 1519

Vasco Núñez de Balboa was a rogue Spanish conquistador who spent much of his time clashing with authority. His greatest achievement—the discovery of the Pacific Ocean—was accomplished during an expedition he undertook purely on his own initiative. Born into the minor gentry, he served as a page to the Lord of Moguer. In 1501 he took passage to the New World on a supply ship that stopped at several ports and at one point passed close to the Indian village of Darién (in modern Panama).

De Balboa became a planter on Hispaniola but soon ran up huge debts. To escape his creditors, in 1510 he smuggled aboard a supply ship bound for San Sebastián in Colombia. While stopped at what is now Cartagena, a ship arrived commanded by Francisco Pizarro (*see pages 98–101*), who reported that Indians had wiped out the settlement of San Sebastián. Sailing to investigate, the supply ship was shipwrecked but Pizarro rescued its crew. De Balboa told Pizarro about Darién and Pizarro sailed there, defeated the local Indians, and established a settlement.

The settlement prospered and, in 1511, de Balboa founded a second settlement nearby,

Right: Vasco Núñez de Balboa, the first European explorer to see the Pacific.

Santa María la Antigue del Darién. The Spanish sent Diego de Nicuesa to govern the colony, but after driving him off, de Balboa continued as unofficial governor of the Darién colonies for another two years. During this period he heard of "great waters" to the west and requested assistance from the Spanish crown to mount an expedition. However, since he also heard that he was to be sent back to Spain to face charges, de Balboa had to go ahead without royal approval.

Seeing the great waters

On September 1, 1513, he and Pizarro set off up the coast with a small flotilla and 190 Spaniards, several hunting dogs, and Indian porters. By luck, de Balboa anchored 120 miles up the coast at the narrowest point of the isthmus of Panama. Leaving half the force to guard the boats, he led the remainder south into the jungle. After three days, he reached an Indian village where he secured guides to help him find the "great waters." After several more days the expedition reached the ridge of low mountains called the Sierra de Quareca, where they had to fight off an attack by hostile Indians. De Balboa retaliated, attacked their village and killed or tortured everyone they could capture.

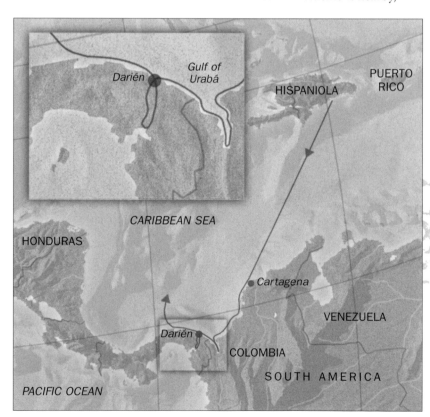

The Spaniards continued through the mountains until they reached a plateau on September 27, 1513. De Balboa climbed ahead of the rest, and so, staring out to the west, became the first European to set eyes on the Pacific Ocean, the "great waters" mentioned by the Indians. A thanksgiving was held, a cross was erected, and de Balboa claimed all the surrounding lands and the Mar del Sur (South Sea) in the name of the King of Spain.

Fighting off Indian attacks, de Balboa's men continued to hack a westbound track through the jungle toward the sea. On reaching the ocean, de Balboa waded in, carrying the flag of Spain, and claimed the entire ocean and its surrounding lands for Spain. To avoid hostile Indians, the conquistadors took a different route back to their ships. On the way they encountered a regional chief called Tubanama (possibly the origin of the name "Panama"), who de Balboa captured and then ransomed for plunder. On January 18, 1514, the fever-ridden Spaniards returned to Darién, only to find that in their absence the Spanish crown had sent a governor, Pedro Arias de Ávila

The new governor was extremely wary of de Balboa, and tension grew. When de Balboa announced plans to build two ships on the Pacific coast to explore Mar del Sur the crisis worsened. Hundreds of slaves cut a route west through the jungles and mountains to the Pacific coast, and there de Balboa established a shipyard near the present day Panamanian town of La Palma. A trial voyage revealed the Pear Islands in the Gulf of Panama, and de Balboa returned to build more ships.

De Ávila, now convinced that de Balboa was creating his own province, sent Pizarro to bring him back to Darién. De Ávila had the conquistador tried and convicted for treason, and on January 21, 1519, Vasco Nuñez de Balboa was beheaded. However, his achievements ensured that his name would be remembered long after his rival was forgotten.

Below: De Balboa and his men ransom an Indian chief in return for plunder. "A splendid maxim by an Indian on the Christian greed." Copper engraving by Theodore de Bry.

PEDRO *de* ALVARADO

1485 *to* 1541

D e Alvarado was the second in command of the small army of Hernán Cortéz that crushed the Aztec Empire in 1519. He became a conquistador-explorer in his own right and conquered hitherto undiscovered territory in both Central and South America that helped to make Spanish control absolute, from Mexico to Peru. Like many conquistadors, Pedro de Alvarado was born in Estremadura, the same frontier province where his near-contemporary Vasco Núñez de Balboa was raised. In 1510, de Alvarado arrived in Santo Domingo on Hispaniola with his four brothers. Together they ran a plantation, and Pedro slowly rose in importance in the local community. In 1518 he was appointed commander of a ship that formed part of Juan de Grijalva's expedition to the Yucatán Peninsula. The expedition was a minor success, and de Alvarado acquired a reputation as a conquistador.

By 1519 he was in Santiago de Cuba, and joined Hernán Cortéz (*see pages 118–121*) when

Below: Pedro de Alvarado, Cortéz's deputy and a conquistador in his own right, from a late 16th-century engraving by William Walker.

he sailed from Cuba to invade New Spain (Mexico). De Alvarado's experience proved useful, particularly in the early stages when Cortéz was selecting a suitable landing place. Following the landing at Vera Cruz and the subsequent march on the Aztec capital of Tenochtitlán (now Mexico City), de Alvarado rose to become second-in-command of the expedition under Cortéz.

In 1520, when Cortéz returned to Vera Cruz to combat the challenge to his authority posed by Panfilo de Narváez (*see pages 56–57*), de Alvarado was left in charge of Tenochtitlán. During his administration he mistakenly tried to put an end to the practice of human sacrifice and the massacre of hundreds of Aztec nobles. His actions sparked an Aztec revolt against the Spanish. When Cortéz returned he found his garrison under siege and his whole conquest in jeopardy. Cortéz pulled back from the city until things had calmed down, then returned to restore order. Tenochtitlán fell after a bitter siege, and Cortéz saved his reputation. De Alvarado's impetuosity had almost cost the Spaniards an empire.

Allied with Guatemalans

By 1523 Spanish rule was complete, the Aztec religion was crushed, and Cortéz was free to rid himself of his troublesome deputy. He authorized de Alvarado to undertake an expedition to explore and conquer the territories south of the Yucatán peninsula. De Alvarado gathered a force of conquistadors, war dogs, and Indian slaves, then marched south from Tenochtitlán through the territory of the Mixtec to Tehuantepec in Oaxaca. His progress to this point was not impeded, and he now stood on the

border of Aztec influence, facing unknown territories and peoples to the west.

From his camp close to the Pacific Ocean, de Alvarado headed almost due east, into the lands of the Chiapas, who subjected the conquistadors to constant harassment. He negotiated almost impenetrable terrain, crossed two rivers, the last of which was the Rio Usumacinta, then reached the plateau of Guatemala beyond. A wave of smallpox had swept through the region ahead of the Spanish and decimated the Guatemalan people, so de Alvarado was able to establish a temporary camp in the almost deserted city of Quezaltenango, where he was forced to fight off repeated Indian attacks.

Prisoners revealed that two Guatemalan tribes were at war, so he allied himself with the Cakchiquel against their rivals, the Quiché. During the summer and fall he fought his way through Quiché territory alongside his Guatemalan allies, to reach the Quiché capital of Atitlán, which he captured after a brief battle. De Alvarado was now, in effect, the overlord of Guatemala and he established a new capital city; a Spanish settlement built on the site where

Guatemala City stands today.

Leaving a small group of settlers and a garrison, he pressed on further east into what is now El Salvador. Despite the opposition of the Pipiles Indians he reached their capital city of Cuzcaclan, near the site of the modern capital of San Salvador. Short of men and supplies, de Alvarado returned to Guatemala, and eventually to Spain to gather support for a further expedition.

In 1526 he was named Captain General of Guatemala, but instead of returning directly, he sailed to Ecuador in 1534 and launched an expedition to Quito, only to find that Pizarro had beaten him to it. Pizarro paid him to leave and de Alvarado returned to Guatemala. De Alvarado was planning a fresh expedition to the north of Mexico in 1541 when he was killed in a riding accident.

Above: The Spaniards were quick to utilize Aztec slaves to build Mexico City on the ruins of Tenochtitlán.

Above: A Spanish attack on an Aztec temple. The sacrificial element in Central American religions prompted the conquistadors to destroy all traces of their religion.

HERNÁN CORTÉZ

1485 to 1547

The man who conquered the Aztec Empire with a handful of men was the personification of the conquistador and, together with Francisco Pizarro (*see pages 98–101*), he almost single-handedly established a Spanish empire in the New World. He combined skill, cunning, cruelty, and treachery to attain his ends, and mixed conquest in the name of Spain with immense personal profit.

Hernán Cortéz, who was born into the minor nobility, read law at the University of Salamanca, but ended his studies to return home in 1502 for some unrecorded reason. In 1504 he took passage on a ship bound for Hispaniola, where he settled in Azua and became a planter and public notary. In 1511 he moved to Cuba along with its new governor, Diego Velásquez.

Cortéz established a farm and a mining business near Santiago de Cuba, and was soon appointed as the local treasury representative and alcalde (mayor) of the colony. Part of his success lay in his friendship with Velásquez, but this was put under strain when an amorous affair shocked the local community, and political maneuvering led to charges that Cortéz was trying to overthrow the governor. Both incidents were dealt with, one by marriage and the other by pleas and pardons, but the relationship between Cortéz and Velásquez remained sour.

However, Velásquez appointed Cortéz to lead an investigative exploration of the Yucatán Peninsula when the expeditions of Hernández de Córdoba and Juan de Grijalva reported finds of gold and traces of an advanced civilization there. As he was preparing to leave, Cortéz learned that Velásquez was having second thoughts and was about to call off the expedition, probably doubting the reliability of Cortéz in obeying his instructions. Rather than comply, Cortéz slipped out of port on February 10, 1519, then completed his preparations in more secluded ports up the Cuban coast.

Leaving Cuba, he set course for the Yucatán and landed on the island of Cozumel. Here, he set about subduing the population and converting them to Christianity with the interpretive aid of a Spaniard, who had been captured earlier by the Maya. Cortéz sailed north and west around the peninsula into the Bay of Campeche. He landed at the Boca de Términos, where Indians who opposed his landing were beaten off. Soon, local chiefs brought a peace offering of gold, provisions, and women, one of whom, an Aztec noblewoman named Malinche, became Cortéz's mistress and interpreter.

Incited by gifts of gold

The Spaniards sailed along the coast for another 200 miles before landing at a sheltered anchorage. While they were busy building a settlement that they named Vera Cruz, Cortéz received several delegations from Aztec Emperor Montezuma, who was unsure if the Spaniards were gods or mortals. The gifts of gold his ambassadors carried only encouraged Cortéz to invade the Aztec Empire.

He burned his ships to prevent any retreat to

Below: Hernán Cortéz comes face-to-face with the last Aztec emperor, Montezuma II, in 1519.

Below: *Cortéz and his men after the retreat from Tenochtitlán.*

Cuba, fortified his base at Vera Cruz, and gathered supplies for the invasion. He planned to advance on the Aztec capital and subdue any non-Aztec Indian tribes along the way to use as allies, a strategy designed to preserve his Spanish force as much as possible. The horse was his secret weapon. Since the animals were unknown in the Americas, they gave the conquistadors a psychological advantage.

On August 16, 1519, Cortéz marched inland toward the mountain plateau to the west. After leaving a garrison in Vera Cruz, his small army consisted of about 600 infantry, including men armed with crossbows and arquebuses (an early form of gun), and just over a dozen cavalry. It was a small force with which to take on the might of an empire.

His plan started to unfold. The army left the swampy coastal plain, climbed the mountains and defeated the Tlaxcala Indians on the high plateau beyond. After their defeat, Cortéz made them his allies, and they remained loyal to him throughout the conquest of Mexico. Next, Cortéz moved southwest and west to the city of Cholula, a city allied with the Aztec, which he captured through subterfuge. By killing the leading citizens, who may otherwise have caused trouble, he ensured its loyalty. Continuing northwest, he came upon a fertile plateau and gazed down into the heart of the Aztec Empire. Cortéz stood on the brink of an incredible triumph or an ignominious defeat.

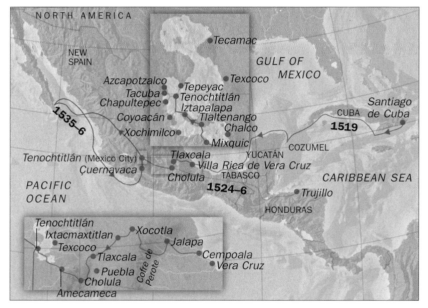

Above: Cortéz employs trickery to seize Montezuma and take him prisoner.

Unopposed entry

Cortéz and his conquistadors entered the valley, crossing through the snow-covered mountain ridge beyond, the pass flanked by the volcanoes of Iztaccihuatl and Popocatépetl. As the conquistadors descended into the flat country beyond, more Indian allies joined Cortéz. Montezuma sent another ambassador, but the Spanish were not to be deflected from their advance on the Aztec capital of Tenochtitlán. By this time they had reached the southern edge of Lake Chalco, one of the string of lakes in the valley that were fringed by city-states under Aztec control.

Continuing along the lake's southern side, they passed by the causeway linking the island city of Cuilahuac with the shore and continued to Iztapalapa, the point where Lake Chalco and Lake Texcoco met. A far longer causeway stretched before them, part of a network linking Tenochtitlán with the shore.

On November 8, 1519, watched by the entire population, Cortéz entered the Aztec capital unopposed. Montezuma was there to meet the Spanish troops. Gifts were exchanged, and the Spanish were housed in the palace of Axayacatal. It was clear that the Aztecs still looked on the invaders as gods, but Cortéz knew this state of affairs could not last. We do not know whether Montezuma bowed to the inevitable and saved face by maintaining that the Spanish were divine beings or whether he truly believed it.

Both sides were in a predicament, and the next few weeks would decide the future of Mexico. Cortéz was effectively trapped in Tenochtitlán, surrounded by thousands of potential enemies. When two Spanish envoys were killed outside the city, Cortéz had to act swiftly to maintain the initiative. During the leaders' next meeting, Cortéz persuaded Montezuma to visit the Spanish quarters, where the emperor was taken prisoner. With control of Montezuma, Cortéz and his men had control of the empire, at least for the time being. Because the Aztec regarded Montezuma as a god, they would not attack the Spanish for fear of the emperor's safety.

Smallpox claims an empire

During this uneasy period, Cortéz learned that Pánfilo de Narváez (*see pages 56–57*) had landed at Vera Cruz with orders from Cuba's governor, Velásquez, that Cortéz should return to Cuba. By entering into secret negotiations with Montezuma, de Narváez gave Cortéz the excuse he needed. Cortéz launched a surprise attack on his rival and captured de Narváez. His men joined Cortéz.

With de Narváez a prisoner, Cortéz returned to Tenochtitlán and found the city in revolt and the Spanish besieged. He forced Montezuma to appear in public to appeal for an end to the violence, but the emperor was stoned by his own people and later died of his wounds. The Spanish fought their way out of the city on June 30, 1520—"Nochetriste," Night of Sorrow— and retreated to Tlaxcala. Cortéz was determined to recapture the city although almost half of his force had been lost. He was assisted by an outbreak of smallpox that devastated the Aztec population during the winter.

In May 1521, Cortéz led his force back to

Left: *The temple of Teoccalli in Tenochtitlán surrenders to Cortéz. Although superior war technology overcame much heavier odds, Aztec buildings like these overawed the Spanish conquerors.*

Below: *"Cortéz's victory over the Indians of Tabasco." Painting by an unknown Spanish artist.*

Lake Texcoco and, using prefabricated warships, gained control of the city's approaches. A methodical siege and a steady approach to the city paid dividends, and Tenochtitlán was recaptured on August 13, 1521, after bitter fighting. Cortéz was now firmly in control of the lands of the former Aztec Empire.

The conquered land was named New Spain, and Cortéz built his new capital of Mexico City on the ruins of Tenochtitlán. By the end of 1522, legal wrangling in Spain between Velàsquez and representatives of Cortéz was resolved in the conquistador's favor, and he was appointed Governor of New Spain. Expeditions over the next few years ensured the loyalty of the hinterland and extended Spanish control to the Pacific Coast and as far south as Guatemala. In 1524, Cortéz led an expedition to establish a Spanish settlement at Trujillo in Honduras.

By 1535 Cortéz was growing tired of government and explored to the northwest as far as the Gulf of California, then built ships and explored the peninsula of Baja California before returning to New Spain by way of the Tres Marias Islands off Mexico's Pacific coast. Cortéz went to Spain in 1540 and, after campaigning in North Africa against the Barbary Corsairs, returned to Seville, only to die of dysentery on December 2, 1547.

CONQUEST OF CENTRAL AMERICA

JUAN *de la* COSA
1460 *to* 1510

Juan de la Cosa was the cartographer responsible for the magnificent *Mappa Mundi*, a world map produced in 1500, just eight years after Columbus first sailed across the Atlantic. De la Cosa, an explorer in this own right, payed particular attention to the Gulf of Urabá. He was born in Puerto de Santa Mariá, a small port on the Gulf of Cadiz. His father was a Basque seaman and, although de la Cosa modestly credits Columbus with teaching him the basics of seamanship, navigation, and cartography, his roots indicate that he would have been immersed in these essential nautical subjects from an early age.

He accompanied Columbus on his second voyage in 1493 as a seaman, and proved a proficient mariner. By the time de la Cosa returned in 1496, he had experienced the Caribbean at first hand, since Columbus had ranged from Dominica to Cuba. On his return, de la Cosa gathered whatever cartographic information he could from Spanish and Portuguese mariners and began work on drafts of his *Mappa Mundi*.

In 1499 he accompanied Alonso de Ojeda's expedition (*see pages 94–95*) to the northern coast of South America as it charted the Venezuelan and Colombian coasts and built on information supplied by Columbus in his fateful 1498 voyage. On his return, de la Cosa combined his new information with that gathered by Pedro Álvarez Cabral (*see pages 68–69*) and Amerigo Vespucci (*see pages 92–93*) for his great cartographic achievement.

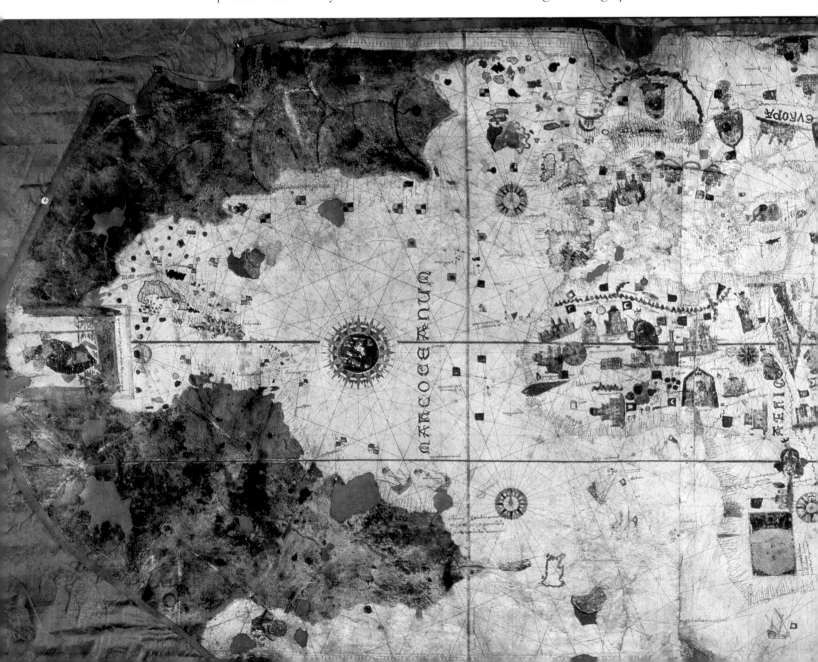

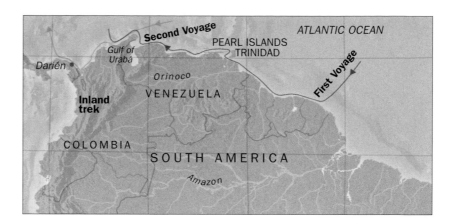

When it was produced in late 1500, the *Mappa Mundi* was the first map ever to show the three newly discovered New World territories; the northern section of North America, the Caribbean islands, and the eastern coast of South America. The map was a cartographic *tour de force* and its production probably altered mankind's vision of the world more than any other map produced before or since.

Chasing rumors of gold

In 1501, de la Cosa revisited the coast of Colombia with the expedition of Rodrigo de Bastidas. De Bastidas went on to explore the coast of what is now Panama, including the Gulf of Urabá, which formed the southeastern corner of the Panama isthmus. On his return, de la Cosa petitioned the Spanish court for the right to stage a fresh expedition to the region, which he considered held great promise for settlement and exploitation. His map had made

him a favorite of the court, particularly with Queen Isabella, and he was granted the royal support he required.

In 1504 he sailed from Spain to make landfall on Margarita Island off Venezuela's Pearl Coast in September. After trading with local Indians for pearls, he headed west toward the Gulf of Urabá. He came across the survivors of the expedition of Cristobal Guerra on the way, a venture that had suffered from shipwrecks and disease, and de la Cosa gave them whatever assistance he could.

He established a camp on the gulf and led several expeditions inland in search of gold. Indians he encountered told him tales of gold further inland and on the opposite side of the Gulf of Urabá, at Darién. The promise of inland gold was underlined when he found a chest filled with gold masks, ceremonial jewelry, and drums in an abandoned Indian village at the foot of the Colombian mountains.

The danger of Indian attack was too strong for him to attempt a deeper penetration inland, so he returned to the Gulf of Urabá. De la Cosa crossed the gulf to chase rumors of gold around the Indian village of Darién. Although the Spanish raided far inland, no gold was found. While this was taking place, the remaining ships of Cristobal Guerra's expedition arrived in the Gulf of Urabá. Both these vessels and those of de la Cosa were too unseaworthy to leave, and it took both groups almost a year to construct new vessels. De la Cosa led these ships to Spain, arriving in Seville in March 1506 with a mere 60 men, the survivors of both expeditions.

In 1509 he sailed with Alonso de Ojeda (*see pages 94–95*) on a new expedition to the Colombian coast, where the Spanish made an abortive raid on an Indian village near present-day Cartagena. The local Indians rose up and overwhelmed the invaders. Wounded by a poisoned dart, Juan de la Cosa died on de Ojeda's ship on February 28, 1510.

Left: *Juan de la Cosa's* Mappa Mundi *(World Map), is the oldest known depiction of the lands Columbus discovered. But it is also the first map to show the Americas in relation to Europe and Africa, and the Indian Ocean. In pale outline in the center are the coastlines of Europe and Africa. To the right is the Caribbean, Gulf of Mexico, the top of South America, and the North American coast as for north as the Carolinas. This is also the map referred to on page 79.*

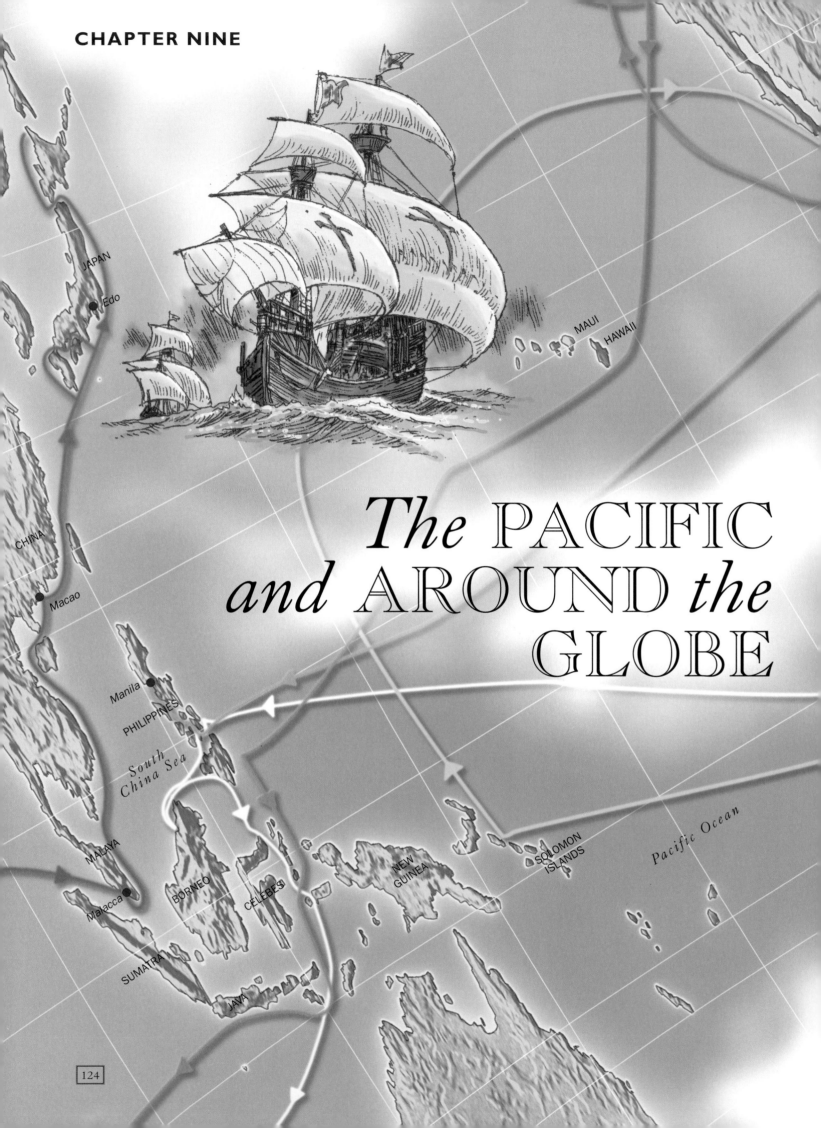

CHAPTER NINE

The PACIFIC and AROUND the GLOBE

JAPAN

Edo

MAUI   HAWAII

CHINA

Macao

Manila

PHILIPPINES

South China Sea

MALAYA

BORNEO

CELEBES

NEW GUINEA

SOLOMON ISLANDS

Pacific Ocean

Malacca

SUMATRA

JAVA

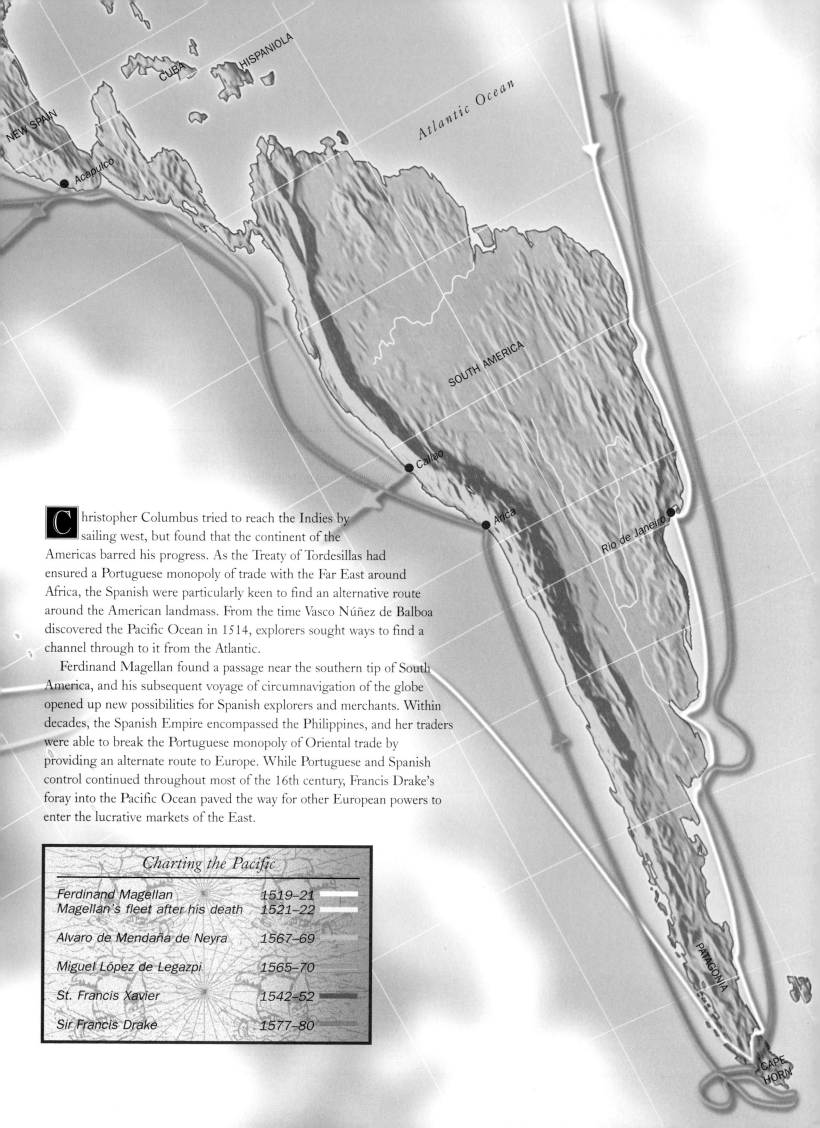

NEW SPAIN

Acapulco

CUBA

HISPANIOLA

Atlantic Ocean

SOUTH AMERICA

Callao

Arica

Rio de Janeiro

PATAGONIA

CAPE HORN

Christopher Columbus tried to reach the Indies by sailing west, but found that the continent of the Americas barred his progress. As the Treaty of Tordesillas had ensured a Portuguese monopoly of trade with the Far East around Africa, the Spanish were particularly keen to find an alternative route around the American landmass. From the time Vasco Núñez de Balboa discovered the Pacific Ocean in 1514, explorers sought ways to find a channel through to it from the Atlantic.

Ferdinand Magellan found a passage near the southern tip of South America, and his subsequent voyage of circumnavigation of the globe opened up new possibilities for Spanish explorers and merchants. Within decades, the Spanish Empire encompassed the Philippines, and her traders were able to break the Portuguese monopoly of Oriental trade by providing an alternate route to Europe. While Portuguese and Spanish control continued throughout most of the 16th century, Francis Drake's foray into the Pacific Ocean paved the way for other European powers to enter the lucrative markets of the East.

Charting the Pacific		
Ferdinand Magellan	1519–21	
Magellan's fleet after his death	1521–22	
Alvaro de Mendaña de Neyra	1567–69	
Miguel López de Legazpi	1565–70	
St. Francis Xavier	1542–52	
Sir Francis Drake	1577–80	

FERDINAND MAGELLAN
1480 to 1521

Below: Magellan consults with his officers after sighting the entrance to the westward passage (Strait of Magellan).

erdinand Magalhães (Magellan) is remembered for leading the first expedition to successfully circumnavigate the globe and for opening up the Pacific Ocean; he died during the attempt. Where, 30 years earlier, Christopher Columbus failed, Magellan succeeded in finding a route to the Orient and the Indies by sailing west from Europe. His father, Dom Ruy Magalhães, was an aide to King John II of Portugal, so Ferdinand was born into a family of minor Portuguese nobility. The youngest of three children, he left his agrarian roots to study in a monastic school when he was seven. After five years he became a page at the Royal Court, part of the train of

Queen Dona Leonor, and his education was expanded to include navigation, mathematics, and cartography. It is an indication of the importance the Portuguese placed on maritime skills that the court maintained a school for these nautical sciences.

In 1495, when Manuel I succeeded John II, the young nobleman came under the new king's patronage and was sent to sea in command of trading voyages to Africa and possibly beyond. In March 1505, Magellan accompanied the Portuguese Viceroy of the Indies, Francisco de Almeida, when he sailed to take up his new office. De Almeida combined a policy of trade with brutal attacks on rivals such as the Persians, and eventually consolidated Portuguese control over the waters surrounding the Indian subcontinent. Magellan participated in Almeida's campaigns against the Indian Muslims, and he was even wounded during an engagement at Cannanore, on the Malabar Coast.

He recovered in time to participate in an assault on the Muslim ports of East Africa, the aim of which was to capture rival Muslim trading posts and replace them with Portuguese ones. By 1507, Magellan was back on India's Malabar Coast, where he helped to defend the Portuguese stronghold of Goa against attack from Malays and pirates. The brutal campaign lasted well into 1510, but the fortress held out and Magellan was promoted.

He returned to Portugal in 1512 and participated in a campaign against the Moors in Morocco in the following year. Once again he was badly wounded, and would remain partially lame for the rest of his life. A whiff of scandal marred his service in Africa: he was accused of lining his own pockets and trading with the Moors. Although the charges were unproven, he fell from favor with King Manuel I, who snubbed Magellan, calling him "clubfoot."

Planning the great voyage

He retired to northern Portugal, where he met mariners and cartographers who spoke of a possible route around the southern tip of the Americas. Intrigued, Magellan moved to Spain, where he lobbied to be given command of a

Inset: *Ferdinand Magellan, from a contemporary engraving.*

Above: *Magellan's ships creep through the strait, led by ships' boats testing the depth of the channel.*

voyage of exploration to test the theory. He married Beatriz Barbosa, the sister of an old colleague, and settled in Seville where he continued his lobbying and eventually gained the interest of the young King Charles I of Spain. The idea of a westerly route to the Indies appealed to Spain because the terms of the Treaty of Tordesillas (1494) denied her access to the region by the easterly route around South Africa. The king gave his support, and Magellan launched himself into the planning of the project. Sanlúcar de Barrameda, close to Seville, was selected as the base port of the expedition, and the town soon became a hive of activity.

Five ships—the *Victoria*, *Trinidad*, *San Antonio*, *Concepción*, and the *Santiago*—crewed by 250 seamen, both Portuguese and Spanish, made up the company. All the ships were under 130 tons in weight, yet they carried stores sufficient for a voyage lasting two years, and trade goods and a substantial armament ensured that they were

ready for anything. On September 20, 1519, Ferdinand Magellan in the *Victoria* led his small fleet out of the harbor and set course for the Canary Islands. The most ambitious voyage of the Age of Discovery was underway.

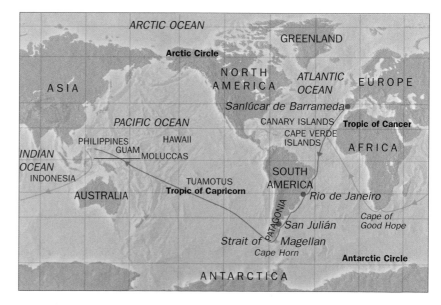

Above: *Diego Ribero's world map of 1529. Apart from the region surrounding the isthmus of Panama, the Pacific coast of the Americas remains uncharted.*

Below: *The* Victoria, *Magellan's flagship and the first vessel to circumnavigate the globe.*

Mutiny in the Atlantic

When choosing his crew, Magellan had made a fundamental mistake: the crewmen were largely Spanish, while the complements of ships' officers were mostly Portuguese. Friction was apparent even before the expedition sailed, but once Magellan passed the Canary Islands and ventured out into the South Atlantic, matters came to a head. Juan de Cartagena, the Spanish captain of the *San Antonio*, acted as a ringleader for the discontented Spanish, and confronted Magellan. It appeared that the Spanish were willing to kill their Portuguese commander, but Magellan somehow managed to defuse the situation, and Cartagena was placed under arrest.

Bad mid-Atlantic storms, followed by a spell in the doldrums, did not help the crews' low morale, so it was probably with some relief that Magellan made a landfall in Brazil in early December. By December 15 the fleet was at anchor in a bay Magellan called Porto de Santa Lucia (now Rio de Janeiro). After taking on water and provisions, the expedition continued down the South American coast. In mid-January 1520 the fleet reached the mouth of a wide channel, and Magellan sent Juan Serrano in the *Santiago* to investigate. It turned out to be the estuary of a river, now known as the Rio de la Plata (River Plate).

Magellan pressed on, and reached the bleaker coastline of Patagonia (southern Argentina), during what was fall in the Southern Hemisphere. The region's name was derived from the natives' skin footwear, which resembled *patas* (animal paws). On the last day of March 1520, the expedition anchored in a secure harbor (now San Julián)

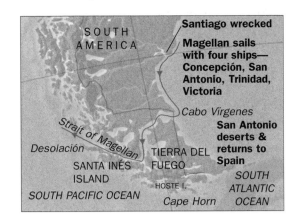

and set up a winter camp. The sailors were further south than any European had gone before, and they had no idea of what lay in the surrounding countryside. Fears of monsters were increased when they encountered penguins, llamas, and strange birds for the first time. It was also discovered that their food supplies were critically low thanks to corrupt suppliers back in Spain. The friction among the crews was exacerbated by anxiety about the situation.

In late April a second Spanish captain led a revolt. Gaspar de Quesada freed Juan de Cartagena and tried to incite a mutiny on the promise that he would lead the Spanish seamen back home. Most of the crew sided with Magellan, the revolt was crushed, and de Quesada was executed. Magellan explored Patagonia for a few months, but he lost the *Santiago* when she ran aground and, by October, he felt it was time to move on. The unfortunate de Cartagena was left marooned in Patagonia when the expedition sailed southward.

The Strait of Magellan

Toward the end of October, Magellan found that the coastline was curving out to the southeast. Where the curve began, he discovered the mouth of another channel heading west, and he sent the *San Antonio* to investigate. Instead of probing the channel, its crew deserted and sailed back to Spain. Reluctant to continue to the southeast, Magellan led his three remaining ships up the strait that would later bear his name. To the north lay Patagonia, while on the southern side Magellan encountered a desolate region that appeared to breathe fire; probably from volcanoes. Appropriately, the explorer named this southern landmass Tierra del Fuego (Land of Fire).

It was not an easy channel to traverse, they encountered whirlpools, contrary tides and currents, and inhospitable cliffs on either side for much of the 350 miles of the passage. Finally, on November 27, 1520, Magellan and his expedition reached the end of the strait, at a point he named Cape Desire. He had reached the South Sea, and in honor of the event and the calm weather, he renamed it the Pacific Ocean, wishing that it would "always be as calm and benevolent as it is today."

Magellan had found a western route into the

Below: View in the Strait of Magellan, a 19th-century engraving of a 16th-century event.

Pacific and the to Orient, which undoubtedly lay beyond, although the treacherous waters around Tierra del Fuego, including Cape Horn to the south, would deter many seasoned mariners from regularly attempting the journey. What now had to be determined was whether it was possible to cross the Pacific Ocean safely and reach the Orient.

Right: On arriving in the archipelago he named San Lazaro, Magellan raised a cross to claim it for Spain. Today, a fragment of the original is encased in a larger cross and mounted in its own rotunda in the center of Cebu City. The ceiling is decorated with scenes from Magellan's life, and the building remains a tourist attraction.

Across the Pacific Ocean

The exact route taken by Ferdinand Magellan across the Pacific remains unknown. As scurvy and malnutrition slowly took hold, the ships' crews ate rats and boiled oxhides. By the New Year there was still no sign of land, although Portuguese maps in his possession indicated that he should have reached the region of the Spice Islands. By January 20, 1521, he had thrown his maps overboard. He would have been even more disgusted if he had known that he was not even halfway across the Ocean.

The following day a lookout spotted land, probably the islands known as the Tuamotos. He named the landfall San Pablo, and the

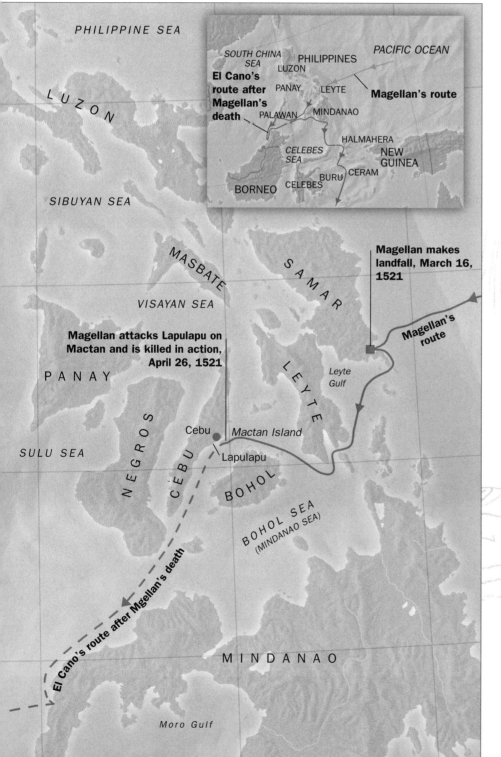

starving sailors gathered what supplies they could before continuing to sail northwest. They crossed the equator on February 13. By March 4, Magellan made another island landfall on Guam among what are now known as the Marianas Islands. He named the islands the Ladrones (Thieves) after the inhabitants tried to rob his landing parties. Despite this interference, the sailors acquired fruit, rice, and meat, and slowly their health was restored. Within a week they set sail again, heading toward the southwest. On March 16, 1521, Magellan made another landfall, this time in a large group of islands. He named the archipelago San Lazaro, since it was first sighted on a Saturday, the day of Lazarus. He had arrived in what the Spaniards would later rename the Philippines.

In San Lazaro archipelago

The Spanish expedition had reached the island now known as Samar, in the northeast of the archipelago. Since food sources were plentiful, Magellan allowed his men to gather provisions, trade with the inhabitants, and recover their

strength. The local islanders appeared friendly, but to Magellan's aroused interest, although they seemed to be poor, some wore gold jewelry. Magellan questioned the people and discovered that the source of the gold was thought to be another island, Leyte.

On March 28, the expedition moved to Leyte to be greeted by islanders who spoke a dialect similar to Malay. To Magellan, this was proof that they had reached the Indies. A celebratory Easter Mass was held in the company of the local raja (chief), Colambu, who expressed an interest in their Christian religion. While some officers argued that they should sail in search of the Spice Islands, Magellan kept the expedition in the archipelago, hoping to find more gold and make more converts. Colambu, who appeared willing to become a Christian, took Magellan to meet another chief on the neighboring island of Cebu, who also declared that he was willing to embrace Christianity.

It is probable that Magellan was being used. By being baptized, the chieftains may have felt that they could rely on the Europeans' help against their enemies. Magellan then ordered that all local chiefs should embrace Christianity or face the consequences. One chief, Lapulapu of Mactan, an enemy of the Cebuano converts, refused to obey, so Magellan made an example of him. On April 26 Magellan led an expedition against Lapulapu, with 60 men and 1,000 Cebuano allies, but it was a disaster. During the retreat to their boats, Magellan was killed.

Other likely successors were also killed in local revolts over the next few weeks, and, following a rudderless period when the Spanish crewmen acted almost like local pirates, Juan Sebastián de la El Cano was elected expedition leader. He had the rotten *Concepción* burned, then sailed off to the west with the *Victoria* and *Trinidad* around Mindanao to Borneo. In November 1521, El Cano made the harbor of Ternate in the Spice Islands. Leaving the *Trinidad* and her crew to repair their ship and follow on behind, El Cano set course for the Strait of Malacca and the Indian Ocean. After rounding the Cape of

Good Hope in May 1522, the *Victoria* was on the last leg of her journey. She limped into the harbor of Sanlúcar de Barrameda on September 6, 1522, almost three years after setting out on the voyage. The *Trinidad* also tried to sail home, but her completely Spanish crew were imprisoned by the Portuguese, who considered them interlopers.

Magellan never reached the Indies proper, and he never returned home, but he was posthumously credited with leading the first voyage of circumnavigation in history. His actions opened up a wealth of possibilities for Spain and, in only decades, the Spanish would incorporate San Lazaro and its lucrative spice trade into its overseas empire.

Above: "The Battle of Mactan" by Carlos Francisco, glorifies Magellan's unsuccessful attack on Lapulapu.

Below: A 20th-century depiction of the crew of the Victoria *returning to Spain after their voyage of circumnavigation. The sailors are led by Juan Sebastián de la El Cano.*

MIGUEL LÓPEZ *de* LEGAZPI

1510 *to* 1572

Miguel López de Legazpi carved out a Spanish province from the Philippines, and turned the archipelago into a bustling trade center. One of the last of the conquistadors, he combined military ability with diplomatic tact and administrative flair, and his exploration was brilliantly followed by firm consolidation of his gains. We know almost nothing about his early life, except that he was born in the Basque town of Guipúzcoa. It may be that, like a number of conquistadors, he had humble roots, and in later years he deliberately obscured his origins.

By his mid-20s he had settled in New Spain (Mexico), soon after the conquest of Mexico by Hernán Cortéz. In his early years in the province he served as a soldier and took part in expeditions to quell native revolts, including the Mixtón War, but as far as is known, he never participated in any expeditions of discovery. For the next 20–30 years he served in both a military and an administrative capacity in the province. Since Portugal had secured a route around Africa and established a monopoly of trade with the Far East, Spain thought it could achieve the same ends by establishing a secure Asian base and creating a trade route between it and New Spain. The Archipelago de San Lazaro, discovered by Ferdinand Magellan a little over 40 years earlier, seemed an ideal location.

Since Magellan's voyage, Spain had dispatched no less than four unsuccessful expeditions to San Lazaro. The commander of the last of these, Ruis Lopez de Villalobos, renamed the islands Felipinas, in honor of the Prince of Spain, Don Felipe, soon to be King Felipe II (Philip II).

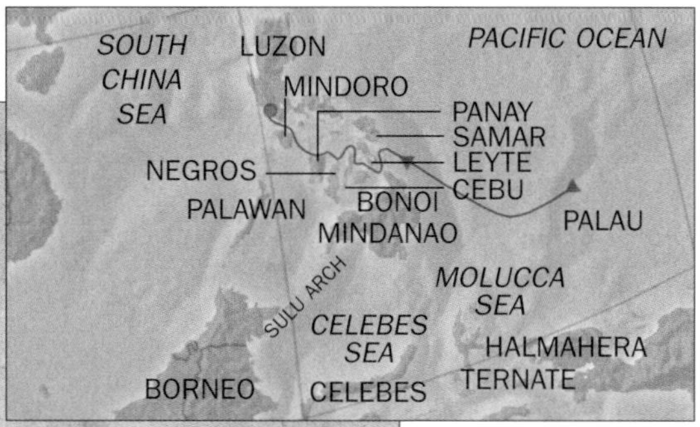

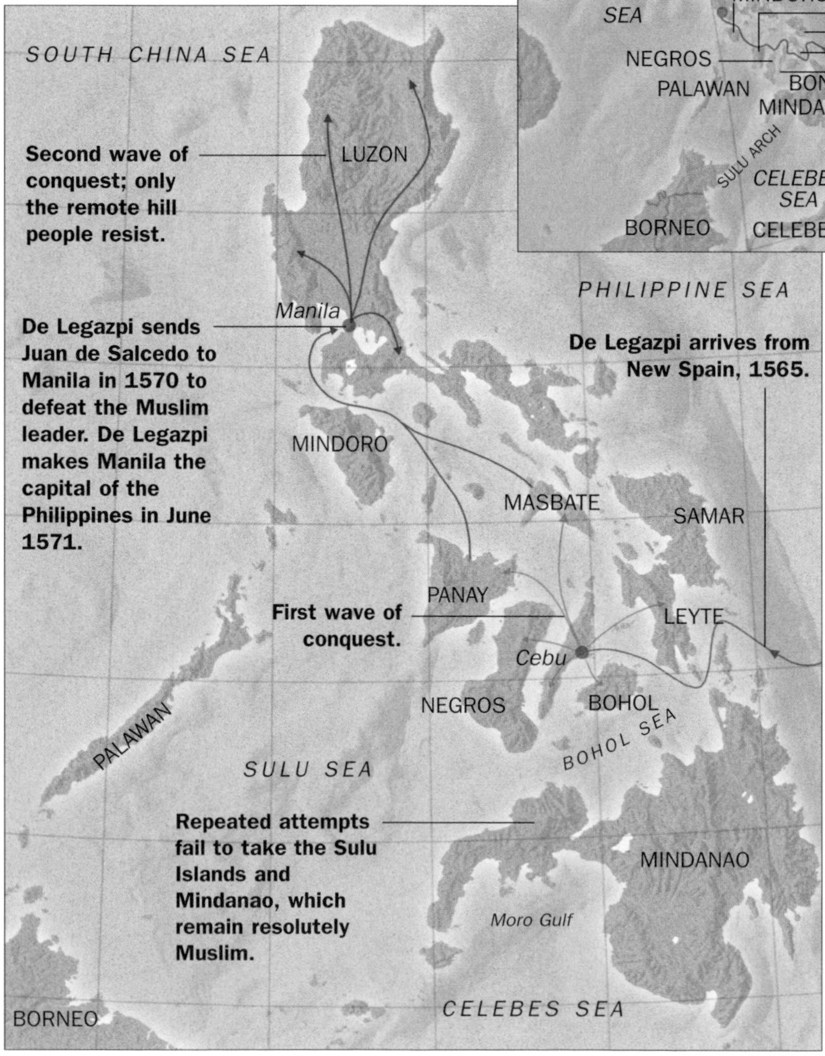

The fifth expedition had the triple aims of subduing the islands, bringing Christianity to the inhabitants, and establishing a trading colony. De Legazpi was chosen to lead it and was awarded the appropriate titles and concessions from Philip II.

On November 21, 1564, de Legazpi sailed from the New Spain port of Acapulco (some accounts say the port of embarkation was Navidad) with five ships and 400 men, a combination of sailors and conquistadors. Apart from a handful of Jesuit priests, he also carried Andrés de Urdaneta as an advisor. An Augustinian monk, de Urdaneta was also an experienced mariner who had already visited the Moluccas, where he was stranded in the Spice Islands for five years. He served as pilot to de Legazpi, and was responsible for all the expedition's mapping tasks.

Pacifying the Philippines

In February 1565 de Legazpi's fleet arrived in the Philippines. They were aware of the basic geography of the islands from accounts produced by the survivors of Magellan's

Map labels (inset):
SOUTH CHINA SEA — LUZON — MINDORO — PANAY — SAMAR — LEYTE — CEBU — NEGROS — PALAWAN — BONOI — MINDANAO — PALAU — PACIFIC OCEAN — SULU ARCH — CELEBES SEA — MOLUCCA SEA — HALMAHERA — TERNATE — BORNEO — CELEBES

Map labels (main):
SOUTH CHINA SEA

Second wave of conquest; only the remote hill people resist. — LUZON

De Legazpi sends Juan de Salcedo to Manila in 1570 to defeat the Muslim leader. De Legazpi makes Manila the capital of the Philippines in June 1571. — *Manila*

MINDORO

PHILIPPINE SEA

De Legazpi arrives from New Spain, 1565.

MASBATE — SAMAR

First wave of conquest. — PANAY — LEYTE

Cebu

NEGROS — BOHOL — BOHOL SEA

PALAWAN

SULU SEA

Repeated attempts fail to take the Sulu Islands and Mindanao, which remain resolutely Muslim. — MINDANAO — *Moro Gulf*

BORNEO — CELEBES SEA

expedition as well as those from the subsequent four failures. After an initial exploration of Mindanao and Leyte, the Spanish were approached by an embassy from the prince of Cebu. It had been reported to the prince that these strangers breathed smoke and ate rocks, so he did not want to offend them. His spies had clearly seen them smoke tobacco and eat hard ships' rations. De Legazpi entered Cebu City, and the conquistadors then took over the whole island, easily subduing any resistance by the Cebuanos. De Legazpi now had a secure base in the center of the Philippine archipelago.

From 1565 until 1570, de Legazpi and his men followed an organized plan of exploration and conquest. After reconnaissance and mapping, the conquistadors would land on an island and neutralize the local leaders through alliance or detention. Once military rule was established, the missionaries would set about pacifying the island. Using this method, the conquistadors' rule was extended over the islands of Leyte, Bohol, Negros, Masbate, and Panay.

The opportunity to conquer the largest island, Luzon, came in 1570 when a rift occurred between the Muslim factions there. De Legazpi sent a small force to the island,

commanded by his grandson, Juan de Salcedo. The Spaniards landed near Manila, captured the city, and signed a peace treaty with the Filipinos that also gave them control over the idland of Mindoro.

In June 1571, de Legazpi established a city council and made Manila the capital of the new Spanish province. The old conquistador became the island's first governor and pacified Filipino resistance through diplomacy before he died the following year. Spain now had a firm foothold in Asia and, thanks to the cartographic work of de Urdaneta, it had also mapped out a secure two-way trade route to Europe via Mexico, a shipping lane that would soon be called the "Manila Galleon" route.

Above: *The Jesuits were quick to convert the Cebuano people and, within a decade of their arrival, churches like this one at Argau, Cebu Island, sprang up all over the pacified Philippines.*

133

ALVARO *de* MENDAÑA *de* NEYRA

1541 to 1595

De Neyra was the nephew of the Spanish viceroy of Peru, Lope Garciá de Castro. Rumors of a rich continent to the west—*Terra Australis Incognita* (Unknown Land of the South) —had reached Peru, and the de Castro decided to send his relative across the South Pacific to investigate and sample the wealth to be found.

De Neyra sailed from Lima's port of Callao on November 19, 1567, with 150 men in two ships, the *Los Reyes* and the *Todos Santos*. The expedition appears to have been poorly planned—although slaves were carried to help build a settlement and there were priests to convert any natives they might meet, they carried insufficient supplies for a voyage across the Pacific Ocean and back.

The expedition headed west-southwest into the Pacific, a course that took them between the archipelagos of the Marquesas and the Tuamotu island groups. Probably due to contrary currents, they veered around onto an approximately westerly heading. On January 15, 1568, de Neyra's crew spotted a large island—probably Nui, now part of the Tuvalu island group to the north of Fiji. The same contrary currents made landing difficult, and when the Spanish tried to send boats ashore to replenish supplies of food and water, hostile islanders in canoes met them and showered them with arrows. De Neyra recalled the boats and they sailed on.

Three weeks later the expedition made a second landfall, almost running aground on a line of reefs that fringed the eastern shore of what was probably the atoll of Ontong, Java. Skirting around the reef but unable to make landfall, the Spanish eventually came to a strip of land that de Neyra believed to be the edge of the elusive Southern Continent. He named the place Santa Isabel, after the saint whose holiday marked their departure from Peru.

Further exploration revealed that they had landed on the northern coast of a long island, not a landmass. The Spaniards had been at sea for a week short of three months.

The inhabitants seemed friendly, and were prepared to exchange food for Spanish trade goods. Although the local chief, Bilebanara, accepted the offered beads, he and his people

Above: Alvaro de Mendaña de Neyra was sent in search of the fabled Southern Continent—and gold. He found neither, but added to Spain's knowledge of the South Sea islands.

Right: A 16th-century map showing the Philippines and the East Indies, with New Guinea to the right and the hint of a mysterious, undiscovered continent, "Australis," to the south. Despite its Spanish origins, this version of the original is overlaid with some English descriptions and names.

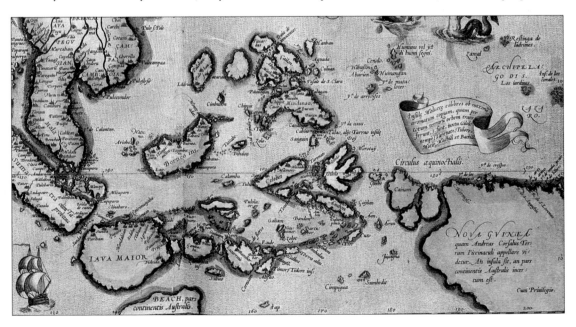

never returned. After several days, de Neyra sent a group of soldiers and sailors into the hinterland to find either the chief or the much-needed supplies. Despite strict orders to avoid conflict, the party encountered hostile villagers and a skirmish ensued. Throughout their stay, some natives remained friendly to the Spanish, while others made travel through the forests fraught with danger.

Solomon's gold

By late March, de Neyra's men had constructed a brigantine small enough to sail through the treacherous reefs off the shore. They first used it to explore Santa Isabel, and it became clear they had landed on an island in an archipelago. The Spanish ventured further and further afield in their craft, exploring and mapping wherever they went. In this manner they discovered the islands of Guadalcanal, Tulagi, Florida, Malaita, and San Cristobal, but failed to find the Southern Continent.

In early August, de Neyra held a council and asked the crew to vote on how they should proceed. Although many wanted to continue exploring the archipelago in a quest for gold, and others, including de Neyra, wished to sail further southwest, the majority elected to return to Peru. Consequently, on August 15, 1568, the Spanish headed east across the Pacific, and arrived in Callao in July 1569.

To help him raise another expedition, de Neyra exaggerated the benefits of what he

named the Solomon Islands (because it was believed that these were the source of the gold King Solomon used to decorate the temple at Jerusalem). At first, interest was low but he finally succeeded in 1595, and his wife accompanied him. On this voyage, they reached the Marquesas Islands and discovered the archipelago of the Santa Cruz Islands, but they never found the Southern Continent. De Neyra eventually died of a fever on the Santa Cruz islands, and the expedition sailed on to the now-Spanish-owned Philippines under the resolute command of his wife. The islands he discovered would remain untouched by Europeans for another two centuries.

Above: The Solomon Islands received their name from the notion that they were the source of the gold King Solomon used to adorn the temple at Jerusalem. It is not known whether de Neyra really believed this myth, but propogating it helped to finance his second expedition.

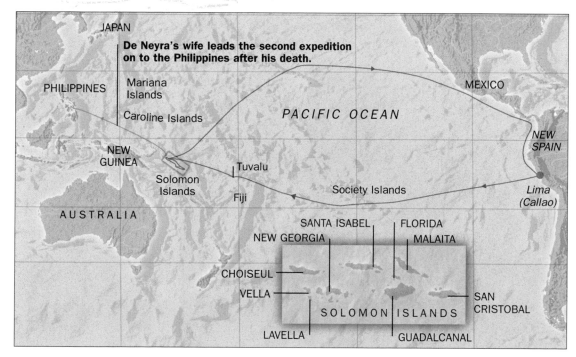

JAPAN

De Neyra's wife leads the second expedition on to the Philippines after his death.

PHILIPPINES

Mariana Islands

Caroline Islands

PACIFIC OCEAN

MEXICO

NEW GUINEA

NEW SPAIN

Solomon Islands

Tuvalu

Fiji

Society Islands

Lima (Callao)

AUSTRALIA

SANTA ISABEL

FLORIDA

NEW GEORGIA

MALAITA

CHOISEUL

VELLA

SAN CRISTOBAL

SOLOMON ISLANDS

LAVELLA

GUADALCANAL

St. FRANCIS XAVIER

1506 to 1552

As a Jesuit, Francis Xavier combined the role of missionary with those of explorer and observer. The Catholic Church called him the "Apostle of the Indies" and later canonized him. As a younger son of a noble Basque family, Xavier was expected to follow a career either in the military or in the church. From 1520 he received ecclesiastical training until, at the age of 19, he traveled to France to study theology at the University of Paris.

There, he met fellow Spanish theologian Ignatius Loyola. An ex-soldier, Loyola's army-trained mind had conceived of an exceptional religious order that would be run with military precision and ruthless dedication. The Order's followers would live their lives in imitation of Christ and embrace the notions of poverty and celibacy. At first reluctant to accept this extreme concept, Xavier was eventually won over and, in 1534, joined Loyola to found the Society of Jesus, together with four other students.

Once Xavier's studies were completed he traveled to Venice, where he was ordained, and then to Rome—along with his fellows of the Society of Jesus (or Jesuits, as they came to be known)—to receive the Pope's blessing to become a missionary. King John III of Portugal needed missionaries to spread Christianity throughout India and the East Indies, and Xavier was one of those chosen. He took a ship to Lisbon and from there to India.

Xavier arrived in Goa in early May 1542.

Right: Panel from Xavier's tomb in Goa that shows a scene from his life.

The city on the Malabar coast was the center of the Portuguese overseas empire, and the seat of the Diocese of Goa, which had authority throughout the Indian subcontinent and the Orient. For the next few years he served as a missionary on India's southeastern coast and in Ceylon, living among the local Parava pearl fishermen and learning their ways.

Good-hearted cannibals

He was transferred to a colony of Macuan people around Cochin on the lower Malabar coast, then in 1547 he moved on to Malacca on the Malay peninsula. From here, he went throughout the Spice Islands (now called the Moluccas) in small trading vessels to perform missionary work among tribes that most Europeans considered hostile. For the next two years Xavier traveled throughout the Indonesian archipelago, living with pirates, cannibals, and even tribes of headhunters. He remained unharmed and even described the people he met as simple but good-hearted.

At Ternate in the Moluccan Sea he encountered Anjiro, a Japanese trader. Anjiro became a Christian and convinced Xavier that

route had been established between Macao and Kyushu's ports.

On August 15, 1549, accompanied by Anjiro, Xavier disembarked in Kagoshima, on the south coast of Kyushu. He spent two years in the country, traveling, preaching, and recording what he found. He described the Japanese as the best people he had so far encountered, and was surprised at the level of sophistication he found in their civilization. Converts were made, including several feudal lords who declared their support for the Jesuit, although their zeal proved short-lived.

Xavier returned to

Above: Detail from a Japanese folding screen depicting a harbor scene that records the arrival of exotic-looking Portuguese merchants.

Left: Anthony van Dyck's portrayal of the canonized St. Francis Xavier and, below, his statue overlooking the strait at Malacca.

Christianity would only flourish in the Far East if a mission were to be sent to Japan. In early 1549 Xavier persuaded his superiors to send him there. Japan's first accidental contact with Europeans had been only five years earlier, in 1544. It came about after a Portuguese vessel from the trading settlement of Macao, in the Chinese province of Guangdong, was blown off course by a typhoon north through the East China Sea, and driven ashore near Nagasaki. The Kyushu islanders were pleased to receive the European traders and, at the time Xavier was petitioning to travel there, a small trade

Goa in 1551 to elicit more support for his mission, but on the return voyage he was taken ill and died in December 1552 on the island of Changchuan, near Macao (although Malacca lays claim to relics and his name is still revered there). Because of his missionary work, the Church made him a saint in 1622, but of his legacy, it is the records he kept of everything and everyone he met for which he is most widely remembered. The Jesuits added to their massive catalog of information and gave Europeans a better understanding of India and the Far East, and of the peoples who lived there.

JAPAN *in the* 16*th* CENTURY

Opposite: Detail of a screen depicting Jesuit priests and Portuguese merchants. The Japanese are fascinated with the physique and outlandish dress of the Namban jin (Barbarians from the south).

Portuguese seamen reached Japan in 1544, and returned with stories of rich ports and an advanced culture. But Japan maintained tight control of all foreign trade, so Europeans were only able to glimpse the country's splendors from the narrow confines of a few ports, from where they were no threat to Japanese economic or cultural stability. Outside the ports, power struggles between samurai warlords dominated the political arena.

Chinese chroniclers in the first century AD described Japan as a land where communities cultivated rice paddies and metallurgical centers thrived. In the next century the Yamato clan rose to preeminence, ruling the country from their central capital of Nara. When Buddhism reached Japan in AD 538 it was adopted as the state religion, although the Shinto religion was still practiced.

By the sixth century, complex legal codes had

been adopted, and a Japanese bureaucracy supported the ruling dynasty. The ruler (shogun) established a new administrative capital at Kyoto. A tendency toward the devolution of power to regional administrators in the tenth century led to rebellions by the nobility, particularly in the east of Japan. This conflict created a warrior cult that would dominate Japanese society for the next millennium.

In the 12th century, the shogun's central power was effectively replaced by regional control in the hands of the aristocracy, and the shogunate became a prize to be fought over. In 1156 local rulers called upon warrior clans to solve a dispute, and this led to the establishment of a warrior elite (samurai) at court, based around a clan system. While the aristocracy retained control of state bureaucracy, the samurai made all the decisions.

The 13th century was a period of stability, despite two failed invasions by the Mongols, but in the 14th century civil war broke out between the northern Ashikaga clan and rival claimants to the shogunate. The war lasted almost 40 years, and ended when Ashikaga Yoshimitsu reunited Japan in 1392. The Japanese economy and agricultural base had been devastated, and harsh taxation led to peasant revolts in the mid-15th century.

Arming the samurai

By the start of the 16th century, the shogun had become little more than a puppet again. The real power belonged to local warlords, who had amalgamated the old Japanese nobility with the leaders of the warrior elite. The result was a nation divided into fiefs based on clan loyalty: the Otomo on the western island of Kyushu, the Chosokabe on Shikoku, the Mori in western Honshu, the Oda near the capital of Kyoto, and the territories of the Imagawa, Takeda, Uesugi, and Hojo clans in eastern Japan.

Japanese feudal culture was based around

Below: Japanese warriors of the 13th century, a period when the Samurai effectively ran the country.

AD 538	1156	1281	1392	1543	1549	1550–60	1570
Buddhism reaches Japan.	Establishment of the Samurai warrior elite.	The Mongols fail in their attempt to invade Japan.	The country is reunited after a 40-year war.	The first Portuguese traders reach Japan.	Francis Xavier, a Christian missionary, arrives in Japan.	Japanese pirates attack the Chinese coast and besiege several cities.	Nagasaki is opened to foreign trade by its local ruler.

samurai who owed allegiance to an overlord. Like its chivalric European counterpart, Japanese feudalism placed an emphasis on bravery, honor, and discipline. Japan was a battleground for these samurai warriors throughout the 16th century. The only effect the European arrival had on this society was to introduce firearms into samurai warfare.

While the rival clans battled for power and control of the shogunate, cities grew in prosperity under the guidance of a new group of merchant oligarchies. As was the case in feudal Europe, these guilds and mercantile alliances were necessary to grant merchants some degree of power in a land ruled by the noble elite. During the early 16th century—and despite a general antipathy toward sea travel—Japanese merchants ventured as far south as the Spice Islands of the Indies, where they met the first wave of European explorers.

This was the society encountered by the Portuguese; a weak emperor presiding over a feuding collection of warrior clans, while merchants concentrated in cities such as Nagasaki and Hirado were given considerable leeway to trade with whomever they pleased. The same maritime traders appear to have turned to piracy when it suited them; Japanese pirates dominated the waters around Korea for much of the 16th century.

Piracy apart, the Japanese had much in common with the Portuguese merchants they encountered and regular trading missions followed, although contact was largely limited to the two main ports of Kyushu. On the other hand, the Portuguese found that they had even less in common with the samurai—who regarded the foreigners as barbarians—than they did with their own aristocracy.

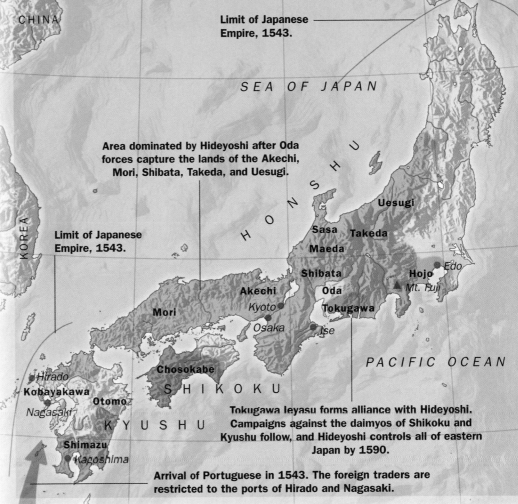

HOKKAIDO

CHINA

Limit of Japanese Empire, 1543.

SEA OF JAPAN

Area dominated by Hideyoshi after Oda forces capture the lands of the Akechi, Mori, Shibata, Takeda, and Uesugi.

KOREA

HONSHU

Uesugi

Sasa · Takeda

Maeda

Shibata · Hojo · Edo

Limit of Japanese Empire, 1543.

Akechi · Oda · Mt. Fuji

Mori · Kyoto

Osaka · Ise

Tokugawa

PACIFIC OCEAN

Chosokabe

SHIKOKU

Hirado

Kobayakawa

Otomo

Nagasaki

KYUSHU

Shimazu

Kagoshima

Tokugawa Ieyasu forms alliance with Hideyoshi. Campaigns against the daimyos of Shikoku and Kyushu follow, and Hideyoshi controls all of eastern Japan by 1590.

Arrival of Portuguese in 1543. The foreign traders are restricted to the ports of Hirado and Nagasaki.

1587	1593	1603	1609	1612–32	1637–41	1641	1720
Christianity is banned.	Japan invades Korea.	The Tokugawa Shogunate begins to restrict Japanese trade with Europeans.	A Dutch trading base is established on Hirado Island.	Systematic persecution of Christians begins.	Portuguese traders are expelled from Japan.	All Westerners are banned from the mainland.	The import of European books is allowed, thus promoting Western ideas.

CHINA *in the* 16*th* CENTURY

Right: This detail from a Chinese lacquer screen shows Portuguese ships and seamen arriving in China.

China was probably the oldest state in history when Marco Polo arrived at the Imperial court in 1271. Under Mongol domination, the country survived and flourished. Polo's writings fascinated medieval Europe and played a part in the quest for knowledge that led to the Age of Discovery.

Marco Polo was not the only European to

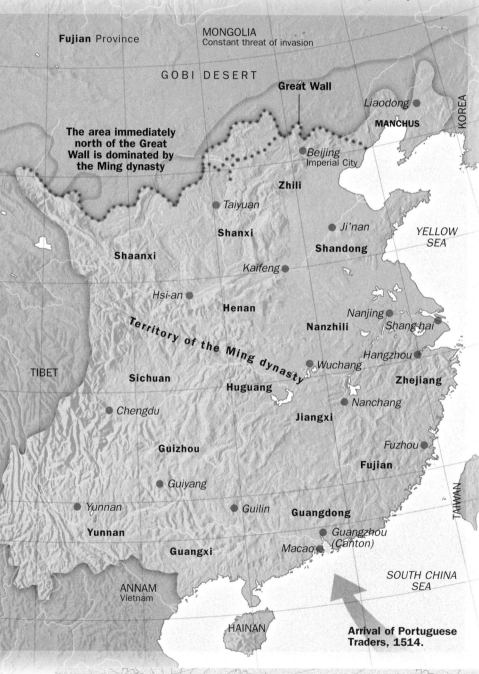

Fujian Province

MONGOLIA
Constant threat of invasion

GOBI DESERT

Great Wall

Liaodong
MANCHUS

The area immediately north of the Great Wall is dominated by the Ming dynasty

Beijing
Imperial City

KOREA

Zhili

Taiyuan

Shanxi

Ji'nan
Shandong

YELLOW SEA

Shaanxi

Kaifeng

Hsi-an
Henan

Nanjing
Nanzhili
Shang-hai

Territory of the Ming dynasty

Hangzhou

TIBET

Sichuan
Huguang

Wuchang

Zhejiang

Chengdu

Nanchang

Jiangxi

Guizhou

Fuzhou

Fujian

Guiyang

Yunnan
Yunnan

Guilin
Guangdong

TAIWAN

Guangxi

Macao
Guangzhou (Canton)

ANNAM
Vietnam

HAINAN

SOUTH CHINA SEA

Arrival of Portuguese Traders, 1514.

visit China in the Middle Ages. As the Venetian was preparing to leave China in 1294, John of Montecorvino arrived at the Imperial court at Khanbalik (Beijing) as a Papal ambassador from Pope Clement V. The clergyman remained and became China's first Christian bishop.

Mongol territories in China had been held by the Yuan dynasty since its foundation by Kublai Khan in 1280, and this grip was retained when the Mongol Empire crumbled. A lasting Mongol innovation was the division of China into provinces, some of which reflected earlier territorial divisions. The Mongols continued to be unpopular rulers and, in 1368, a former peasant named Chu Yuan-chang rose to prominence as the leader of a rebel faction. The Yuan dynasty was overthrown in a 19-year campaign and the rebel became the new emperor and founder of the Ming dynasty, the last dynasty of Chinese descent.

The Ming dynasty, which lasted 250 years,

479 BC							
Death of philosopher Confucious.	Constuction of the Great Wall is begun.	Confucianism becomes the state religion.	Paddle-wheel ships are in use.	Chinese navigators use the magnetic compass.	Chinese ship technology enables longer trade voyages.	Marco Polo arrives at the Imperial court.	Establishment of the Ming dynasty ends Mongol rule.
287 BC	136 BC	c.AD 1130	c.1150	c.1200	1271	1368	

has come to represent a golden age in Chinese history. During this period Chinese society underwent significant change: the emperor instituted a major policy of public works that included irrigation, the construction of dams, forestry on a massive scale, and road building. Farming communities thrived, surplus provisions were produced, markets sprang up, and the economy boomed.

The southern provinces of Fujian and Guizhou were ideally suited to crop production, particularly rice, and became known as the "granary of China." Large plantations were established by landowners, where food was produced on a massive scale. The peasant unrest that would help to end the Manchu dynasty in the mid-17th century arose from grievances about large-scale farming. The plantations also produced cash crops, principally tea and cotton.

Control kills trade

The glut of food drove a need to export produce. Under the Chinese Admiral Cheng Ho (*see pages 39, 61*), voyages of discovery were undertaken between 1405 and 1433 that opened up markets as far away as the West African coast. During the 15th century, Chinese trading junks could be seen in the ports of the Indian Ocean, the Spice Islands, Southeast Asia, and Japan.

At this moment, when Chinese merchants were making their presence felt internationally, Imperial enthusiasm for maritime commerce waned. Part of the reasoning behind this rationale lay in the Imperial taxation system, which was based on land ownership and production and not on commerce and the mercantile centers it encouraged. During the 15th century the success of maritime trading led to a rapid growth in urban centers, which in turn fueled further increases in commercial activity. Because these mercantile communities avoided most taxation, the emperor saw them as a destabilizing influence.

An Imperial edict severely limited Chinese maritime trade in the late 15th century, just in time for Portuguese merchants to arrive in the Indian Ocean and capture the market.

Above: *The Chinese emperor and his court go riding through the grounds of the Imperial Palace.*

The decline also resulted in increasingly common Chinese and Japanese pirate attacks in Chinese waters. Lacking an effective fleet, the Ming dynasty relied on mercenary sea captains, who were almost as bad as the pirates themselves. In 1555, pirates sacked Hangzhou and navigation of the lower Yangtse River was considered unsafe. The emperor's lack of action indicated just how introverted the Chinese court had become.

Chinese war junks—demonstrating that the Europeans did not have the monopoly on naval artillery—drove off Portuguese trading ships trying to reach Chinese ports in 1521 and 1522. Emissaries were sent to the Imperial court, and when the Portuguese were eventually allowed to trade with China, it was on terms imposed by the court. This did not prevent the Europeans from linking up with the pirates of Fujian province, and trading began years before an official Portuguese trading post was established at Macao. The West had established a toehold in China that would be retained until the late 20th century.

1400s	1405–33	1412–15	1422	1431–33	c.1460	1488	1521–2
A rapid growth in urban centers occurs.	Chinese Admiral Cheng Ho sends out ships on voyages of discovery.	Chinese ships explore the Indian Ocean coast as far as Arabia.	A Chinese treasure fleet reaches East Africa.	The last of the Chinese Indian Ocean expeditions sacks Mecca.	Ming China goods are exported to the West.	The Great Wall is partially rebuilt.	Portuguese ships trying to reach China are driven away.

Sir FRANCIS DRAKE

1540 to 1596

Sir Francis Drake is far better known as an Elizabethan "Sea Dog," or privateer, and for terrorizing the Spanish than he is as an explorer. During his voyages he recorded his visits to new territories, particularly those on the west coast of America and in the South Pacific. The scientific by-product of his raiding against the Spanish was a wealth of information that makes him worthy of a place among the most famous explorers of the 16th century.

As a young man, Francis Drake sailed with John Hawkins on his 1566 and 1567 slave-trading expeditions to Africa and the Caribbean. He led his own raiding expedition to the Caribbean in 1570, then repeated the raid in two successive years, returning to England with his hold filled with plunder. However, because England and Spain were at peace at the time, his attacks on the Spanish were considered to be acts of piracy, and Drake went into hiding for two years to escape punishment.

In 1577 he was back in favor at court, and Queen Elizabeth secretly backed a new expedition that would combine research and warfare. Drake planned to sail through the Strait of Magellan and enter the Pacific, a feat that no Englishman had ever attempted. Drake's main purpose was to plunder unprotected Spanish ports rather than to explore

Right: Sir Francis Drake, from an oil painting by Marcus Gheeraetrts the Younger (1561–1635), dated 1591.

new territories, but the details of the voyage would be meticulously recorded in order to benefit future English raiders. He sailed from Plymouth in December 1577 aboard his flagship, the *Pelican* (which he renamed the *Golden Hind*), together with four other ships. Drake had already circulated rumors that his destination was Egypt, so his crews were surprised when they sailed past Gibraltar and

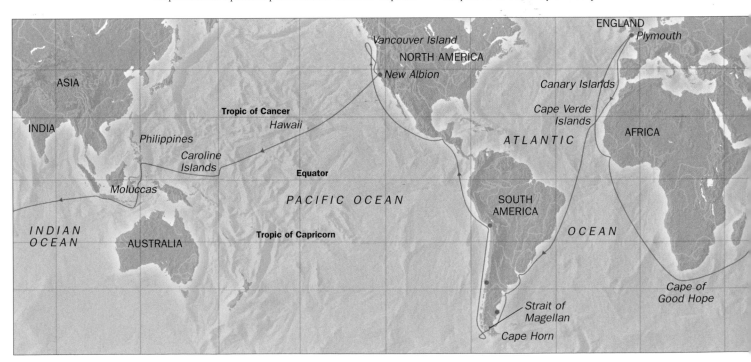

down the African coast to arrive at the Cape Verde Islands. On the way, he captured a Portuguese ship to encourage his men with plunder. Drake then led his small fleet southwest across the Atlantic to Brazil, making landfall in April 1578.

Raiding in the Pacific

Drake sailed down the coast, but a storm off Cape Horn sank some ships and forced others to return home. On her own, the *Golden Hind* sailed north up the Pacific coast of South America and sacked Valparaíso in Chile. In March 1579 Drake captured the Spanish treasure ship *Cacafuego*, whose holds were filled with silver and gold. Drake then explored the American Pacific coast as far north as Vancouver Island. In the late spring he turned south again, to make landfalls in present-day Oregon and in California. The anchorage in California was named Drake's Bay (situated north of modern San Francisco), and he claimed the hinterland for England, calling it New Albion.

In July 1579 he decided to return home by sailing west across the Pacific. The sailors saw no land for more than two months until they sighted the Caroline Islands. Native hostility forced

Drake to press on. He touched on Mindanao in the Philippines before heading south in search of the fabled Spice Islands (Indonesia). Locals helped him to navigate the waters of Indonesia, and local rulers traded with the Europeans and allowed Drake to repair the *Golden Hind*. He decided against extending the return voyage by sailing to China, and instead sailed through the Indonesian archipelago, recording what he encountered, before crossing the Indian Ocean bound for Africa. Almost three years after it had set out, the *Golden Hind* limped back into Plymouth in September 1580. The voyage brought him fame, wealth, and the admiration of the queen, who knighted him in 1581.

Four years later Drake resumed his war with the Spanish by raiding the Caribbean, then participated in the defeat of the Spanish Armada in August 1588. Sir Francis Drake returned to the Spanish Main in 1595, but an attack on Puerto Rico was repulsed and, although Drake captured Nombre de Dios, his attempted attack on Panama was defeated. Drake died at sea in February 1596. Considered a national hero, he is remembered as one of England's greatest sea captains. He should also be remembered for his work as an explorer.

Below: *A reconstruction of the* Golden Hind, *the tiny flagship used by Drake during his voyage of exploration.*

GREENLAND

*Davis
Strait*

Frobisher Bay

Hudson Strait

Hudson Bay

LABRADOR

St. Lawrence

Seeking a Way

Jacques Cartier	1534 1535–36	
Martin Frobisher	1576 1578	
John Davis	1585 1587	

Henry Hudson

Only 23 years after John Davis's second voyage to find a northwest passage, this ill-fated English explorer made another attempt. His voyage of 1610–11 failed to find a northerly way to the Pacific Ocean, but did discover the vast subarctic bay, now known in his honor as Hudson Bay. He never returned home: his crew mutinied and cast him, his teenaged son, and seven loyal crew members adrift in a small rowing boat to perish in the icy wastes.

CHAPTER TEN

ICELAND

Atlantic Ocean

NEWFOUNDLAND

NOVA SCOTIA

The NORTHWEST PASSAGE

hen Ferdinand Magellan rounded the southern tip of America and entered the Pacific Ocean, he gave the Spanish a westerly route to the East Indies, where they could challenge the Portuguese, who held the easterly South African route. For centuries, the notion of a northwest passage through the Arctic waters of North America dominated the minds of English, Dutch, and French explorers. By finding a route free from either Spanish or Portuguese control, the northern European powers could match their rivals' monopoly of trade with the Orient and the Indies.

During the 16th century several expeditions attempted to find the passage, but all were thwarted by ice, storms, or simply by dead-ends. Explorers operated in some of the most inhospitable waters in the world, where an error could easily result in death. Although they failed in their goal, explorers such as Jacques Cartier and John Davis helped to define the geographical extent of the North American continent. The discovery of the elusive northwest passage would remain an unfulfilled challenge for another three centuries.

JACQUES CARTIER

1491 to 1557

I n the early 1530s, Francis I was looking for an experienced seaman to lead a French expedition of discovery to the Americas and Jacques Cartier's name was put forward. By the time Cartier left his home of St. Malo in Brittany, he was already highly regarded as an experienced seaman and navigator. The bustling port traded throughout Europe, and it has been suggested that Cartier may have joined an earlier expedition to America in 1524, led by Giovanni da Verrazano (*see pages 88–89*). In 1533, Francis I had the Treaty of Tordesillas (1494) amended by Pope Clement VII. Previously, it had excluded French explorers from the Americas, but the amendment granted freshly discovered land to whichever nation found it first. France was keen to join the European land-grab in America.

Below: Jacques Cartier, from a 16th-century engraving.

Cartier sailed from St. Malo in April 1534 with a commission from the king, two ships, and 61 men. This small force would change the political landscape of North America forever. Cartier's original brief was to find a new source of precious metals and to find a northwest passage

to the Far East. Within three weeks, the ships made Newfoundland, which was already well known by French fishermen who harvested the area of the Grand Banks. Floating ice forced Cartier to repair damage to his ships, but they were ready to proceed by late May, and sailed northwest up the Newfoundland coast. It was a desolate place, where Cartier records that he "saw not one cartload of earth, though I landed in many places."

In June he reached the Straits of Belle Isle between Newfoundland and Labrador. He decided to sail through the passage to the southwest and made note of "very steepe and wild hills." He had discovered a landlocked body of water (the Gulf of St. Lawrence) that held promise of a passage through the American landmass.

On July 1, the expedition made landfall on the northern shores of what is now Prince Edward Island. Sailing on to the west and north, Cartier encountered the local Micmac Indians at Chaleur Bay. The French traded with the Indians and, after finding the bay was a dead end, they continued north. On July 21 Cartier ordered that a 30-foot-high cross be erected on the Gaspé Peninsula to claim the territory for France. He went on to explore Anticosta Island

in the middle of the Gulf before, by consensus of the crew, he returned to France.

Although Cartier had achieved neither of his two objectives, he had succeeded in claiming new territory for France. He was given a hero's welcome, and Francis I commissioned a second, larger expedition.

Québec and Montréal

In May 1535, Cartier sailed from St. Malo with three ships, and reached Newfoundland seven weeks later. This time he avoided the inhospitable coast and pressed straight on to the Straits of Belle Isle. On August 10, on the feast of St. Lawrence, he named the bay after the saint (the appellation was later applied to the whole Gulf and the St. Lawrence River). With help from local Indians, he discovered the mouth of the massive St. Lawrence River in mid-August. From here he headed west into the American continent. Because of its initial width, he was certain that this would prove to be the northwest passage he was seeking.

Cartier called his discovery La Grande Rivière. Natives told him it led to the fabulously wealthy kingdom of Saguenay, which he imagined to be the Orient. He pressed on up the river. On September 8 he reached the native village of Stadacona (now Québec) where, for political reasons, Chief Donnaconna tried to entice the French to stay. Cartier, who had no intention of becoming embroiled in local infighting, left some men behind and continued on his way with a reduced party. They reached Hochelaga (now Montréal) a week later, where the local Huron Indians appeared friendly. Cartier's spirits were dashed, however, when he climbed a nearby mountain and saw rapids that blocked further passage to his ships. Cartier sailed back down the river and rejoined the rest of his party. The French suffered a disease-laden winter on the banks of La Grande Rivière, consoling themselves with the Huron tales of a fabulously wealthy hinterland beyond the rapids. Cartier became increasingly convinced that the land was worth exploring further.

Above: This map of the east coast of North America from Labrador to Cape Florida, and featuring the mouth of the St. Lawrence River, was made before 1547 and based on Cartier's discoveries of 1534–41. The map is seen from an unusual angle: the Atlantic Ocean is at the top, with the Azores visible (1), the Gulf of St. Lawrence is toward the bottom left (2), and Florida can be seen at the extreme top right (3).

Above: *A 19th-century illustration showing Cartier and his men exploring the St. Lawrence river by canoe.*

A new French colony

Any further exploration would have to wait. First, he needed to return to France for fresh men, ships, and supplies. He kidnapped Chief Donnaconna and other key Hurons and took them with him to France so that the French king could hear their stories at first hand.

Back in France, Chief Donnaconna's tales of fabulous wealth, gold, and spices in the wilds of what is now Canada excited Francis I's interest. The king commissioned a second expedition, which would be the largest the French had yet assembled, but war with Spain delayed the project until 1541. Cartier assembled five ships and 1,000 men, including soldiers and colonists, but at the last moment, Francis I placed another favorite, Jean-François de Roberval, over Cartier, who then sailed as second in command.

The expedition left France in May and promptly ran into problems. Roberval and three of the ships became separated from the others during heavy weather. Cartier pressed on with the remainder of the fleet and arrived at Stadacona in late August. Chief Donnaconna had died in France along with all but one of

Cartier's captives, so the French told the Hurons that although Donnaconna had died of too much good living, the others refused to return to Stadacona, and were living in the lap of luxury. This story hardly convinced the Hurons, but their new chief, Agona, was relieved that his rival had been removed. Cartier, who felt it would be wise to establish a new fort and settlement some way off from the native village, ordered the soldiers and settlers to remain behind to develop the new colony—Charlesbourg Royal—while he set off in the ships to explore the wilderness.

Trouble strikes

They reached the rapids and falls around Hochelaga, but local guides failed to show the Frenchmen the Ottawa River, which Chief Donnaconna had said was the route to Saguenay. Rapids blocked the French advance at every turn, so Cartier gave up the attempt and returned to Charlesbourg Royal. He returned just in time to avert a disaster. During his absence, animosity between the settlers and the Hurons had erupted into full-scale warfare.

Attacks had been made on the disease-ridden settlement, and Chief Agona had gathered his warriors for an all-out attack. Cartier's reinforcements forced the Hurons to back down temporarily, but the lack of Roberval and his ships made the situation desperate.

Heavily outnumbered, Cartier had little option but to abandon the colony. The settlers and soldiers embarked and, in June 1542, the two remaining ships sailed down the St. Lawrence. When Cartier docked at the anchorage of St. Johns in Newfoundland to replenish his water supplies, he discovered Roberval and the other ships. Roberval, who had wintered in Newfoundland, ordered Cartier to return to reestablish the settlement, but the explorer had endured enough. He refused, and slipped away one night with his two ships to return to France. Roberval went on with his remaining force to see the situation for himself, and built a winter camp near the abandoned settlement. The rapids around Hochelaga also foiled him, and he returned across the Atlantic the following summer, arriving back in September 1543.

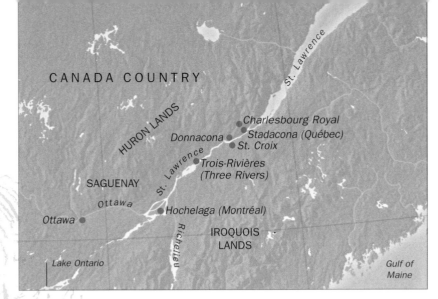

Cartier was forgiven his act of mutiny, and the king gave him his two ships as a reward. The explorer retired to his estate outside St. Malo, where he died in September 1557. His dreams of a fabulous lost land of Saguenay had come to naught, as had his hopes of finding a northwest passage. Mineral samples the colonists brought back proved to be worthless, and the whole enterprise did nothing to swell the coffers of France. What it did achieve, however, was the establishment of a French claim to Canada, and it led directly to the development of New France as a colony.

Below: Cartier and his crew on the St. Lawrence. Details from a map of 1536 or 1542 by Pierre Descaliers.

MARTIN FROBISHER

1540 to 1594

Martin Frobisher's career as an explorer is less well known than his role as one of Queen Elizabeth's band of "Sea Dogs," those men renowned for privateering and naval exploits against the Spanish. But he led three expeditions in an attempt to find a northern sea route to the Indies.

Frobisher was born into the minor nobility in northern England, but he chose to go to sea at about the age of 13. His first voyages were slaver expeditions; on one he was captured, first by African tribesmen, then by the Portuguese, who eventually released him.

By the early 1560s he had established himself as a master mariner and led privateer attacks against French and Spanish shipping. Although his actions were often illegal, he was rewarded with a royal commission in 1571 and continued to serve his own interests as well as those of the crown for the next two years, combining duty and profit. A change in the political climate made it unwise to continue as a privateer, so Frobisher looked for other profitable avenues.

Since the expedition of Jacques Cartier 40 years before, geographers had speculated about the existence of a northwestern passage through the northern waters of the Americas to the Pacific. Frobisher organized a small expedition to find the route. It consisted of two ships, the *Gabriel* and the *Michael*, plus a small pinnace (or launch). In June 1576 Frobisher sailed north as far as the Shetland Islands, then headed for Greenland. Storms separated the ships, and the *Michael* returned home, while the pinnace was lost at sea.

Right: Martin Frobisher, detail of an oil painting by Cornelius Ketel (1548–1616), dated 1577.

Below: Arctic scene featuring Frobisher's ship.

With a skeleton crew of 18 men, Frobisher reached the coast of Greenland. A second storm snapped the *Gabriel*'s mizzenmast, putting the vessel at risk. The debris hung over the side and threatened to swing the ship's beam onto the waves, where she could be swamped. Frobisher ordered the mast cut away, and the vessel was saved. The storm passed and Frobisher turned west into uncharted waters.

On August 11, 1576, he sighted Baffin Island, a large landmass north of the Canadian Labrador coast. Frobisher found an inlet that he thought might be the start of the strait leading to the Pacific and began to explore it. In the process the Englishmen came into contact with local Inuit hunters (Eskimos) and the two peoples traded with each other.

Mistaking the Hudson Strait

The Inuit offered to lead Frobisher up the channel now known as Frobisher Bay. What happened next is unclear, but it is probable that a group of sailors in a ship's boat were sent to explore with the native guides. They never returned; it is likely that they fell out with their

guides, who killed them. The capture of an important Inuit hostage failed to resolve the desperate situation.

With his crew reduced to just 13 seamen and faced by a potentially hostile local population, Frobisher had little choice but to turn back for England. On his return, he displayed the Inuit hostage, a kayak, and a local rock, which was believed to contain gold. The publicity generated support for a second expedition in the following year, but it also returned empty handed, save for a few worthless mineral samples.

Undeterred, Frobisher sought further backing for a third expedition. One investor convinced others of the potential of finding gold on Baffin Island, and the Cathay Company was formed as a mining venture to fund Frobisher's new expedition. In the summer of 1578, the explorer returned to Baffin but missed Frobisher Bay in fog. Instead, he entered what became known as the Hudson Strait. He called it Mistaken Strait and was tempted to explore further, but his backers had funded a mining expedition, not a voyage of discovery.

He returned to his anchorage of two years previously and extracted ore samples, then returned home via Greenland. Unfortunately the ore contained no gold, the Cathay Company failed, and Frobisher returned to privateering. For the next decade he attacked Spanish shipping, and was knighted after his participation in the Spanish Armada campaign of 1588. He died following a battle with the Spanish off Brest in 1594 and his dreams of discovering the Northwest Passage died with him. However, his expeditions paved the way for further attempts to find a northern route around America.

Below: During Frobisher's second journey to Baffin Island in 1577, he and his men encountered hostile Eskimos. Contemporary watercolor.

JOHN DAVIS

c1550 to 1605

John Davis was an associate of Walter Raleigh, founder of England's first (though unsuccessful) colony in North America. As a youth, Davis went to sea on privateering and trading voyages and, by his late 20s, he was an experienced ship's captain and a master navigator; he invented the Davis Quadrant, a navigational tool that accurately determined the observer's latitude.

After several commercial voyages, he allied himself with Raleigh and Adrian Gilbert, brother of the explorer Humphrey Gilbert. The three mariners formed a trading company, supported by the mathematician John Dee, Secretary of State Sir Francis Walsingham, and English merchants and financiers. Their primary aims were to find a northwest passage to the Pacific and to secure a monopoly over the trade route.

In early June 1585, John Davis set sail from Dartmouth in the county of Devon with two tiny ships, the *Sunshine* and the *Moonshine*. On July 20, lookouts sighted Greenland's eastern coast and they followed the landmass south around its southern tip, which Davis named Cape Desolation (now Cape Farewell). Continuing up Greenland's western coast, he anchored at an inlet he named Gilbert Sound (now Godthåbfjord), where he encountered the local Inuits (Eskimos).

On the first day of August he headed west to Baffin Island, making landfall north of Frobisher Bay at the mouth of what is now Cumberland Sound. He thought this might be the much sought-after Northwest Passage, but the threat of winter ice forced him to return home without exploring further.

The following year Davis led a second attempt. His original ships were joined by a larger vessel, the *Mermaid*, and a pinnace. He headed directly for Gilbert Sound, where his friendly relations with the Inuit ensured a safe forward base. Two ships were sent to scout up the eastern coast of Greenland to try to find a way through the arctic ice, but they were unsuccessful, and returned to England.

Davis, with the *Mermaid* and *Moonshine*, explored the water between Greenland and Baffin island, which was named the Davis Strait. The ice worried the English sailors, so Davis sent the *Mermaid* home with all those who were reluctant to continue. No passage was found, so the *Moonshine* returned home before winter, her holds filled with fish to demonstrate the abundance found in the waters of the strait. In all these voyages, Davis charted and recorded everything he saw, creating a unique record of early Arctic exploration.

Serving the East Indies

A third expedition was sent in 1587, consisting of three ships. Two were sent purely to establish a fishing station at Gilbert Sound, while Davis crewed the pinnace *Ellen* with the more adventurous mariners and set off to explore the Greenland coast. He reached just beyond the latitude of 70°N, where ice floes and contrary winds prevented him from continuing northward. He named the region Sanderson

BAFFIN BAY

Arctic Circle

GREENLAND

Exeter Sound

Baffin Island

Foxe Basin

Davis Strait

1585   1587

HUDSON STRAIT

Ungava Peninsula

ATLANTIC OCEAN

LABRADOR

HUDSON BAY

NEWFOUNDLAND

NORTH AMERICA

Above: *John Davis's ship ice-bound in the Arctic wastes.*

Hope (now Umanak), after his main investor, then crossed the Davis Strait, keeping just ahead of the advancing pack ice. He explored Baffin Island as far as what is now the Hudson Strait, where he was encouraged by the strong current. He was unaware that this was the body of water that Frobisher had discovered and named Mistaken Strait nine years before.

On his return to England, the imminent war with Spain prevented the dispatch of any other expeditions, and it would be over 20 years before Henry Hudson (*see page 144*) continued the exploratory work of Davis and Frobisher. Davis fought in the Spanish Armada campaign of 1588, then became a highly successful privateer under the patronage of Elizabeth I.

He participated in the disastrous 1592 expedition led by Thomas Cavendish that attempted to find an entrance to a northwest passage from the Pacific. Instead, Cavendish died at sea in the South Atlantic and Davis returned home, discovering the Falkland Islands on the return voyage. The expedition ruined him financially, but he served the Crown in two naval campaigns in 1596–7 before participating in the first Dutch expedition to the East Indies in 1598. He later piloted the first voyages of the English East India Company, until he was killed during a surprise attack by Japanese pirates off Malaya in 1605. Davis's contribution to the understanding of the Arctic was immense and, together with his pioneering work on navigation, made him one of the most distinguished mariners of the late 16th century.

HUGH WILLOUGHBY *and* RICHARD CHANCELLOR

c.1516 *to* 1554

c.1520 *to* 1556

H ugh Willoughby and Richard Chancellor took a different view of the northern route to the Orient; instead of heading west they went east, along the northern coast of Russia. The quest was the same—to chart a sea route that could be monopolized by the nation who discovered it. In this case, the route would be known as the Northeast Passage.

Willoughby was an experienced military officer in Henry VIII's army, but intrigue led him to lose his lucrative garrison command in 1550, and he sought a new avenue for his endeavors. At the time, the Portuguese held a monopoly of trade with the Orient by maintaining a string of forts along the West African coast. The development of an alternative route was an appealing prospect for English financiers and merchants. Although Willoughby had no nautical experience, he considered himself a suitable candidate to command a voyage to discover an alternative route around the north of Europe.

The Company of Merchant Adventurers was a business cartel masterminded by John Dudley, Duke of Northumberland. The group agreed to fund Willoughby's expedition on the advice of the explorer Sebastian Cabot (*see pages 84–85*), the group's governor and advisor. While Willoughby was placed in command of the expedition, Richard Chancellor was appointed as pilot and navigator. Little is known of Chancellor, although he was regarded as an experienced and competent mariner.

The expedition of three ships left England on May 10, 1553, with Chancellor in the *Edward Bonaventure* and Willoughby in the *Bona Esperanza*, in company with the *Bona Confidentia*. Two months later, in mid-July, the small fleet was scattered by a violent storm in the Norwegian Sea. Chancellor sailed on to a planned rendezvous at the northern Norwegian harbor of Vardö and waited for the other ships.

Willoughby led the two remaining ships around northern Norway into what is now called the Barents Sea. Willoughby's diary records frequent changes of course, but by late August the two ships reached a landmass on a north-south line, which was named Willoughby's Land (now the two islands of Novaya Zemlya).

Fated with death at sea

A leak in the *Bona Confidentia* forced Willoughby to retrace his route until he reached the mouth of the Arzina River, near the present-day city of Murmansk. There the ships were trapped by ice and the sailors had to prepare for the winter as best they could. Food supplies were plentiful, but the crews were unprepared for the Arctic cold. In the following spring, Russian fishermen found the ships, but every man aboard had frozen to death, including Hugh Willoughby. The commander's last diary entry was in January 1554. The bodies were eventually repatriated to England.

Below: Men of Richard Chancellor's expedition hunt polar bears in the Barents Sea.

Richard Chancellor had waited at Vardö for a week before continuing in the *Edward Bonaventure*. In early August he entered the White Sea and explored southward. At the mouth of the Dvina River he found a Russian fishing harbor at Kholmogory. The initial alarm caused by his arrival was succeeded by friendship, and the sailors and fisherman traded with each other.

Chancellor and his men wintered in the port, and even answered a summons from Tsar Ivan (the Terrible). The resulting visit to Moscow cemented the details of a lucrative trade deal between Muscovy (Russia) and England and, when Chancellor returned home in the spring, he had something to show for his voyage.

A charter of monopoly was granted to the Company of Merchant Adventurers, which became the Muscovy Company. In late 1555 Chancellor led a second expedition of two ships to establish a market in Muscovy and an English Embassy was founded in Moscow. The *Edward Bonaventure* was returning in the following summer with both Chancellor and the Russian ambassador

aboard when it was hit by a violent North Sea gale. The ship was wrecked off the Scottish coast and, although the ambassador survived, Chancellor and most of his crew were drowned.

There were other attempts to find a northeast passage to the Pacific, but the region was considered too inhospitable and the course was abandoned. Russia and England maintained good trade relations and the Muscovy Company used the route to develop overland trade links with Persia.

Above: *A depiction of the men of Willoughby and Chancellor's doomed expedition preparing to spend the winter on the coast of the Barents Sea.*

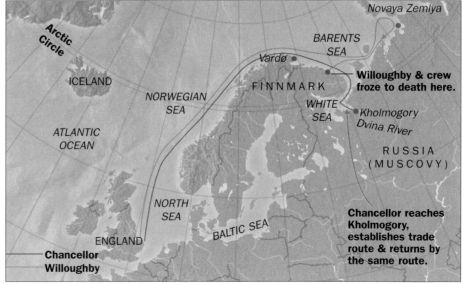

The ARCTIC WASTE

Right: The waters of the Davis Straits appear tranquil, but sudden storms and the danger of floating ice belie the calm appearance of these arctic seas.

When Christopher Columbus discovered the Americas in 1492, he was trying to find a sea route to the Indies. Although the islands and landmasses of the Caribbean basin blocked his way, he died convinced that he had achieved his goal. By a geographical quirk, North and South America existed as an unbroken barrier of land stretching almost from pole to pole. To the south, explorers found that they could enter the Pacific only by traversing the treacherous Strait of Magellan, or by braving the seas off Cape Horn further to the south. Even today it is considered one of the worst maritime passages in the world, so for centuries mariners sought an alternative northerly route.

By the time Roald Amundsen fought his way through these northern waters to reach the Pacific Ocean in 1905, work was underway on the Panama Canal to make the journey around South America unnecessary. As early as 1534, King Charles I of Spain had ordered a survey of the Panama Isthmus to see if it would be feasible to cut a canal through from the Gulf of Mexico to the Pacific Ocean. But in the 16th and 17th centuries, in the absence of such a passage, a voyage around the top of the continent was considered the only viable alternative to a voyage around Cape Horn.

The extreme environment of the Arctic wastes was the greatest barrier to finding a passage. Maritime explorers of the Age of Discovery were completely unprepared for the conditions they encountered. During Martin Frobisher's expedition of 1578, an English chronicler reported the extremes: debilitating cold, icy snowstorms, and a glaring sun that hurt the eyes, followed by periods of complete darkness.

During the 16th century, mariners wore simple woolen clothing, insufficient to provide much warmth in freezing conditions. The crewmen sailing with Martin Frobisher and John Davis resorted to hunting for game to provide skins for warm clothing, while trade with the local Inuit provided an alternative source of protective attire.

An unfinished world

The fate of the White Sea expedition led by Hugh Willoughby in 1553–4 highlighted the problem: when the expedition was trapped by ice, the entire crew froze to death. The survivors of the first expeditions to find the Northwest Passage spoke of a forbidding region filled with majestic icebergs, an almost surreal light, and a

Below: Dutch mariners prepare to build shelters as their ship lies trapped in the ice. Detail from a painting by Gerit de Veer.

landscape that looked like "a world unfinished by the hand of its Creator."

Climatic extremes are not confined to temperature. The waters surrounding Newfoundland and Greenland are subject to some of the worst gales and storms imaginable, particularly above the latitude of 60°N. Although 16th-century vessels could be as seaworthy as many later craft, their limited sail plans and crude rudders made these sailing conditions seem even worse. Their hulls were unprotected and therefore vulnerable to damage from ice. Observers in the Frobisher and Davis expeditions noted the seasonal pattern of ice movement and learned to avoid the advance of solid ice in the fall, and the threat of loose icebergs and smaller ice floes in the spring that could rip their wooden vessels apart.

Similarly, ice threatened to crush the hulls of trapped ships. During the expedition of the Dutch mariner William Barents in 1596, two Dutch ships were trapped in ice off the northern coast of what is now Russia. Although the crew tried to keep the ice from the hulls, the ships were raised out of the water by the pressure, causing irreparable damage. The crews were forced to establish shelters on shore, using parts of their vessels as building material. One sailor described the winter as one of "great cold, poverty, misery, and grief." Certainly they were the worst conditions a 16th-century mariner could expect. Problems created by a lack of suitable provisions, particularly fresh fruit and vegetables, added to the suffering, and meant that scurvy and malnutrition were commonplace.

Because the Arctic was a region where the physical challenges proved too much for explorers of the time, the Northwest Passage remained undiscovered for over three centuries after Frobisher and Davis gave up their attempts to find it.

Above: The pack-ice spreads south every winter, threatening to entrap wary mariners. These small floes in the Arctic Sea will eventually solidify into an ice sheet.

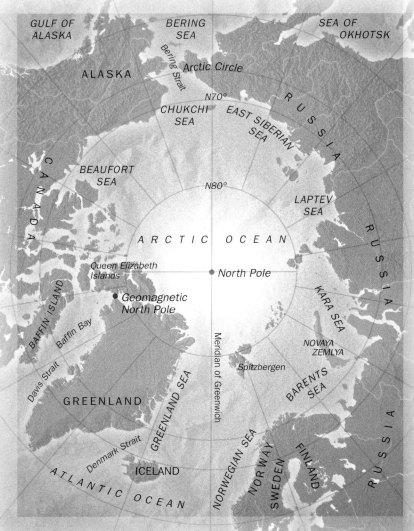

GULF OF ALASKA

BERING SEA

SEA OF OKHOTSK

ALASKA

Bering Strait

Arctic Circle

N70°

CHUKCHI SEA

EAST SIBERIAN SEA

RUSSIA

BEAUFORT SEA

N80°

LAPTEV SEA

CANADA

ARCTIC OCEAN

RUSSIA

Queen Elizabeth Islands

North Pole

Geomagnetic North Pole

KARA SEA

BAFFIN ISLAND

Baffin Bay

NOVAYA ZEMLYA

Davis Strait

Meridian of Greenwich

Spitzbergen

GREENLAND SEA

BARENTS SEA

GREENLAND

RUSSIA

Denmark Strait

ICELAND

NORWEGIAN SEA

NORWAY

SWEDEN

FINLAND

RUSSIA

ATLANTIC OCEAN

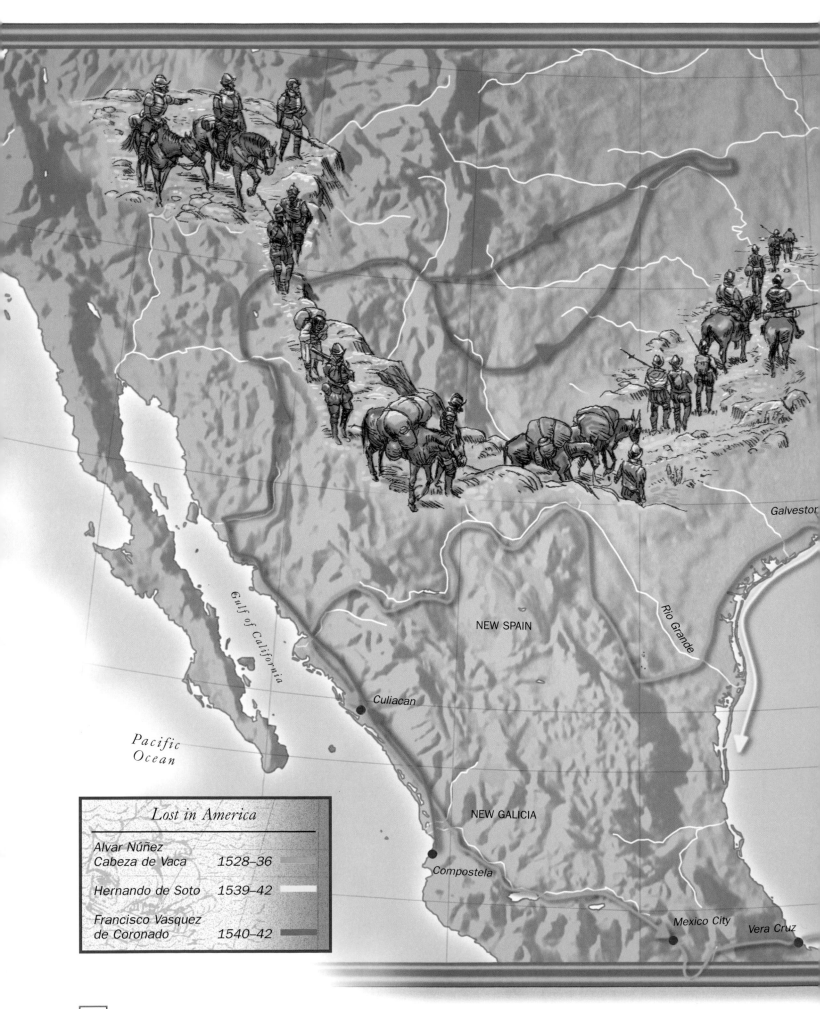

Lost in America

Alvar Núñez
Cabeza de Vaca   1528–36

Hernando de Soto   1539–42

Francisco Vasquez
de Coronado   1540–42

Gulf of California

Pacific
Ocean

NEW SPAIN

Rio Grande

Galveston

Culiacan

NEW GALICIA

Compostela

Mexico City

Vera Cruz

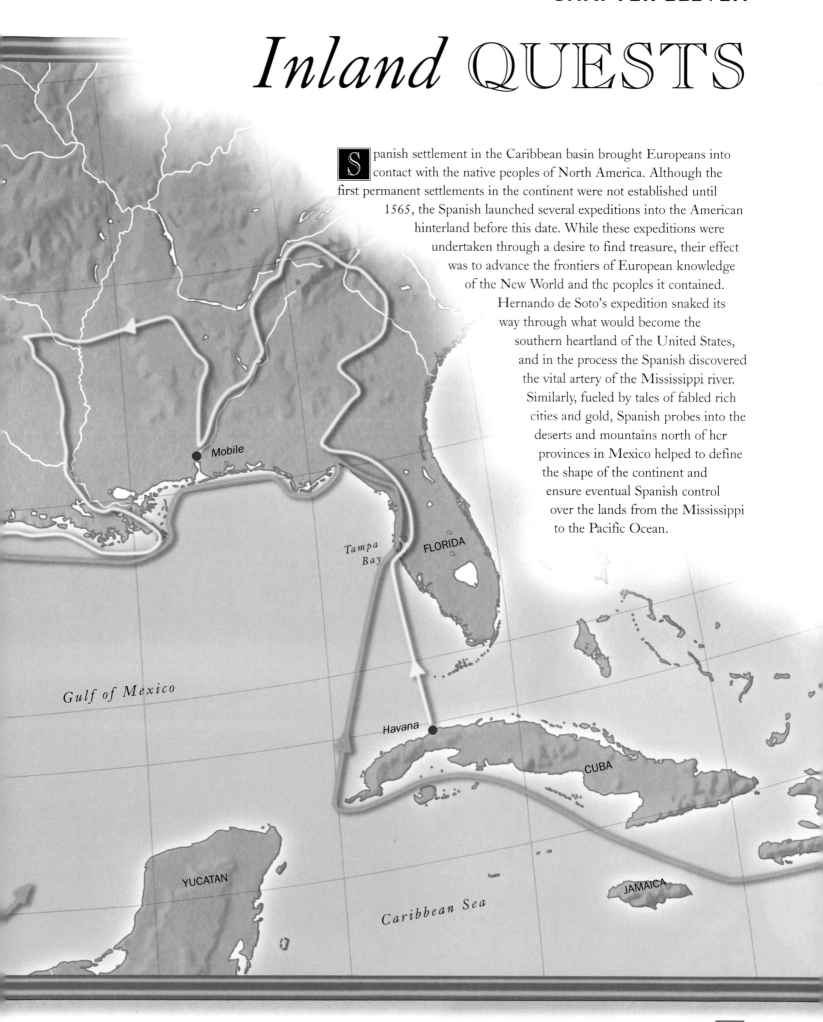

panish settlement in the Caribbean basin brought Europeans into contact with the native peoples of North America. Although the first permanent settlements in the continent were not established until 1565, the Spanish launched several expeditions into the American hinterland before this date. While these expeditions were undertaken through a desire to find treasure, their effect was to advance the frontiers of European knowledge of the New World and the peoples it contained. Hernando de Soto's expedition snaked its way through what would become the southern heartland of the United States, and in the process the Spanish discovered the vital artery of the Mississippi river. Similarly, fueled by tales of fabled rich cities and gold, Spanish probes into the deserts and mountains north of her provinces in Mexico helped to define the shape of the continent and ensure eventual Spanish control over the lands from the Mississippi to the Pacific Ocean.

Mobile

Tampa Bay

FLORIDA

Gulf of Mexico

Havana

CUBA

YUCATAN

JAMAICA

Caribbean Sea

HERNANDO *de* SOTO
1496 to 1542

Hernando de Soto was born some time between 1496 and 1501. In 1514, during his teens, he reached the New World as part of the entourage of Pedro Arias de Ávila, the newly appointed Governor of Panama. De Ávila was to supersede Vasco de Balboa as local governor (*see pages 114–115*), but his arrival at the struggling settlement of Darién caused friction. Fearing that his rival wanted to create his own province, de Ávila sent troops to arrest him, and de Balboa was executed in January 1519.

While this was happening, the young de Soto was serving his military apprenticeship under veteran Spanish captains commanded by de Ávila. These included Francisco Fernández de Cordóba, who de Soto served under during the conquistador's 1524–7 exploration and conquest of what are now Nicaragua and Honduras. In 1531 de Soto opted to join Francisco Pizarro on his conquest of Peru (*see pages 98–99*). Since de Soto and his men were used as an advanced guard, they were the first to discover the Inca civilization and meet the Inca king, Atahualpa. Over the next three years Pizarro conquered the entire Inca Empire, and de Soto became a trusted lieutenant.

On his return to Spain in 1536 a wealthy man, the Spanish monarch made him a marquis and a member of the order of the Knights of Santiago. While in Spain he married Isabella de Bobadilla, the daughter of his old Panamanian mentor, Pedro Arias de Ávila.

Despite the trappings of wealth, Hernando de Soto still sought glory. After extensive petitioning, he was appointed Governor of Cuba and granted the right to explore and conquer the territory known as La Florida. Volunteers flocked to his standard, and the conquistador sailed to Havana in April 1538 with a powerful force of about 350 infantry, 200 cavalry, and a dozen priests to convert the natives.

Striking against the natives

The expedition made its final preparations in Havana, and on May 18, 1539, de Soto and his conquistadors sailed from Cuba and headed to the northwest. They landed on the southern side of what is now Tampa Bay 12 days later, probably at Shaw's Point, near the modern city of Bradenton.

Speculation surrounds their exact route, but the version given here represents the current view of most leading Spanish colonial historians. In the 1930s the United States De Soto Commission combined archæological evidence with four contemporary Spanish accounts of the expedition to produce what was considered the definitive itinerary. Recent archæological evidence seems to support their findings.

On nearby Terra Ceia Island, the conquistadors established a protected camp in a Timuacan Indian village and readied themselves to go inland. About the second week of June 1539, de Soto marched his men north, although they had to swing slightly inland due to

Below: Hernando de Soto, from a contemporary engraving.

constraints of the terrain. They struggled across the Santa Fe and Suwannee rivers, turned to torrents by the heavy rain. Timuacan Indians also threatened them, but de Soto preferred preemptive tactics and attacked Indian villages he encountered along his route if the locals seemed at all unfriendly. In one of these attacks, the Spanish captured Juan Ortiz, a survivor of the doomed 1528 expedition of Pánfilo de Narváez (*see pages 56–57*). He joined de Soto and acted as an interpreter.

The expedition continued north to the Indian town of Apalachen, in the lands of the Apalachee Indians (near the present-day Florida State capital of Tallahassee), where the Spaniards wintered. De Soto has been criticized for his treatment of Indians he encountered here (*see also page 170*), destroying settlements, killing many, and using others as slaves. Probably in order to speed the Spaniards on their way the Apalachee told them of a wealthy land called Cofitachequi to the northeast. The Spaniards took the bait and set off in search of gold on March 3, 1540.

First they headed northwest, then north, discovering a succession of rivers. At the Flint River the conquistadors went upstream into what is now Georgia, then continued northeast to the Ocmulgee River, which they forded and followed upstream to reach the site of the modern city of Macon, Georgia. Cofitachequi was reported to be to the northeast, so they marched on until they reached the Savannah River, south of modern Augusta.

Above: *The Everglades, the "river of grass" that fascinated the early Spanish explorers.*

Left: *De Soto and his men stand beside the waters of the Mississippi, the first Europeans to cast eyes on one of the greatest rivers in the world.*

Fools' gold

The Queen of Cofitachequi sent canoes to ferry de Soto and his men across the Savannah and guides took them to the Indian capital. There was no sign of gold, but the Indians told de Soto to go northwest beyond the Appalachian mountains, where there were richer lands. De Soto heard what he wanted to hear and, as the expedition trekked off, the Indians were pleased that he had believed them.

The conquistadors went inland, through what is now South Carolina toward the mountains near the site of Franklin, North Carolina and descended into the Tennessee River valley at modern-day Chattanooga. Nearby they encountered the Chiaha Indians, reputed to own gold in great quantities. There were provisions in plenty, but no sign of any gold.

The Chiaha helpfully pointed de Soto toward the lands of Chief Cosa, a leader, they told him, of a powerful people. De Soto led his men south into modern Alabama and they found the chief on the Coosa River. In what was becoming a familiar pattern, Cosa in turn passed them on to Chief Tuscaloosa of the Choctaw Indians. Trade with the Choctaw produced food but sill no treasure, so de Soto and his men followed the Alabama River downstream.

As they traveled south, they encountered hostile Choctaw and Mobile Indians, who fought a vicious battle with the conquistadors; De Soto's men won—but it was a pyrrhic victory. Out of food and ammunition and their clothes reduced to rags, the Spanish troops found themselves in dangerous territory, with no hope of fresh supplies.

Although they had almost reached the mouth of the Alabama River, they headed north again, seeking a place to winter. De Soto led them to the Tombigbee tributary of the Alabama River to reach the village of Pontonoc, in what is now northern Mississippi. Although the break was welcome, they were still subject to attack by Choctaw Indians.

A grueling expedition

They headed west in April 1541 and crossed the Yazoo River. Marshes slowed progress but de Soto was spurred on by tales of a vast river to the west. On May 8 they reached the Mississippi, just south of its junction with the tributary White River, at what is now Rosedale. Four barges were built and the conquistadors crossed the river and continued west, over the lower reaches of the Arkansas River to reach the Saline River at Hot Springs, south of the modern State capital of Little Rock, Arkansas.

The grueling terrain of forest and swamp was taking its toll, especially as much of the march had been conducted during a summer drought. De Soto's small army had been reduced to about 300 men, and most of the horses had died. The Spanish established another winter camp on the Oachita River at a Tula Indian village called Utiangue. Here, the force survived a brutal winter and resumed its journey on March 6, 1542.

De Soto follwed the Oachita downstream, heading southeast, hoping it would lead them back to the Mississippi River and the sea. They entered what is now Louisiana, but close to the confluence of the Oachita and Red Rivers bad weather forced them to halt, and de Soto came down with a severe fever. He died on May 21, 1542, close to the spot where the city of Natchez, Mississippi was built. To prevent Indians from finding the body, it was weighted down and dropped into the river, a fitting though lonely resting place for a great conquistador.

Luis de Moscoso, de Soto's successor, led the party to the west, hoping to reach the Spanish territory of New Spain. The attempt was a failure, although it almost reached Brazos River in modern Texas. They retraced their steps and spent winter on the banks of the Mississippi. During the winter they built boats and, in July 1543, sailed down the river and into the Gulf of Mexico. After following the coast, sailing west, they finally linked up with Spanish colonists in New Spain in September 1543.

Although de Soto and his men failed to find wealth, they traversed 4,000 miles through what are now the southern States of the USA, recording and mapping what they saw. One of the most epic journeys ever undertaken, it greatly helped the Europeans understand the new continent.

Left: *De Soto discovering the Mississippi, 1541, painting by Oscar E. Berninghaus.*

AMERICAN CULTURES
of the SOUTHWEST

The tribes in the southwest of North America were protected from the first impact of Europeans by inhospitable geography. The period of isolation ended when Francisco Vasquez de Coronado (*see pages 168–169*) scoured the region for gold and the elusive Seven Cities of Cibola. However, the natives were so poor that further Spanish conquest was discouraged.

The geography of the region is varied, containing a large, arid plateau to the north cut by the Colorado River and its tributaries. Further south, a desert region extends into

The people de Coronado encountered were a mixture of relative newcomers and civilizations that had been there for thousands of years. To the northwest the Havasupai on the lower Colorado River near the Grand Canyon shared their northern border with the Indians of the Great Plains. Tribes sharing the same basic cultural and linguistic traits, such as the Mojave and Yuma, occupied the region between the Havasupai lands and the Gulf of California.

The Athabascan Navajos were relative newcomers to the region. They began migrating from the northern plains to the southwest in the century before the Spanish arrived, a movement that continued while de Coronado passed through their territory. The Apache, another group of new arrivals, settled in the modern border region of Mexico, New Mexico, and Arizona. The Navajos settled in an area that was also the homeland of a more established people, who spoke a tongue known as Utaztecan. These included the Hopis, Pimas, and Zuñis, all of whom had been living in the region for centuries.

Further to the east in modern New Mexico

Above: *Cliff Palace, Mesa Verde, was once hub of a Colorado chiefdom of the Pueblo and Basketmaker Indians some 900 years ago.*

Mexico, crossed by a handful of small rivers. The mountains of New Mexico develop into the plains of modern Oklahoma and the Texas panhandle and create a terrain that would discourage all but the most gold-hungry Spanish adventurer. Despite the seemingly arid and infertile nature of the land, this region had been in constant human habitation for some 9,000 years before the arrival of the Spanish.

c.2500 BC	c.500 BC	c.200 BC	c.AD 500	c.700	c.700–900	c.900	900–1300
The first farming cultures develop in the region.	Improvement of farming and irrigation techniques spread agriculture.	The first traces of Anasazi culture date from this time.	The Anasazi construct cliff dwellings from hewn rock.	The Hohokam, the Mogollon, and the Anasazi have all emerged by this date.	Pueblo people live in houses above ground-level in Arizona.	Hohokam culture flourishes in Arizona and New Mexico.	Villages are linked by a 250-mile-long road network in the Chaco Canyon area.

were the Pueblo Indians, named after their distinctive townships. These people shared a common heritage with their Utaztecan-speaking neighbors, although the various Pueblo groups spoke different dialects of the language.

Rise and fall of tribes

Because of a dry climate and a lack of modern development, a wealth of archæological information regarding these southwestern cultures has survived. The original inhabitants were nomads, maintaining themselves by hunting and gathering. The first farming settlements can be traced to c.2500 BC; about 500 BC technological improvements in corn production allowed farming to become more widespread, and several of the communities began to settle in small villages.

By AD 1100 the permanent settlements had grown into substantial towns, with their own infrastructures of art, manufacture, and worship. These settlements were most commonly found in the Pueblo regions, but by the 16th century they were in decline, as arable land became less fertile and made a more scattered population a necessity. Towns were abandoned, while the incursions of tribes such as the Navajos threatened to take away valuable land.

De Coronado was drawn north by the legend of the Seven Cities of Cibola, a land of rich and plenty. What he found were seven townships of the Zuñis, none of which possessed any wealth, and all of which were in decline. The Spanish encountered similar colonies of mud huts based around religious centers in the Pueblo and Hopi regions—instead of lands filled with gold they found only base metals and subsistence economies.

The new arrivals, the Apaches and Navajos, were less fragmented than their city-based neighbors and their tribes maintained a degree of political and military unity. This discouraged the conquistadors, who preferred to occupy cities in search of treasure, rather than chase nomadic warriors.

The mid-16th century was, therefore, a period of change in the region, with new groups

Left: *The Pueblo Indians who the conquistadors met lived poorly compared to their forebears, who had constructed towns like this in the cliffs of Arizona. This example from Canyon de Chelly was built about AD 1066.*

arriving just when the older cultures were fading. While the Spanish took full advantage of the disunity they encountered, they also noted that the region had nothing to offer to a permanent European settlement. Apart from an influx of Jesuit missionaries, the Native Americans of the southwest were largely left undisturbed for another two centuries.

Below: *A cotton shirt of the Anasazi culture from the Pueblo period of about AD 700–1200. Unlike later Navajo weaving, Pueblo weaving was a task done by men.*

1060	c.1300	c.1300	c.1350	1534–6	1540	1540	1541
The Mogollons build multi-room structures.	Anasazi farming cultures are in terminal decline after a period of drought.	Navajo and Apache Indians prey on the weakened Anasazi.	Most cultures in the region have returned to a hunter-gatherer existence.	De Vaca navigates through the region with the help of local Indians.	Spaniards led by Coronado reach the seven cities of Cibola in what is now New Mexico.	Lopez de Cardenas, one of Coronado's men, discovers the Grand Canyon.	The region becomes part of New Spain, although it is too arid to colonize.

ALVÁR NÚÑEZ CABEZA de VACA

1490 to 1556

Although Alvár Núñez Cabeza de Vaca, born into an Andalusian military family, never set out to be an independent explorer, his achievements helped to reveal the full extent of the North American continent for the first time. From the age of 20, de Vaca participated as a young officer in the Spanish campaigns of the Italian Wars (1494–1529). In 1512 he took part in the Battle of Ravenna, and continued to serve in both Spain and Italy until 1525. Following the overwhelming Spanish Imperialist victory at the battle of Pavia in 1525, de Vaca turned his attention to the prospects offered in the New World. He sailed on Pánfilo de Narváez's 1527 expedition as treasurer of the force (*see pages 56–57*).

De Vaca was stranded on Trinidad during a hurricane that struck his ship while he was ashore, but he was found and rescued by de Narváez. In April 1528 the expedition anchored in the present location of Tampa Bay, on Florida's western coast. De Narváez sent his ships ahead to rendezvous with his expedition later, while he led his men inland.

After passing through much of Florida, the conquistadors found that they had missed their rendezvous and were stranded on the shores of the Gulf of Mexico. De Narváez ordered his men to build barges and, in late September, the flotilla began its journey west along the shores of the gulf, bound for New Spain. Off the Mississippi delta a storm scattered the flotilla. In November two barges, including the one carrying de Vaca, were wrecked on Galveston Island, in what is now Texas, and the other three

craft were lost, along with Pánfilo de Narváez.

De Vaca took charge of the 90 survivors that were left of the 300 conquistadors who had set sail. The local Indians were friendly and provided information about two of the other barges; one was cast ashore and the survivors massacred, another was stranded on a reef—Indians found the castaways had starved to death. De Vaca and his men could count themselves as being relatively fortunate.

Powerful medicine

As they were preparing to walk south along the shore toward New Spain, de Vaca fell ill and was left behind with the local Indians. He survived and was taken south by his benefactors, a captive they believed was imbued with special powers. The Indians moved southwest through what is now Texas until they reached the vicinity of the Rio Grande. By the time they crossed it and entered New Spain, de Vaca had formed close ties with the Indians. Late in 1534, they came across the only three survivors from the group that had walked south in 1529: Andres

Above: *Although merely a footnote in de Vaca's story, the Moorish slave Estevanico had a sufficiently interesting life that there are now several societies that honor his memory. After returning to Mexico, Estevanico acted as guide to Marcos de Niza's expedition to the Zuñi Indians (see page 170).*

Right: *Alvár Núñez Cabeza de Vaca set out as a conquistador, but misfortune cast him in the role of true explorer.*

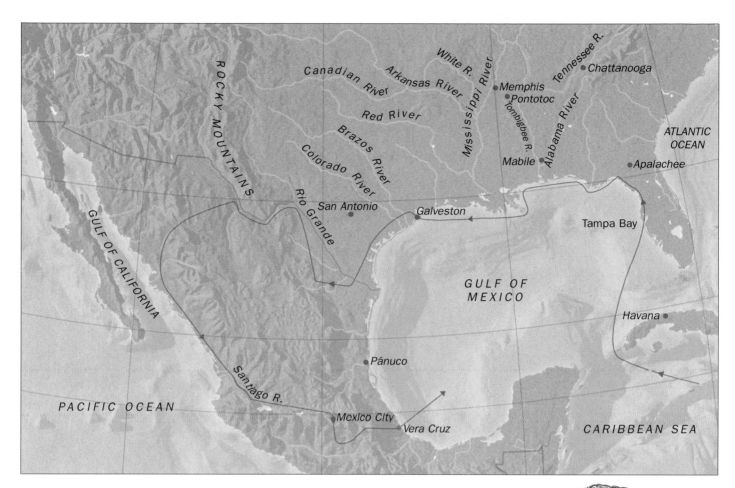

Dorantes, Alonso Castillo Maldonado, and a Moorish slave called Estevanico.

De Vaca decided to leave the Indians and join the three Europeans, who wanted to head east to avoid the worst of the Sierra Madre mountains and the hostile coastal tribes. However, some of the Indians elected to accompany them as guides. They walked west then northwest into what is now New Mexico and Arizona, and to a point on the west-flowing Gila River near the present city of Phoenix, Arizona. De Vaca turned southwest and eventually reached the Gulf of California.

The guides told everyone they encountered that de Vaca was a powerful medicine man, which probably accounts for their safe passage through hostile territories. In the spring of 1536, north of the Spanish settlement of Culiacan, they met a Spanish slave-raiding patrol. De Vaca prevented them from seizing his Indian compatriots, and the Spanish accompanied the patrol back to Mexico City, arriving there in July 1537.

De Vaca was a hero and, on returning to Spain, he wrote an account of his travels, *Los Naufragios* (The Shipwrecks), published in 1542. In 1540 he was appointed governor of the Spanish settlements on the Rio de la Plata in modern Paraguay, but he was ousted in a coup and sent home. His last years were spent in poverty in Seville, a tragic end to a conquistador who had endured so much. He died in 1556.

Above: *Indians of the coast of California.*

FRANCISCO VÁSQUEZ *de* CORONADO
1510 to 1554

Francisco Vásquez de Coronado led an expedition in search of lost cities and gold. He failed to find either, but recorded a wealth of information about the peoples and places that he encountered in the southwest corner of North America. De Coronado left his aristocratic family when he was in his 20s to seek fame and fortune in the New World. He arrived in Vera Cruz in 1535 on the staff of the new viceroy of New Spain, Antonio de Mendoza. Already considered for high office, de Coronado married Beatriz de Estrada in the year after his arrival. His new wife was wealthy and proved an invaluable political asset. Shortly afterward, the viceroy appointed him Governor of New Galicia, an important province of New Spain on the Pacific coast, with its provincial capital at Compostela.

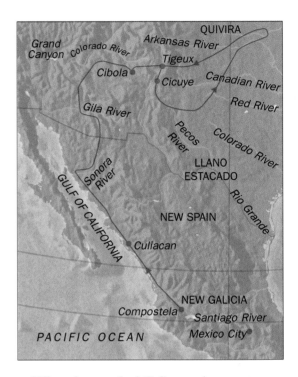

When Father Marcos de Niza's expedition to the north (*see page 170*) returned with tales of the Seven Cities of Cibola, full of immense wealth, de Mendoza ordered de Coronado to organize an expedition to investigate. In January 1540, the conquistador marched north along the Gulf of California at the head of 340 Spanish soldiers and 300 Indian allies, along with slaves and herds of cattle, and Father Marcos.

Above: *Francisco Vásquez de Coronado's name became synonymous with searching for gold. He found none, but his conquistador trek opened up vast tracts of the American hinterland for future generations of Spanish.*

When they reached Culiacan, the most northerly outpost in New Spain, de Coronado left the supply column to follow and pressed ahead with a fast-moving force. Up the Sonora River he crossed into what is now Arizona and descended into the valley of the Gila River, the territory of the Apache Indians.

Heading northeast, the Spanish sighted the first of the seven cities of Cibola on July 4, 1540, in what is now northern New Mexico. Instead of a wealthy city, the conquistadors found adobe huts forming the Zuñi Indian pueblo (village) of Hawiku. Patrols revealed the other six cities of the Zuñi confederation were equally destitute, and Father Marcos was sent home in disgrace. The first pueblo was turned into a winter camp, and the supply column was brought up.

During winter, de Coronado sent out several patrols to investigate the area. One scouting party discovered the Colorado River, running through the Grand Canyon. Another, sent to the east, reported that there were larger villages along the Rio Grande River, so de Coronado moved his winter quarters to Tiguex, north of the present-day city of Albuquerque, New Mexico.

Led astray by the "Turk"

Despite constant Indian attacks, de Coronado continued to send out patrols, and one of these brought back a Plains Indian they called the "Turk." He told them about a land with gold and an abundance of wildlife to the north, called Quivira. On April 23, 1541, de Coronado led his men across the Pecos river at Cicuye (now Pecos), around the Sangre de Cristo Mountains and down onto the plains. This was the prairie of what is now northern Texas, and the Spanish were amazed at the bison and the endless sea of grass. The local Tejas Indians possessed no gold, and it appeared that the Turk had lied, so

de Coronado had him executed.

Sending most of the expedition back to Tiguex, de Coronado went north with 30 horsemen on one last search for Quivira. At the Red River in modern Kansas they encountered Quivira (later Wichita) Indians for the first time. Again, there was no gold to be found, only small huts, a handful of Indians, and a poor climate. De Coronado turned south for Tiguex, taking Quivira guides to show him a shorter route back, a path that would one day become the Santa Fe Trail.

The Spanish wintered in Tiguex and, in April 1542, began their long march home. De Coronado had been injured during the winter; unable to exert his customary control, the expedition fell apart as it reached New Spain, when soldiers, Indians, and slaves deserted in droves. When de Coronado reached Mexico City to report the failure of his expedition, he had scarcely a hundred men left under his command.

De Coronado remained Governor of New Galicia for another two years, when he moved to Mexico City to take a seat in the city council. He never recovered from the failure of his expedition or from his injuries, and died in 1554, unaware that his expedition had revealed large parts of North America for future explorers, and that he would be remembered as one of the great explorers of his day.

Above: Across the Pecos River, de Coronado and his men were astounded to see the endless plains alive with herds of bison.

In SEARCH *of* MYTHS

S panish conquistadors were driven by a quest for military glory and personal esteem, as well as by pure greed and religious conviction—motivations that became the defining forces for the conquest of the New World. In the early decades of conquest when the Americas were still mostly unexplored, stories of hidden treasures in the form of lost cities, mountains of gold, and even fountains of youth were widespread.

The Spanish encountered an environment that was completely alien when they reached the New World. The first native peoples they met appeared to be primitive, but soon they stumbled upon impressively advanced civilizations in Central and South America. It seemed possible that other, even more developed cultures might exist in the vast interiors of the two continents. Early on in the Spanish conquest, Native Americans understood that

Below: Hernando de Soto became so obsessed with his search for hidden Indian treasure that he took to torturing the natives for information. Sensibly, most of them provided directions to the next village.

greed was the driving force behind the invasion. They learned to tell the Spanish what they most wanted to hear, in the hope that the invaders would go elsewhere in search of the treasure or lost cities they craved.

One of the first occasions was in 1513, when Carib Indians on Puerto Rico told Ponce de León about a land to the north called "Bimini" that contained gold in abundance and a fountain that restored the youth and health of anyone who bathed in it. De León was well into middle age when he heard the tale, and decided he had to find the land (*see pages 86–87*). In March 1513 he sailed north, probably much to the relief of the Caribs who he had spent five years exploiting. De León found neither his gold nor the fountain of youth, but the legend was too attractive to disappear, and was resurrected during de Soto's march through the southeast of the North American continent in 1539 (*see pages*

There were neither Fountains of Youth nor pots of gold to be found in North America. While those who conquered Central and South America did find treasure, such as this gold Chimu mask, left, explorers to the north found only humble Indian crafts, such as this decorated mortar, below, which to the eyes of the conquistadors had no value.

160–161). Throughout the de Soto expedition, the natives he encountered used the same tactic; they sent him in search of fabulous gold and rich tribal lands elsewhere. His expedition became, in effect, a treasure hunt across America, where the line of march was decided by the stories concocted by local tribes.

The Seven Lost Cities

Another goal of the de León expedition was the discovery of the Seven Lost Cities of Antilia, which had been described by Indians and even included on a contemporary world map in Europe. The rumors had also reached New Spain, and an expedition was sent to investigate. Three priests led by Father Marcos de Niza were accompanied by the Moor Estevanico (*see page 166*), who had survived de Vaca's military conquest (1528–36). Estevanico went on as a guide, sending back reports of progress to the priests, who learned that the cities existed but were called the Seven Cities of Cibola, and that two wealthy lands, each with a further seven rich cities, lay beyond. Estevanico was captured on entering the first of the cities of the Zuñi and killed. The priests, who were some days behind, promptly turned on hearing the news, and fled back to New Spain. Although they never saw

the Zuñi cities, these small adobe towns became the Lost Cities, and a major expedition led by Francisco de Coronado was sent to find them. Once again, he found no rich cities, only desert villages and an arid land.

Some rumors turned out to be true. The rich land Pizarro heard of called "Birú" was the Peru of the Inca, and it did indeed contain a mountain of silver at Potosi, as his Inca captives had told him it would. Similarly, the hinterland of Colombia and Equador did contain emeralds and gold for the taking, and

these and the Peruvian silver found at Potosi formed part of the riches that the Spanish shipped back home. These discoveries fueled the mythology and wild tales, but within a few decades it became apparent that most of the stories were unfounded.

CHAPTER TWELVE

MAPPING *the*

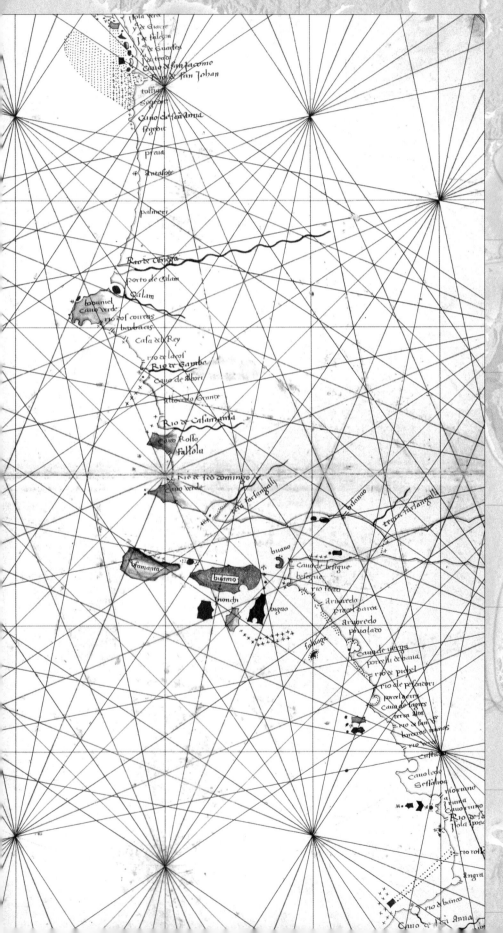

The Charting of Africa

By the time this chart (left) by Graziolo Benicasa was produced in 1473, Prince Henry the Navigator had been dead for more than a decade. His legacy continued in the detailed cartography still being undertaken off the treacherous coast of West Africa; vital information for Portuguese mariners sailing between Lisbon and the Guinea coast.

An element of mystery still surrounds these 15th-century Portuguese charts, since very few have survived to the present day. The navigational center established by Prince Henry at Sagres was an institution shrouded in secrecy, and although navigational and cartographic information was avidly collected there during the Prince's reign, little information was disseminated beyond its walls. Certainly, by the 1460s other European cartographers had seen a number of Portuguese charts, as this example testifies. Graziolo Benicasa was one of the Italian cartographers whose reputation for accuracy grew following Prince Henry's death. The Northern Italian ports such as Genoa and La Spezia became the new mapping capitals of the Mediterranean, although much of their information came from Portuguese mariners.

New information

It was at this time that a new breed of world maps appeared. Produced by northern Italian cartographers, they incorporated the African discoveries made by the Portuguese and placed them in a wider setting. Gradually, the Portuguese control of information was relaxed, and by the early decades of the 16th century,

DISCOVERIES

fresh information from Portuguese sources was used to regularly update maps and charts produced throughout Europe.

The two charts shown here are both examples of this diffusion of knowledge: the first shows a section of the West African coasts, with the Cape Verde Islands in the top left of the chart and the Bissagos islands in the center. This important work marks shoals close to the mouth of the Gambia River, information that

Portuguese mariners would probably have preferred to keep to themselves. The second work (below) dates from a century later and represents a detailed view of the Cape of Good Hope, as well as the islands and reefs surrounding Madagascar. Although less detailed than the first more practical chart, it contains information vital to any mariner making a passage between Madagascar and the East African coast.

Opposite: *Cape Verde to Cape Rosso, with the Gambia River, from the Benicasa Chart of 1473.*

Below: *The Cape of Good Hope, from the Joan Martines Chart of c.1578.*

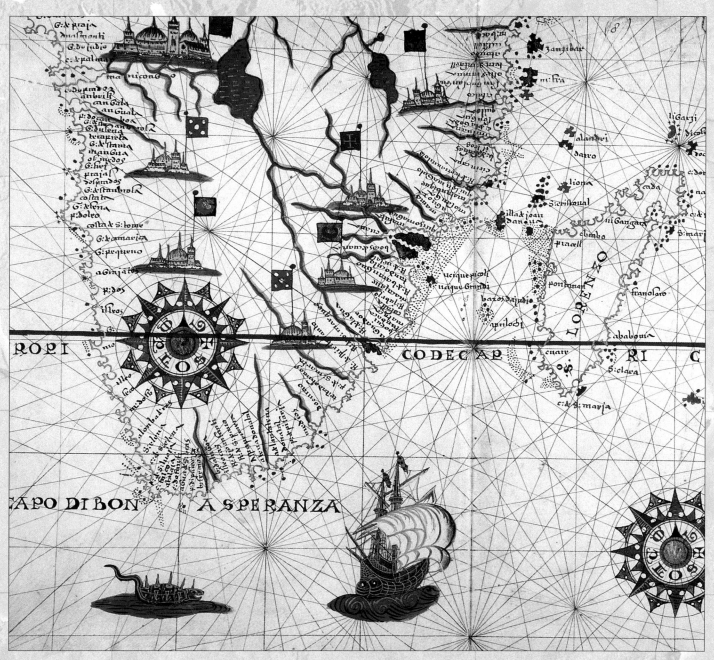

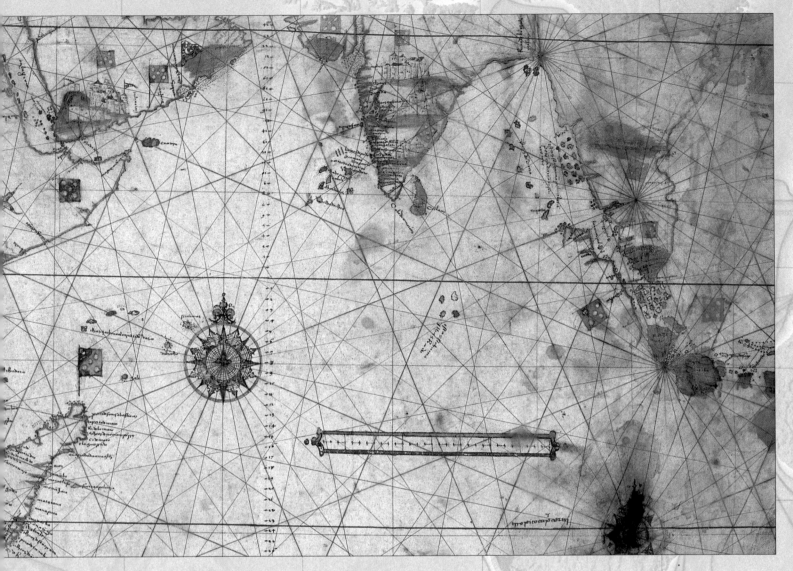

Lands of Silks and Spices

Above: *India and the route to Malacca, from a Portuguese chart of 1518.*

The impetus behind most of the expeditions undertaken during the Age of Discovery was the desire to find a trade route to the Indies. The voyage of Vasco da Gama and the Treaty of Tordesillas placed this region within the orbit of the Portuguese. The Indies—the Spice Islands—lay close enough to Portuguese bases in India for her merchants to monopolize the trade. As a whole new continent lay between the Spanish and that goal, it would take the Spanish another half century to gain a foothold in the Orient.

These two maps illustrate the development of the Indies trade. The first (above) was produced by the Portuguese within a decade of the establishment of their control of the Indies, and the second was drawn up at the time Spain established herself in the Philippines, so breaking the Portuguese monopoly of the spice trade.

The first map is limited to the passage between Goa and Malacca, with Portuguese emblems denoting that both the Indian subcontinent and the lands and islands of the

Indonesian archipelago were controlled by her. The lands of the Spice Islands proper, lying to the east of Malacca and Sumatra, are only depicted in a vague manner, demonstrating that the Spice Islands themselves had still to be explored and mapped. The second chart, part of a world atlas of 1573 depicts the extent of Portuguese trading in the Far East. Japan and the coast of China are shown, although the geographical details of Japan and the Asian mainland to the north and northwest are still vague. Within the next decade, Jesuit missionaries would furnish the information required by cartographers to complete their survey of Japan and its environs. Similarly, although the Chinese coastline is charted in some detail, the western line of the Philippines archipelago is only crudely delineated. Spanish conquest and settlement would also fill in these important gaps. By contrast, the heart of the Spice Islands, the Moluccas, have been mapped with some accuracy, reflecting the vital importance of the region to Portuguese merchants.

Below: *China and Japan from the Vaz Zdourado atlas of 1573.*

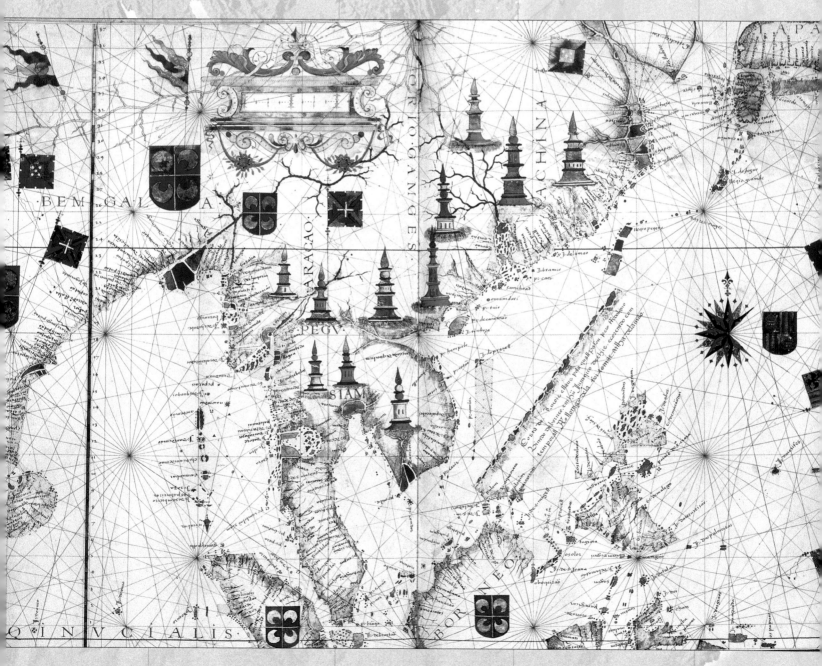

Beyond the Western Sea

When Columbus sailed from Spain in 1492, he thought that nothing lay between him and the Orient. Instead, he found a new continent. Over the next ten years two areas were explored: the Caribbean and Newfoundland. These two maps, created within a year of each other, show these new discoveries in different ways. The first (below), part of Giovanni Contarini's World Map of 1506, was the first printed map to show any part of the New World. The cartographer did not share Christopher Columbus's views about what he had found. While Columbus remained convinced that he had discovered part of the Orient, Contarini portrayed the lands as

entirely new territories. In the lower corner of the map, Hispaniola and Cuba are portrayed in the center of a vast ocean, roughly midway between Europe and China. It also depicts the inhospitable landmasses of what were probably Labrador and Newfoundland as a northern extension of the Asian continent. To the south of Hispaniola and Cuba lies Terra Crucis, the northern coast of South America, while between it and the Asian mainland the cartographer has placed Japan.

The Johannes Ruysch World Map of 1507 (opposite) covers the same geographic area, and again, Terra Nova or Newfoundland is shown as

Below: *Giovanni Contarini World Map, 1506 (detail).*

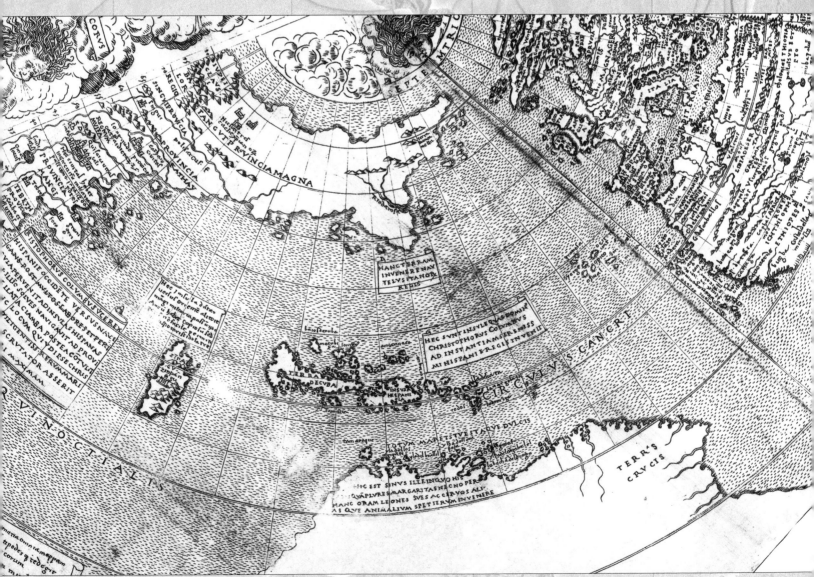

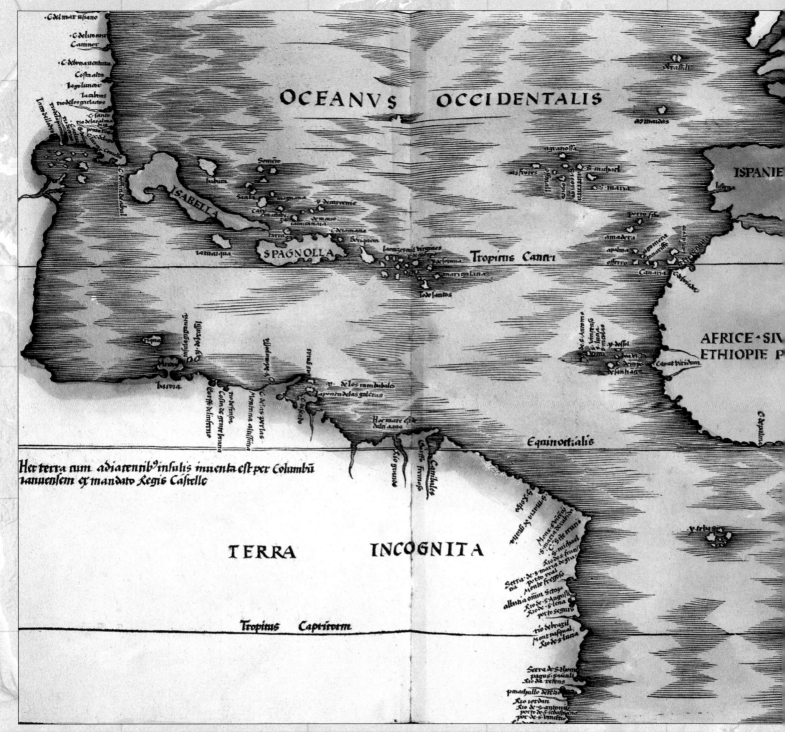

Map text labels (partial):

OCEANVS OCCIDENTALIS

ISABELLA

SPAGNOLLA

Tropicus Cancri

Equinoctialis

ISPANIE

AFRICE·SIV
ETHIOPIE P

Hec terra cum adiacentib'insulis inuenta est per Columbū
Ianuensem ex mandato Regis Castelle

TERRA   INCOGNITA

Tropicus Capricorni

part of Asia, as is Greenland. While the depiction of the rest of the Asian mainland and offshore islands is largely fictitious, based on a combination of earlier maps and the writings of authors such as Marco Polo, the depiction of the New World is based on the latest discoveries. Like the Contarini map, the discoveries of Columbus are shown to be islands half way between Asia and Europe. In this version the discoveries include the Antilles. The northern coast of South America is also depicted in more detail than on the Contarini map. Clearly cartographic knowledge had developed to the point where the claims of Columbus could be refuted, but there was still no clear understanding that the New World constituted two whole new continents.

Cathay
INDIA superior
Quinsai
FRANCISCA
C. Britonum
Exteriores
Terra florida
Oceanus occidentalis
Medera
Archipelagus 7448 insularū
Fortunate inf.
Chamaho
Panuco- Inf. Tortucarū
Iucatana
CVBA
Inf. Hesperidum
AFRI
Temistitan
Hispaniola
Antille
Seriana
Dominica
S. Jacobi
Jamica
inf. pdonum
Berigu
PARIA sabundat auro & margaritis
Sinus Atlanti
Catigara
Nuw
India Atlatica quam vocant Brasilij & Americam
Caribali
Inf. infortunate
Welt
Calenfuan
Regio Gigantum
7. infule Mar queritarū
Mare pacificum
Fretum Magaliani

The New World

Above: The Americas by Sebastian Münster, 1544.

By the middle of the 16th century, cartographers were able to produce a reasonably accurate interpretation of American geography. The two versions shown here date from within two years of each other, but are completely different in both their perceptions and their accuracy. Sebastian Münster was a highly influential cartographer whose *Cosmographia* became one of the most widely published collection of printed maps of its time. Although he incorporated many discoveries made over the previous 30 years in his work, it was still outdated. Unlike the world maps of Cabot and Gastaldi published within a few years of the Münster map, the German cartographer had little opportunity to gain access to the latest Spanish or Portuguese charts. The result was a work that was hopelessly inaccurate. Basic cartographic depictions of the central islands of the Caribbean were ignored and scales distorted to produce a continent centered on Cuba and the Yucatán peninsula, shown as an island. Given that the map was produced after the conquest of both Peru and Mexico, there is no reason the geographical information produced by the conquistadors was not incorporated in the work.

By contrast, the world map produced by Giacomo Gastaldi in 1546 reflected the latest information available at the time of production. It included the Strait of Magellan through the southern tip of South America, and Ferdinand Magellan's voyage is also reflected in the incorporation of Pacific islands and the Philippine archipelago. The basic geography of South America is reasonably accurate, although specific details such as the course of the Amazon River and the extent of the Andes are incorrectly shown. In North America, the fabled Seven Cities of Cibola are located to the north of Mexico City, while the Gulf of California and the Sonora Peninsula are depicted for the first time, both features reflecting the discoveries made by the conquistador Coronado. Like many earlier maps, the continent is portrayed as being linked to the Asian mainland, a misconception that would continue for another 30 years.

Below: *North America from Gastaldi's World Map, 1546.*

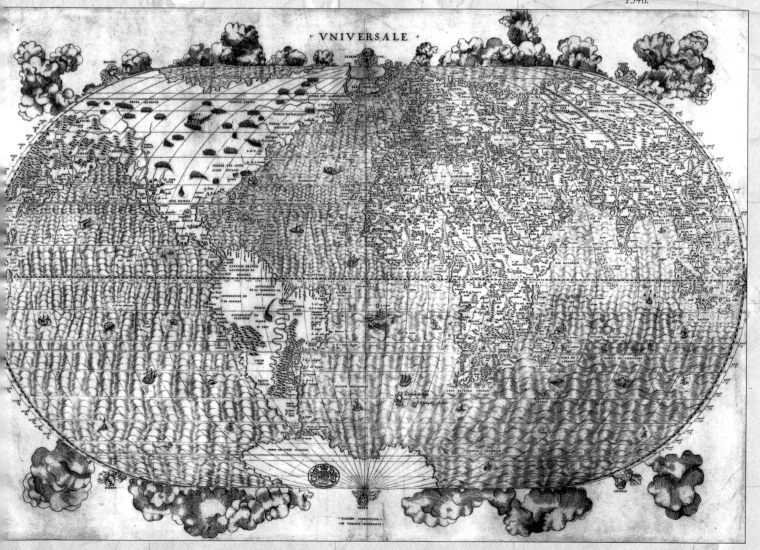

CHAPTER THIRTEEN

The PRIZE and LEGACY of DISCOVERY

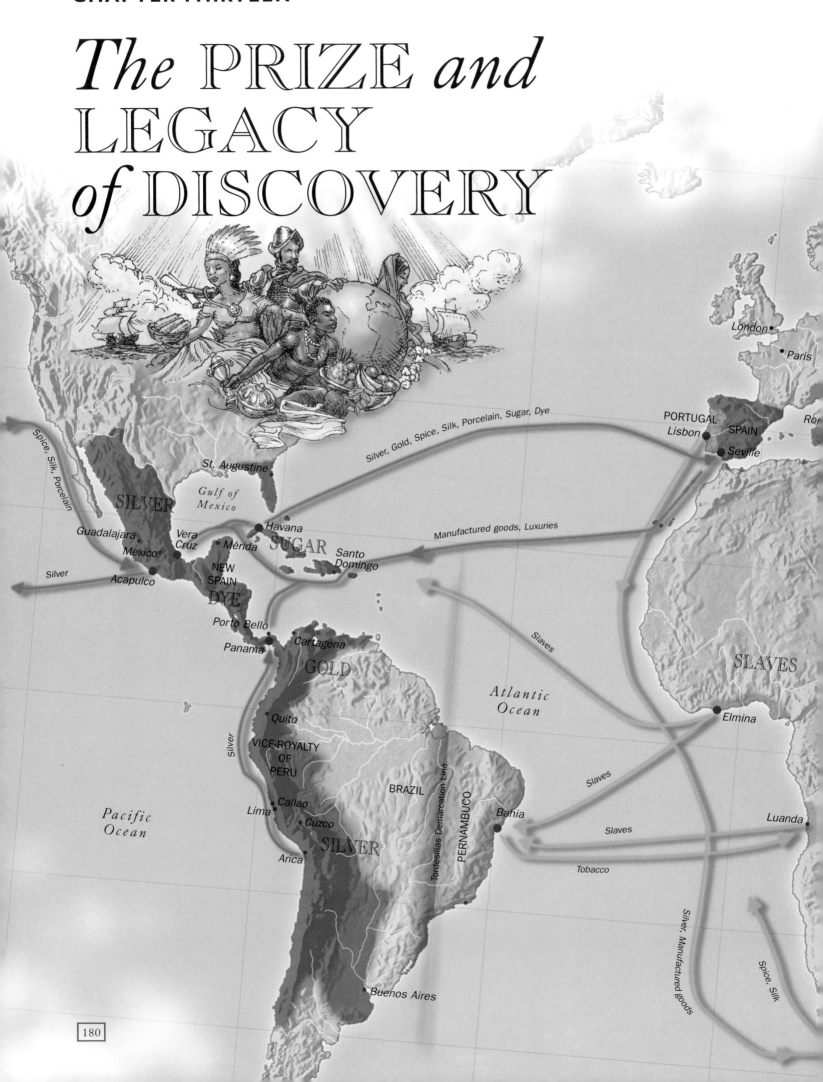

Spice, Silk, Porcelain

Silver, Gold, Spice, Silk, Porcelain, Sugar, Dye

London

Paris

PORTUGAL
Lisbon

SPAIN

Rom

Seville

St. Augustine

Gulf of
Mexico

SILVER

Manufactured goods, Luxuries

Guadalajara

Vera
Cruz

Havana

Mérida

SUGAR

Santo
Domingo

México

Silver

Acapulco

NEW
SPAIN

DYE

Porto Bello

Panama

Cartagena

GOLD

Slaves

SLAVES

Atlantic
Ocean

Elmina

Quito

Silver

VICE-ROYALTY
OF
PERU

Slaves

Pacific
Ocean

Lima

Callao

Cuzco

BRAZIL

Bahia

Luanda

Tordesillas Demarcation Line

PERNAMBUCO

Arica

SILVER

Slaves

Tobacco

Buenos Aires

Silver, Manufactured goods

Spice, Silk

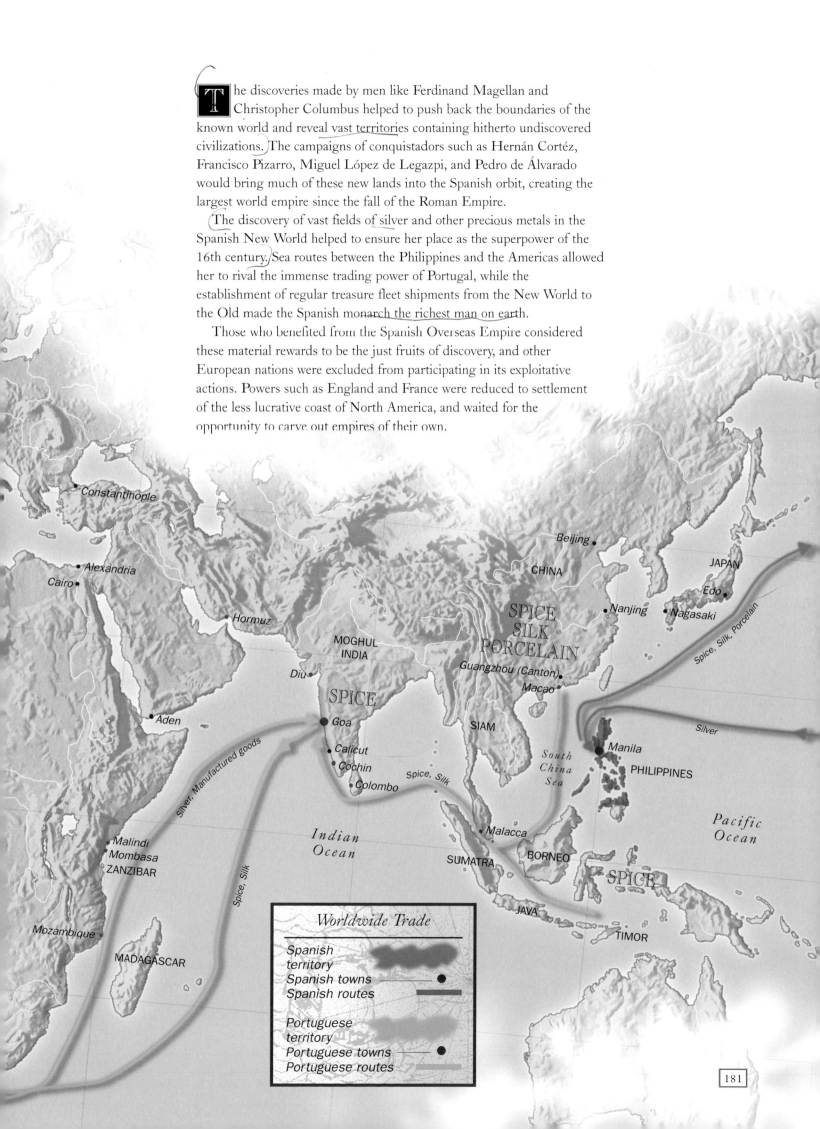

The discoveries made by men like Ferdinand Magellan and Christopher Columbus helped to push back the boundaries of the known world and reveal vast territories containing hitherto undiscovered civilizations. The campaigns of conquistadors such as Hernán Cortéz, Francisco Pizarro, Miguel López de Legazpi, and Pedro de Álvarado would bring much of these new lands into the Spanish orbit, creating the largest world empire since the fall of the Roman Empire.

The discovery of vast fields of silver and other precious metals in the Spanish New World helped to ensure her place as the superpower of the 16th century. Sea routes between the Philippines and the Americas allowed her to rival the immense trading power of Portugal, while the establishment of regular treasure fleet shipments from the New World to the Old made the Spanish monarch the richest man on earth.

Those who benefited from the Spanish Overseas Empire considered these material rewards to be the just fruits of discovery, and other European nations were excluded from participating in its exploitative actions. Powers such as England and France were reduced to settlement of the less lucrative coast of North America, and waited for the opportunity to carve out empires of their own.

Constantinople

Alexandria

Cairo

Hormuz

MOGHUL INDIA

Diu

Aden

SPICE

Goa

Calicut

Cochin

Colombo

Silver, Manufactured goods

Spice, Silk

Indian Ocean

Malindi
Mombasa
ZANZIBAR

Mozambique

MADAGASCAR

Spice, Silk

Beijing

CHINA

SPICE
SILK
PORCELAIN

Nanjing

Guangzhou (Canton)

Macao

SIAM

South China Sea

Malacca

SUMATRA

BORNEO

JAVA

TIMOR

JAPAN

Edo

Nagasaki

Spice, Silk, Porcelain

Silver

Manila

PHILIPPINES

Pacific Ocean

SPICE

Worldwide Trade

Spanish territory
Spanish towns
Spanish routes

Portuguese territory
Portuguese towns
Portuguese routes

The SPANISH NEW WORLD EMPIRE

Below: *With an abundance of natural mineral resources, Inca artisans used gold, silver and precious jewels lavishly. To the Spanish conquistadors, Peru truly was a treasure trove.*

When Christopher Columbus returned from the Americas in March 1493, the tension between Spain and Portugal became critical because both nations wanted control of the newly discovered lands. Conflict seemed almost inevitable. The Pope intervened, and under the terms of his 1494 Treaty of Tordesillas, a line was drawn through the Atlantic. Spain was given a free hand in the lands to the west of the line, Portugal to the east. It was thought that this gave Spain control over all of the New World in much the same way Portugal controlled Africa. However, at the time of the treaty, no one had discovered South America and the fact that a southern landmass projected to the east of the line. It was later realized that the Portuguese sphere of influence also included most of Brazil, which duly became Portugal's only colony in the New World.

Within a decade it became clear that the islands Columbus had discovered formed part of a new continent that now belonged to Spain. Spanish settlement began in the islands but gradually the Spanish expanded their influence to include Central America and the northern coast of South America. As a result, the Caribbean basin became known as the "Spanish

Opposite: *Spanish treasure from a treasure galleon sunk off the Florida Keys is displayed alongside more modern American maritime artifacts.*

Main. By the 1520s, the most lucrative part of this New World territory was Mexico, carved from the Aztec Empire by Spanish conquistadors.

The subsequent development was even more important, as it would produce a long-term financial windfall for the Spanish crown. During the early 1530s, Pizarro conquered the Inca Empire in Peru and discovered that the land contained metallurgical resources hitherto only dreamed of. Within a decade, Spanish mines had been established to extract large quantities of silver from Peru, and of these, for more than a century Potosi was the largest single source of silver in the world. The lure of these mountains of silver led to the partial depopulation of the Spanish Main's colonies when settlers flocked to Peru. The adoption of native slave labor in the Peruvian mines and the import of African slaves to work on the Caribbean plantations averted the crisis.

The voyage of circumnavigation led by Ferdinand Magellan was the next stage in the creation of an empire. It demonstrated that a sea route existed around America to the Orient, thereby achieving the original goal of Christopher Columbus. Because the passage around the southern tip of South America was hazardous, the Spanish established ports on the Pacific Coast of her New World territories. Although these were primarily designed to facilitate the flow of silver from Peru to the Spanish Main, they also provided the opportunity for further Spanish development of the Pacific. By the 1550s, these ports had formed part of the greatest maritime trading enterprise the world had seen.

Bringing the treasure home

Every year a convoy of ships left Seville in the south of Spain bound for the Spanish Main. Once there it split up to visit the various ports of the region before recombining at Havana in northern Cuba for the transatlantic voyage home. These annual fleets transported settlers, tools, and luxury items needed by the New World colonists. They returned with cargoes of silver, gold, spices, and precious stones. Silver was shipped from the ports of Peru to Panama, where it was transshipped onto pack mules for the journey across the isthmus to the ships waiting off the Caribbean coast.

Similarly, valuable cargoes were stockpiled in warehouses in Vera Cruz in New Spain (Mexico) and Cartagena in New Granada (Colombia) for the annual Spanish convoy. In the 1570s, a new leg was added. The Spanish conquest of the Philippines in 1571 provided a market in the Far East, and every year Manila galleons shipped silver from New Spain across the Pacific and returned with spices, silks, and porcelain purchased in the Philippines.

Within a century of 1492, Spain was the richest country in Europe, and the wealth of her overseas empire helped her to become a European military and political superpower.

However, to maintain this power she was increasingly reliant on the steady stream of silver. When it dried up, Spain quickly became a European backwater, although she resolutely clung to her overseas empire and vestiges of her former glory until the 19th century.

Above: A 17th-century map. By this stage, the Spanish controlled most of South America, all of Central America, and large swathes of North America.

THE PRIZE AND LEGACY OF DISCOVERY

The PORTUGUESE SEABORNE EMPIRE

Trapped between the Atlantic Ocean and hostile neighbors, Portugal was a small and a relatively poor country at the start of the 15th century. Over the next hundred years the Portuguese pursued a policy of maritime expansion down the African coast and into the

Portuguese discovered the Cape Verde archipelago and rounded West Africa to reach Guinea. Following Prince Henry's death in 1460, Portuguese explorers discovered the Gold Coast and the Congo River. The final phase extended the frontiers south to the Cape of Good

Right: *Calicut in the 16th century, the center of the Portuguese trading empire on the Indian subcontinent.*

Indian Ocean, and established the first world trading empire (the Spanish emphasis was more on plunder). Further expansion took her to the Far East and the markets of China and Japan— an amazing achievement by a small country.

Blocked from the North African coast by the Moors, Portugal outflanked her enemies by sailing around their shore to establish settlements in West Africa. The settlement of the Azores and the discovery of the island of Madeira (1419) provided stepping stones and an extra source of royal income. Loans from European financial houses to fund Prince Henry the Navigator's program were augmented by profits from the Madeira sugar trade. Henry's plan went in four phases. First was the exploration of the Moroccan coast (after the capture of Ceuta in 1414), the Canary Islands, and Cape Bojador in the 1430s. In the second, in the 1450s, the

Hope and beyond it to the coast of East Africa in the 1480s and 1490s.

Commanding East-West trade

In 1498, Vasco da Gama sailed around Africa and reached India at an opportune moment. The Chinese trading presence in the area had ended just prior to da Gama's arrival due to a new Chinese imperial policy regarding foreign trade (*see pages 140–141*). If it could bypass the Arabs, Portugal had a free hand in the Indian Ocean. During the next decade the Portuguese bought, traded for, or captured a string of fortified settlements and ports around the Indian Ocean, including Sofala in Mozambique, Mombasa in East Africa, Hormuz and Socotra on the Arabian coast, and Goa, Calicut, and Ceylon on the Indian subcontinent. The Portuguese also established

trading settlements on the West African coast, which become conduits for the slave trade. Portuguese plantations on Madeira and the Canary Islands needed a steady supply of slaves, but by the mid-16th century the Portuguese also became the main purveyors of African slaves to the Spanish colonies of the Americas.

The capture of the city of Malacca on the Malay Peninsula guaranteed Portugal's monopoly of the spice trade, and further remote colonies were established at Bantam in Java, Brunei on Borneo, and in the Moluccas. Large fleets (the Carreira da India) sailed between Lisbon, Goa, and Malacca, bringing peppers and spices to Europe in quantities that undercut the Arab-Venetian spice route, yet provided a vast source of wealth for the Portuguese crown and its merchants. Another trading outpost in Macao in China and one in Nagasaki, Japan created an additional trade in Oriental porcelain, tea, silk, and cotton. Although Arab trade continued, despite the best efforts of Portuguese commanders to obstruct it, the competition did little to damage the virtual monopoly enjoyed by the Portuguese during the 16th century.

Portugal was too small a country and her resources too stretched to maintain this sprawling trade empire. In 1580 she united with Spain in a doomed 60-year dynastic experiment. While the Spanish used Portuguese resources to develop their own American empire, Dutch and then English merchants infiltrated the Eastern markets. By the mid-17th century the Dutch had almost completely taken over the spice

trade, while the English were about to do the same in India. Most of the Portuguese settlements survived into the 18th century, but the heady days of her trading empire were over.

Below: *A carrack of the late 15th century, typical of the Portuguese vessels that first established the lucrative spice trade between Portugal and the East Indies.*

A WORLD *brought* TOGETHER

We witnessed the 500th anniversary of the discovery of the Americas by Christopher Columbus in the final decade of the 20th century. The rapid colonization of both halves of the American continent, to the great detriment of the indigenous populations, has characterized this half a millennium. It has been a period of substantial migration, with many millions traveling to the New World in the hope of finding a better life, while still more millions of slaves made the journey involuntarily. The slow social and cultural amalgamation of these groups of people has rarely been easy in any of the former colonies, and the process continues today.

The Age of Discovery precipitated a transitory movement of people, goods, and ideas throughout the world, and gave birth to the political and technological society we know today. The result is a global society with a huge and rapidly expanding population, with people from all parts of the world now trading directly with each other. The benefits to humankind are undeniable, and are on a scale that the pioneers of exploration and maritime trade simply could not have foreseen. None of this progress would have been possible without the vision, bravery, and skill of a tiny number of medieval seamen, who conquered their fear of the unknown to push forward the boundaries of human knowledge.

The direct result of the exploration was an explosion in maritime trade, colonization, and the development of European empires. With the collapse of those empires in the first half of the 20th century, the age of European global domination passed, but the legacy of those dynamic yet cruel times can still be seen in the cultures of the modern world. English, Spanish, Portuguese, French, and Dutch are languages spoken by millions of people around the world, and those nations' cultures have blended with the indigenous peoples' to create a vibrant mix.

Creating the United States

The United States of America is often referred to as "the melting pot of nations." Literally every nation and ethnic group is represented to

Below: With the conquistadors came the priests, monks, and Jesuits to bring a "civilizing" ideology to the pagan Native Americans, but in all too many instances, Christian zeal only masked secular greed. The Spanish burn the Indian Chief Hatuey, from a mid-16th-century Spanish engraving.

1776	1811	1811	1816	1818	1821	1821	1821
The 13 English colonies in America become independent and form the USA.	Paraguay declares independence from Spain.	Venezuela becomes an independent republic.	Argentina declares independence from Spain.	Chile declares independence from Spain.	Mexico becomes independent from Spain.	Haiti becomes independent.	Honduras becomes an independent republic.

some degree in the modern U.S. population. This fact reflects the dynamic range of immigration over the past 500 years. In that time North America has been transformed from a wilderness containing a handful of people into a relatively crowded continent with a population larger than that of Europe—the continent that initially colonized it. Although the Native Americans of North America avoided the worst excesses of the Spanish-colonized lands to the south, they also suffered the more pervasive influence of northern European settlers. The lack of immediately exploitable resources led

Above: *Africans transported to the Americas as slaves, from a watercolor by Francis Meynell, "The Slave deck of the Albanez," c.1860.*

Left: *Captain James Cook, explorer and symbol of the British drive to establish a world empire in the wake of the Spanish and Portuguese.*

English, French, and Dutch colonials to follow a policy of slow expansion based on agriculture and commerce. In the long run, it proved to be more profitable than the Spanish approach and even more devastating to the natives who the Europeans encountered.

Equally devastating was the African Diaspora. It has been estimated that over ten million slaves crossed the Atlantic and, as a result, Afro-Americans make up a sizeable portion of the communities of the United States and the Caribbean, both regions where slavery was an economic tool. Afro-American historians are only just coming to terms with the enormous social consequences of the transatlantic slave trade, a historic event whose emotional wounds have still not fully healed. As such, the Age of Discovery can be seen to have affected Africans more than any other group of people, and it led directly to the collapse of the civilizations of West Africa through depopulation and warfare.

Above: *Roald Amundsen (1872–1928), the explorer who made the first maritime journey through the Northwest Passage in 1903. He went on to reach the South Pole, and to explore both the north and south polar regions.*

1821	1821	1822	1823	1825	1830	1841	1854
Guatamala gains its independence from Spain.	Peru gains its independence from Spain.	Brazil declares independence from Portugal.	The United States declares the anti-colonial "Monroe doctrine."	Bolivia declares independence from Spain.	Uruguay is proclaimed a republic.	China cedes Hong Kong to Britain following the Opium War.	The USA uses "gunboat diplomacy" to open Japan to trade.

South of the Caribbean

In South America, the change was equally drastic—perhaps even more so in the early decades of colonization. The first Spanish settlers literally wiped out most of the population of the continent and the Caribbean islands, either through genocide, forced labor, or the unintentional spread of European diseases. The survivors of the great Aztec and Inca civilizations were harnessed to the land, producing food, growing cash crops, and mining the natural resources the Spanish needed to keep their empire financially viable. Even in the early days, the attitude of the Spanish toward the peoples they conquered drew criticism. One such critic was Bartolomé de las Casas, who raised European awareness of Spanish brutality in the New World with his 1540 report to Emperor Charles V entitled *A Brief Account of the Destruction of the Indies*. Bartolomé focused on the *encomieda* system, in which conquistadors were given a free rein to exact labor and tribute as they saw fit. The report resulted in changes in the Spanish colonial legal system that in time enabled equality to develop, but the exploitation and cruelty continued for many centuries nevertheless. In the end, it was religion—often a co-conspirator in the land-grab in the first years—that most helped to unite ethnic groups, together with a gradual transition from a Spanish administration based on isolated colonies to one that ruled large provinces and encompassed entire populations.

By the 17th century, New World Hispanics rather than Old World Iberians increasingly rose to positions of power within the Spanish colonial structure. And in the late 18th century, most of the Spanish overseas Empire, apart from the governors and the military, was run by Hispanics. Over the years, they received a political and administrative training that stood their leaders in good stead during the South American Wars of Independence of the early 19th century.

Across the Indian Ocean

In the Far East, the older civilizations were able to resist Western expansionism to a greater degree. Both Japan and China maintained a tight control over foreign trade, and contact with outsiders was kept to an absolute

Above: A 16th-century illustration of a cayenne pepper plant. The word is said to derive from "cayan," a modification of the Tupi Indian word "kyinha." Explorers of the 16th century discovered many new species of edible plants in the New World that have since enriched the rest of the planet.

The FRUITS of EXPLORATION

Cayenne peppers are native to South and Central America and the West Indies, where they had been grown for thousands of years. The cayenne is not related to the black and white pepper of Asia and Africa, but Spanish explorers seeking black pepper misnamed it. The Spaniard de Cuneo, who accompanied Columbus on one of his voyages of discovery, reported that the natives ate peppers like "like we eat apples!" It is possible he may have mistaken what was being eaten for the milder-flavored capsicum, or bell pepper. The Spanish introduced the cayenne, its many close relatives, and the bell pepper to Europe and the rest of the world.

Kidney beans and peanuts are now grown all over the world, but they originated in South and Central America. The Spanish brought them back from the New World, and the Portuguese introduced them to West Africa and India. Ironically, it was the African slave trade that took these staples to North America.

1885	1886	1901	1903	1918	1931	1939–45	1947
Tanganyika (now Tanzania) is ceded to the German East Africa Company.	Colombia becomes a republic.	Australia becomes a self-governing dominion.	Panama becomes independent.	Tanganyika and other German colonies are seized by the WWI victors.	Canada becomes a self-governing dominion.	World War II seriously weakens the European colonial powers.	India and Pakistan gain independence from Britain.

minimum, which allowed these countries to trade on their own terms. This came to an end in the mid-19th century when the Oriental nations were forced to accept Western commerce as a result of colonial "gunboat diplomacy." By the latter part of the century, the U. S. had joined the ranks of the world's colonial powers, completing the circle from colony to colonizer.

While rival European nations sought control of India and the Spice Islands—the Portuguese, Dutch, and French included—it was the arrival of the English that produced the most lasting impression on the region. The British Empire was created from a framework established by traders such as the English East India Company, and only when colonial aspirations replaced commercial endeavors did the European presence break into the mainstream of Indian, African, or Asian society and politics. Even these influences were largely lost through the collapse of Empire following the end of the Second World War, and the emergent Third World struggled to overcome the legacy of its colonial past.

The discovery and settlement of the New World and the development of global trade over the past 500 years was only achieved through terrible human hardship suffered by both the conquered peoples and, in many cases, by the European colonists. We are among the first generations to reap the benefits brought about by global exploration without having to pay a high price for the progress.

Above: *The Maya and Aztec used rubber for centuries before Christopher Columbus discovered the Americas. It remained a curiosity until the 19th century, when a method for keeping it soft when it became a solid was discovered. Europeans took plants to Asia, and rubber production is now an important economic mainstay for countries such as Malaysia, Thailand, and Indonesia.*

Below: *After its discovery in the Americas by Columbus, tobacco spread to Europe through the Spanish, Portuguese, and British. European traders ensured tobacco's spread to Java, the Philippines, China, and Japan, while the European slave trade introduced it to Africa and the Middle East.*

Potatoes are native to the Andes and were cultivated by the Inca. They came to Europe in the 1500s aboard Spanish ships and rapidly became a principal staple of European diets. During the 1600s, European maritime traders exported potatoes to Asia and to North America.

In Asia, rice was cultivated around 3500 BC, and in Africa around 1500 BC. It was introduced to Spain by the Moors and, from there, the Spanish exported rice to the New World, where it was unknown. Rice is now a staple of Latin American diets.

Corn, or maize, was one of the essential crops of South and Central America. It appears to have been domesticated in Mexico c.3500 BC, where it was used to make flour. It is also the ingredient in modern polenta, a porridge the ancient Romans originally made from pearl barley.

The tomato, which originated in South America, is now one of the most widely grown fruits around the globe. The Inca first domesticated the vine and Spanish monks cultivated plants brought to Europe. Despite its current popularity, 16th-century Europeans did not at first regard it as an edible fruit.

The clove originated in the Far East and was known to the Chinese (as chicken tongue spice) in the 3rd century AD. The use of the clove spread to Europe, and by the 8th century was the most important commodity in the spice trade. The Portuguese claimed a monopoly in the trade when they opened up the Spice Islands, which they maintained until around 1611, when the Dutch took Malacca. Once a preserve of the east, the clove is now widely cultivated in many tropical habitats like Brazil.

Bananas are thought to have originated in Malaysia. First noted by Alexander the Great in India, Spanish explorers took bananas to the New World with them in 1516, when the monk Tomas de Berlanga first planted banana root stocks in the fertile soil of the Caribbean.

1949	1965	1971	1973	1975	1974	1997	1999
Indonesia gains independence from the Dutch.	Rhodesia (now Zimbabwe) declares independence from Britain.	Britain announces its withdrawal "from all bases East of Suez."	The Bahamas become independent from Britain.	Mozambique gains independence from Portugal.	Angola's right to independence is recognized by Portugal.	Hong Kong is returned to China after 156 years of British colonial rule.	Portugal returns its colony of Macao to China.

The EXPLORERS Index